# No Stress Today
# with PSYCH-K®

How to transform stress
into vitality, peace and a
stress-free fulfilling life

Bornem, 11-01-2015

ISBN book: 978-94-91442-73-5
ISBN eBook: 978-94-91442-74-2

Dr. Marina Riemslagh

# No Stress Today
# with PSYCH-K®

## How to transform stress
## into vitality, peace and a
## stress-free fulfilling life

'Marina has written a wonderful book about PSYCH-K®, filled with a treasure trove of stories and results people have shared as their personal experiences. Having used PSYCH-K for over 25 years, I was not *surprised* by these stories and experiences, however I was deeply *inspired* by them. Read this book and be prepared to be both *surprised* and *inspired!*' – Rob Williams, Originator of PSYCH-K®

# Preface
*The purpose of this book*

PSYCH-K originated in 1988 and was transmitted orally. Bruce Lipton, the author of 'The Biology of Belief' is a great advocate. I discovered it myself in 2011. It changed my life. Before PSYCH-K, I felt the constant pressure of having to defend and explain myself. Now I am open and I feel loved. Not only did my inner world find peace but also I can get along much better with my fellow peers. My productivity increased tremendously and I bubble with energy. Every day I reach my full potential. I wish the same for everybody.

This book showcases the real results reached with PSYCH-K. Thanks to the many testimonies we have succeeded.

It was necessary to explain in a rational and understandable way, the additional value of this method that leads to an open way of being. The book answers the question 'why PSYCH-K works'. This is important for practitioners as well as people using it for themselves and is the main surplus value. By using PSYCH-K oneself we are able to communicate with our hidden automatic system (subconscious) and we can reprogram our disturbing habits.

It is fun to use and is like playing a game: you make a move and wait patiently to see what happens. When you hear facilitators talk among themselves – the people who learned the method – it is like listening to children who babble enthusiastically about the level they reached in the latest computer game. It stimulates our self-reflecting thoughts and our creative potential.

I am so happy with this book, just because it is there, and because you the reader has the opportunity to learn to know PSYCH-K.

Marina

# Content

Preface                                                                    5

Introduction                                                              13
   Let's get acquainted                                    13
   Peace is the objective. PSYCH-K® is the process         15
   Learning PSYCH-K®                                       19

'How PSYCH-K® changed my life...'                                        23
   The testimonies and how PSYCH-K® works best             24

What I experience when using PSYCH-K®                                    29

1.  Beliefs Determine our Lives                                 33
   A belief is a conclusion drawn from an experience       33
   Beliefs are the "glasses" through which we see reality  34
   Our beliefs create our current reality                  35
   Beyond guilt and shame                                  37
   Opposite beliefs: inner conflict                        38
   Our beliefs determine who we are                        39
   "I am a believer because this option offers most possibilities"  41
   Beliefs can affect our health                          42

2.  PSYCH-K® Works Quickly and Effectively                      45
   PSYCH-K works quickly and effectively                   45
   Aiming directly at a new future                         46
   Establish communication with the subconscious mind: testing  48
   A straightforward choice: a conscious mind              50
   The whole universe works together in order to help us:
   the super-consciousness                                 52
   Respecting the language of the subconscious mind        57
   We leave the job to the subconscious mind               58

The subconscious mind chooses the procedure to do the job 60
Checking if the transformation has taken place 62
Celebrate! 63
Living freely and fully: taking action 64

3. Trauma 69
Trauma 70
Research and story of a trauma 72
How trauma works on 74
There is no memory of sensory signals 78
Trauma-related behaviour 81
More trauma than we think 83
Trauma-related behaviour in the testimony 84

4. Stress and Total Exhaustion 89
Stress, a testimony 89
The whole brain available 90
Our brain does not function optimally under stress 93
In our subconscious mind it is always now 95
People do not have to divulge their entire soul 96
Three kinds of stress reactions: fighting, fleeing and freezing 98
Fighting reactions 99
Fleeing reactions 99
Freezing reactions 100
Total exhaustion of body and/or mind: the stress reaction
running wild 101
Stopping a derailed stress reaction 105
Experiments 107

5. From Drama to a Learning Opportunity 109
What is drama and how does it work? 110
Working out a solution 113
Choice 116
Opportunity 117

6. PSYCH-K® Principles and Philosophy 121
   Being visible 121
   We are all spiritual beings having a human experience 124
   We live in a universe with a meaning. Events happen for a reason 126
   The message conveyed by the challenges of life 127
   Partnership guides the healing process 130
   Knowing what you do not want is not the same as knowing
   what you do want 130
   'Everything should be made as simple as possible, but not simpler' 131
   The subconscious mind needs different tools 132
   The belief of being separated from the divine is the core of
   all difficulties and challenges in life 132

7. Surrogation 135
   Testimony 135
   Surrogation, a gift to others 136
   Levinas: philosophical background of surrogation 140
   A 'sacred' ritual 142
   'Love thy enemy' 145

8. Peace in Relationships 147
   The power of words 150
   Checking for stress between us 151
   Discovering and transforming the problem 153
   The individual bonding process 155
   The collective bonding process 156
   Relationships are being touched for peace 157
   Relationships with children 159
   Relationship with an 'invisible' twin brother or sister 160
   The relationship with 'abuse' 161
   More relationships in balance 162

9. A Healthy Mind in a Healthy Body 167
   The effect of a previous trauma on our current health 168

We don't have to experience the trauma again in order to
transform it 175
Developing fear and behaving accordingly 178
Transforming allergies 180
'No need of medication to make it through the day' 183
'Smoking is dirty and it stinks' 184
Through PSYCH-K the competence of health workers is expanding 185
The belief may determine whether we live or die 187
Mentally healthy 187
A healthy body as well 188
PSYCH-K effectively activates the self-healing capacity of the body 188
Placebos and nocebos: the power of enhancing and the force
of limiting beliefs 189
Be sure to have healthy beliefs in a healthy body 190

10. PER-K, PSYCH-K® at the Workspace 193
PSYCH-K for working conditions 194
PER-K, how it is taught 197
The impact of beliefs and stress on the quality of work 197
PER-K: from willpower to automatic behaviour 200
Results after a PSYCH-K or PER-K Balance 202
PER-K, areas of application 204
    Exceptional leadership 204
    Excellent management 205
    Top sales results 206
    Effective communication 207
    Team building 208
    Health and well-being 209
    Transforming stress into success 210
One more testimony 211

11. Infinite Possibilities 213
With only 11 Balances we create infinite possibilities 213

Working with children and teenagers 216
PSYCH-K workshops are open to young people from 10 years old
onwards 218
PSYCH-K as a playful way of preparing yourself for getting
what you desire 220
PSYCH-K connects us to the Universal Energy 221
Making Music 223
Understanding a foreign language 224
"Cleaning" a house before the sale 225
Working with horses 226
Working with different animals 229
Asking for money in times of poverty 230
Bothered by heat? 232
No more sickness of heights 233
Insomnia 233
When mourning blocks you … 234
The feeling of panic stays away 235
Nice to practice PSYCH-K together and explore the possibilities 235

12. PSYCH-K® Unleashes Love 237
A Testimony 237
Our system is one 239
From separation to unity 240
Consciously choosing peace freely and responsibly 245
Fine-tuning to the superconscious mind 247
Aligning our subconscious mind to the superconscious mind 249
Learning to listen to synchronicity 249

A Word of Thanks 251

Notes 253

Bibliography 279

# Introduction

*'The question to ask yourself when things are going well is, how much better can it get?'* – Robert Williams

## Let's get acquainted

'How are you?' If you answer 'Fine, thanks' or something similar this book is the one for you: it is possible to keep up this attitude of well-being and expand it to every situation of your life. If this question creates discomfort and problems chances are you will have a better understanding of yourself and of your environment after reading it. If you learn and apply PSYCH-K®, you will have a proven tool to help you evolve from survival to fully living, and you will have more ways to manage your own life even more effectively. 'How are you doing?' creates an opening for the question that is really the issue: what is it I truly want, what is it I deeply long for? These are questions that touch the soul. They steer you away from trauma and drama and they bring you home to who you really are, and who you would like to be. They show the core of who you are and what your true possibilities are.

Let us get acquainted. This book is conceived as a dialogue between you, the attentive reader and myself. So, let me introduce myself. My name is Marina Riemslagh. I am a qualified doctor. I hold a PhD in Relational Ethics. Between 2005 and 2010 I conducted research into 'the why of unethical behaviour of people in the course of their profession'. This doesn't involve extreme forms of bullying at work only. My field of research was much larger. It also included the subtle forms of incorrect behaviour during counselling. One of the results, which will be discussed extensively later, was that professionals mean to do very well. However as soon as something awkward occurs, their automatic programming takes over. Suddenly one changes from having an open perspective to a reactive one.

No matter how hard one tries to do their best and one is aware that their reaction is not adequate, it's as if everything runs on autopilot. What we know and intend to do belongs to our so-called conscious mind; what happens automatically, is triggered subconsciously. You can read more about this in Chapters 1 and 2. The results of my research made me focus on how we can change the subconscious mind, so that what we consciously think and want to do matches what we actually feel and do.

I started my career in nursing. Then I was a group counsellor, a supervisor and a pastor. My education in the medical world has enabled me to have solution focused thinking and acting. I like to know how our body works and it is a joy for me to find out that it functions optimally. As a nurse I was also trained in explaining difficult subjects simply. Sometimes an image or a story calls up more than 1000 words. From my work as a nurse I brought helpfulness and an obvious readiness to answer questions to assist the patients.

For seven years I worked as a counsellor for the Centre of Relationship Development and Pregnancy Problems for women who underwent an abortion[1]. Far too often an abortion is carried out because the man or the woman do 'not want' the child-to-be. They do not stop to think about what they really want. Abortion can be a desperate effort to restore the situation to what it was before the pregnancy, although this situation has already passed[2]. At the moment of the intervention they barely stop to think about how things will feel later, how this abortion may cause painful relationships and can remain a sensitive spot when the topic of children is raised. With what I know and can do now, I would deal with these groups in a completely different way. These years of counselling have made me aware of the fact that focusing on the past can close the door to what essentially is at hand. With PSYCH-K we are able to create a future in which we can accept what has been and – perhaps in the end – become what we want to be. Working with these women has also taught me not to judge.

As a supervisor and educator I have become convinced in the power of words, both encouraging and impeding words. I did not only get an insight into how people learn, but also how different though similar we are. My systemic and group dynamic way of looking at things expanded my capacities for counselling. Each time it struck me how much trouble it takes us to become  responsible for our own lives. How much we are rooted in patterns of being a victim, of 'the other one or the situation is to blame not me'. My own desire to take full responsibility for my own life inspired me to help others as well, in this matter.

As a pastor or spiritual caretaker, rituals became quite precious to me. Wherever words and gestures in love shape the bipolar aspect of our humanity, of our individuality and our belonging together, something of 'the sacred' is touched. We then feel that we 'exist in a holy place'; in something that transcends us in a benevolent way. From nature we learn to inhabit our own space and to respect that of others. Flowers bloom in the most beautiful way when they are 'in the right spot' and also inhabit that spot. The same goes with us: we are called to bloom in our own spot. That is why I could not help but write this book[3].

Due to the limitations of this book it is not possible for you to introduce yourself 'literally'. I would like to know you. I would like to hear your name and I am curious to find out why you want to read this book. Perhaps you could contact me through www.freefullliving.com. I am curious to know your impression of this book and how it contributes to what you know, who you are and what it is you do.


**Peace is the objective. PSYCH-K® is the process**

This book is about PSYCH-K, a method or process to make peace with ourselves, with others and with the Universe – or whatever you may call what surrounds us. Because it is really about peace, we can call PSYCH-K a 'spiritual process'. All side effects, like feeling good, having a fine intimate relationship, making contacts easily, living in a loving environment, working with challenging people, having enough money, sleeping well, being in good health, expressing oneself through a beautiful body, relaxing in due time, ... are part of it. The objective always remains peace, the dynamics by which everything finds its proper place.

*Peace with ourselves*

*Peace with others*

*Peace on this earth*

Peace settles in when our deepest longing (our superconscious mind[4]) matches what we want (our conscious mind) and what we have already experienced in our lives (our subconscious database). If for example someone has been hit or abused during childhood and has stored all kinds of defensive behaviour because of it, this person will stand in his own way (reactions triggered by the subconscious mind). They will want to openly show the talents he or she has (superconscious mind) and choose to follow a certain education or training (conscious mind). If this education matches the person's talents and if this person's automatic impulses enable him or her to realize this longing (and he or she does not counteract him/herself), this feels like peace.

Peace comes into being when we whole-heartedly do what is right for us, when we realize our own being. In the past, finding peace was difficult for me and it required a lot of effort. Now it is simple for me to create peace within myself and with others since I know and use the 'process'.

Peace gives us shining eyes, which easily shows when we are at peace or not. We just radiate. Peace does not mean that we cannot feel sorrow or pain; it only means that we feel what is there and experience this in unity with ourselves and with others. Peace is being balanced. That is why the PSYCH-K procedures are called 'Balances': methods in order to evolve from a situation of dissatisfaction to a situation of peace.

You might call PSYCH-K a way of life. It is a permanent choice to be "my best self". Of course I can let myself go, to complain or feel victimized. This is not what I choose. I want to live in peace and that gives me wonderful satisfaction. This fundamental revolution doesn't happen in one day; I repeatedly choose to experience whatever happens as an opportunity of learning and living. When I made the commitment to do this, I was a bit afraid that my life without drama would not be so exciting. But nothing is further from the truth. I am free and in this freedom so much more can happen. Love is flowing and I can realize whatever I want to, for instance I can write a book J

PSYCH-K does not only mean inner peace, which can be seen as the alignment between the subconscious mind, the conscious mind and the superconscious mind. By applying PSYCH-K it is possible to make peace in all our relationships: with yourself, with others, with nature, with companies, with the universe. The trump of PSYCH-K is that realizing this peace happens automatically and effortlessly.

PSYCH-K is a process with fixed and flexible parts. This process contains some fixed elements with a flexible middle part. Just as an informative book begins with an introduction and ends with a conclusion, every PSYCH-K process or Balance begins and ends in the same way. Every Balance contains the same basic ingredients with flexible additions and variations. The fixed elements are quite simple. The flexible elements can be either simple or more complex.

Firstly, fixed elements establish contact with the subconscious mind, to test the desired change. The superconscious mind is then checked to see if this change is in your highest interest, and engages with the subconscious mind in doing the job, by making sure that what you wanted to change has indeed been realized. The change is then celebrated. Finally, it is required to complete a first step of action for your conscious mind. The flexible elements of the Balances can be movements that make your brain function as a whole, or they can be an addition of energy or breathing.

Every element will be thoroughly dealt with in Chapter 2.

Robert Williams is the originator of PSYCH-K®. His formal education as a professional counsellor and psychotherapist, in addition to his 14 years of experience as a business manager, made it possible for him to understand the value of the gift he received in a series of spontaneous insights in December of 1988-89. The details of this process are described in his book, *PSYCH-K, the Missing Peace in Your Life*. I owe my learning of PSYCH-K and the writing of this book[5] completely to Robert.

## Learning PSYCH-K®

You can learn PSYCH-K by applying the process. It is like cycling, learning to steer and keeping your balance, or learning to change gears when driving. PSYCH-K is a process that you can learn. You can make progress by effectively using the vehicle. Just like in cycling or driving, if you are a stay-at-home couch potato, you will not achieve any speed at all. You can learn PSYCH-K and not make use of the extra possibilities. If you do not practice the Balances, you will stay where you are.

PSYCH-K can be learnt in five consecutive workshops from three to four days each: the Basic, the Pro, the Advanced workshop, the Health and Wellness workshop and the Divine Integration Retreat. All workshops are open to young people who choose to learn this, from the age of 10 onwards, as these processes are quite easy to learn.
In order to get some insight into what can be reached with PSYCH-K I will give you a short description of these five workshops.

Practicing PSYCH-K yourself starts with attending a two or three-day Basic workshop, in order to master the basic elements. You can do quite a lot with this already: you can transform stress in just a few minutes, through several movements or positions within yourself, and help others to transform stress in themselves. You can replace limiting beliefs like 'I cannot write', 'I cannot concentrate when reading' with more supportive beliefs. This could be, for instance, 'I am writing fluently and have a dialogue with the reader', 'I concentrate with pleasure in order to read this book to the very end'. The process can be applied to any belief that may be helpful to you.

After this workshop you can also make the 'translation' between the conscious and the subconscious mind. The content that I am writing and that you are reading is conscious. Subconscious is what happens automatically: my fingers moving across the keyboard, joining the letters while you are reading, looking outside or hearing birds whistling in the background. As soon as we pay attention to something, it becomes conscious; when we don't pay attention the subconscious automatically takes over. The conscious mind and the subconscious mind deal with language in a different way. When we respect the language of the subconscious mind, we can translate an abstract wish of longing into the language that the subconscious mind understands. Then we can bring the wish or longing into action automatically. We will pay attention to this later.

In the PSYCH-K® Pro workshop you will extensively learn to use these basic processes for specific purposes. You will learn to "converse" with your subconscious mind and listen to the messages it reveals. Our subconscious mind can show us where the stress comes from (without needing to re-experience it) and our conscious mind can pay attention to this. In the Pro workshop you will discover what advantages are created by behaving in a certain way and you will transform these advantages so that you automatically drop any awkward behaviours. For instance, scratching my ear, while I was lecturing troubled me. The advantage was that I could concentrate better by this extra bodily impulse. But I myself experienced this behaviour as a nuisance. I have kept the advantage of concentrating, but in my brain I have disconnected it from scratching my ear. The same kind of disconnection can be created with allergies. Allergic reactions are mostly created by stress, which is subconsciously connected with one element or another, like food or pollen. In the PSYCH-K Pro workshop we learn how to transform allergies. You will also learn different ways to access limiting beliefs. Afterwards you can work with friends, colleagues and clients with a lot more self-confidence and you can possibly build up a counselling practice of your own or integrate PSYCH-K into your practice a lot easier.

The Advanced workshop has more sophisticated processes and Balances. We start with a Rapport Balance, where stress is transformed in verbal and non-verbal communication. Using this Balance, you create options whether to stay in contact with someone or not. Besides transformations using movements, you will also learn to work with energy in this workshop. Just like in acupuncture certain points are being touched in order to release this energy. Moreover, you will also learn, through the connection that exists between us as human beings, to contribute to the life of others in a respectful and benevolent way. This process is called 'surrogation'. For instance, it creates the possibility, during a Relationship Balance, to create peace between a partner who is present and a partner who is absent. In order to create peace, the 'foundation of our existence' should be in balance. You can call our basic attitude: 'I want to live', 'I love myself', 'I expect the best to happen', 'I deserve to be happy', 'The universe is governed by Divine Intelligence', ... All these beliefs together are embedded in our system as one whole in about one and a half hour. Then there is another Balance for the attachment to life, in which traumas of birth and the fear of death are being transformed. All this makes the Advanced workshop a life-changing event.

In the Divine Integration Retreat all process will be used to integrate the relationship with the universe, the Divine or whatever you wish to call this natural dynamic. The result is that everything flows effortlessly. I experience unity with the Whole more clearly; I can connect to it and easily work with it while counselling.

In the Health and Wellness workshop, our thinking about disease and health is expanded. Not only are the beliefs that are related to disease being transformed, but also the condition itself. Diseases often contain a message from the superconscious mind. 'Something stuck in my throat' can be an indication that some permanent stress has settled. If the subconscious mind is not capable of lifting this stress through regular relaxation (like sleeping, walking, talking, meditation), in most cases a Balance can transform the blockage that is expressed as a symptom or disease.

Five workshops with increasing possibilities and depth enable us to use PSYCH-K for the transformation of almost any situation in life. By transforming we mean: the stress is taken out of the situation and peace is being installed. Peace doesn't mean passiveness here but action. After the Balances life goes on, and we may be surprised now and then about our ability to realize things that were unthinkable before.

Every chapter of this book brings testimonies from users of PSYCH-K, sometimes during one single session, sometimes after having attended several workshops.

After every story we go in depth to certain aspects of the method. Here comes the first story: F.T. describes what the five workshops have meant to him. Afterwards I will tell you some more about these testimonies and I will close the introduction with an outline of the structure of this book.

# 'How PSYCH-K® changed my life…'

'In March 2012 I had my first experience with PSYCH-K. Preceding a training from Other Life[1], I attended a session with someone in the Netherlands. This was because I did not feel so well…

After the first session, which I attended quite apprehensively, I experienced how fast things can change. I drove back home in such a relaxed state that I thought I should do this ride again. In the one-hour and a half session several themes and one trauma were dealt with. For me they desperately needed to be solved.

Through this experience I became interested in PSYCH-K and I started studying it. In November of that year there was a Basic workshop in the same location as the "Other Life" training where everything had started. Of course I immediately signed up and after two days I was able to practice the Balances that I had learned. (A Balance is the name given to the transformation process). Every day I dealt with problems that bothered me and I noticed that there was a change in my behaviour and perception; it was just great.

After a few months, in April 2013, there was an Advanced workshop in Belgium, where I participated with some more people from the Netherlands and Belgium. Through my positive experiences I wanted to get more out of it.

After this workshop I practiced with several people in order to get the hang of it. This has brought me a lot and I have been able to deal with things that hindered me in my life on a deeper level.

I started applying PSYCH-K with others, friends and family. They also noticed positive changes.

Later that year I also attended a Health and Wellness workshop. This was superb. It gave me even more insights that I am now able to use with myself and with others. Through these insights I can work faster and with more creativity. And this is what I do with great regularity.

At the beginning of 2014 I attended the Divine Integration Retreat, a wonderful experience that I can recommend to anyone who has *attended the Basic and Advanced workshops. By the way, I attended the Advanced workshop a second time. At first I thought it might be superfluous, but it gave me new information to work with. Even if you have completed the Advanced workshop and you have the opportunity, it is certainly worthwhile to do it again. Moreover, repeating a workshop is free of charge. I have also registered for the Pro workshop, the only one I have not attended yet. I certainly do want to, as I want to work with PSYCH-K in a totally professional way.*

*It is wonderful to experience how you can evolve from someone who was depressive and seemed to have little perspective into someone who is brimming over with enthusiasm and is now achieving the objectives that were seemingly unattainable at first. All this thanks to PSYCH-K.'*
*F.T.*


### The testimonies and how PSYCH-K® works best

When I decided to write a book about PSYCH-K, I sent an email to all my Dutch-speaking clients and to all PSYCH-K facilitators in the Netherlands and Belgium and asked them whether they would like to contribute by writing something about their experience with PSYCH-K. Six hundred and seventeen people had followed the workshop before July 2014. Four people reacted that they could not make a statement about the effectiveness of PSYCH-K, because they had attended only one or two sessions. There was one person who did not see any results and all other 77 stories have a positive tone. It is remarkable that more than 10 percent of the people, who followed the workshops, took the time to write a testimonial and to send it in[2]. Perhaps this is because PSYCH-K 'works' so well or maybe because in the Netherlands and Flanders people are not inclined to express their negative experiences in testimonies. Here you will find the four stories.

I.V., E.M. and E.D.B. all had one or two private sessions, M.P. did the Basic workshop.

*'I attended a session concerning headaches and ringing in the ears, only once. I have noticed no difference up till now; the session in itself was quite a pleasant experience.'*
I.V.

*'I have attended two sessions with you. I do not feel that anything has changed.'*
E.M.

*'I would like to help you, but honestly I have to say that I can give too little feedback. I have been there only once and then I did not have a clear before and afterward feeling.'*
E.D.B.

*'I have nothing to report; I have practiced it intensively for some time, but I do not notice tangible results. I really would like to attend the next course, because I probably did not practice it sufficiently and then I totally stopped of course.'*
M.P.

Following the testimonial, M.P. came for a private session. There the block to create results was removed.

If you take individual sessions with a PSYCH-K facilitator, you may sometimes notice a clear improvement in your life after only one session. This is obvious in the story at the beginning of the second chapter. Maybe you will not notice anything. The changes are established in our subconscious mind. Because of this 'automatic pilot', it is quite possible that it will not be noticed by the conscious mind. If people attend several sessions, they often experience spectacular results. Other people remain somewhat disappointed. They sometimes come with complex problems and thus expect a universal panacea, which PSYCH-K is not. Whoever attends sessions will be like someone who is sitting on the back of a bike. Someone can bring you to your destination after one or several rides.

You will obtain the best results by learning and applying PSYCH-K yourself, by learning to ride the bike. As soon as you apply PSYCH-K in your daily life, both for transforming stress and transforming limiting beliefs, you will improve considerably. There will be growth. You will dramatically increase your chances of arriving where you want to be.

From people who attended two to five workshops, I only received enthusiastic reactions about what the method had caused in their own lives. I do hope that my enthusiasm and theirs doesn't irritate you as a reader. I wrote down the testimonies exactly as I received them. No part was deleted nor added.

There are also coaches who offer PSYCH-K in their counselling programmes. Here you will have the opportunity to meet professionals: they have gained in-depth knowledge of how they can help. You will then get a combination of their expertise and PSYCH-K. For people with complex problems this is the best way: attending some sessions with a professional who applies PSYCH-K, then learning the method in a couple of workshops, applying the method and attending a session now and then if you encounter any difficulties. Someone who can establish where it is you fail, and who knows how to deal with it, will be quite an added value.

And there is more: the people, who sent a testimony, received the chapter in which it was included. They were able to read the context in which their story was set. The corrections they wanted to make have been done. Therefore, all testimonies are set in a context, with which the writer agreed.

Personally I would write certain testimonies differently. Still, I left the formulation unchanged in order to render the words of the 'hands-on' experts as fairly as possible. Everyone has his/her own experiences and should use their own language to describe them.

**Survey**

This book contains 12 chapters. The first chapters give the theoretical background; the last ones will rather focus on testimonies. Chapter

1 describes beliefs. I will focus more on the workings of PSYCH-K in Chapter 2. Chapter 3 is about trauma, with some added material from my own research. In Chapter 4 stress and total exhaustion are dealt with. As soon as one's vision of beliefs, trauma and stress is expressed, Chapter 5 is devoted to the transformation of dramas in which we tend to live daily and the opportunities of evolution they contain. Chapter 6 is exploring the presuppositions or principles underlying PSYCH-K. In Chapter 7 I will deal with a valuable ritual by which we can contribute to someone else's life, namely surrogation. Chapter 8 is an extensive chapter about peace in relationships with many testimonies. In Chapter 9 "A healthy mind in a healthy body" I will deal with the contribution of PSYCH-K to optimal health. Chapter 10 is about PER-K, which is PSYCH-K for the professional work environment. In Chapter 11 the most incredible testimonies are told. Chapter 12 presents itself under the title 'PSYCH-K unleashes Love'. It is love that creates peace, establishes unity, in short, makes the creation of a friendly world possible.

The book ends with some words of thanks and a bibliography.

# What I experience when using PSYCH-K®

'*I don't do struggle anymore. I choose life, that is in the flow.*' – Robert Williams

As I said, this book contains 77 testimonies of people who are applying PSYCH-K in order to transform their stress, to change the context in which they are living and to create a free and full life. Some terms we use are specific for this method. The procedure that is being used in order to realize this transformation is called a PSYCH-K 'Balance'. The person experiencing the transformations is called the 'partner' and the one who is helping is called the 'facilitator'. We test which beliefs are anchored in the sub-conscious mind, to establish the cause of automatic behaviours. If strong, the kinaesthetic response means the belief statement is true for the subconscious mind. If the response is weak, it is untrue. In the following chapters we will go into it extensively. Let me give you a preview of the testimonies.

K.V.O. came to see me twice for a private session; she already attended two workshops, both the Basic and the Advanced.

'*I already did quite a number of trainings which always gave me new insights. The past is clearer; you have a better understanding about why feelings of sorrow always prevail. You keep on discovering why certain themes touch you or make you sad or angry. So many experiences are triggered by common life. You uncover these experiences through the courses and you learn to see what influence they still have today. You also learn to deal with them in a better way. A lot has been healed. Wonderful things have happened. And still I kept falling back into very deep sadness. It is a sea into which I fell over and over again. Now I am trying to stop doing that. In the meantime I know what it feels like: heavy, deep and endless. The heaviness of life is all you feel then. Although a lot has already been dealt with, the sea remained a presence underneath my skin.*

*I am now trying to stay out of it. No more swimming or fishing … I do not want to burden my children with this heavy undertone either. I rather like to be a glad, positive mother, who brings light into the house, who enjoys life and spreads positivity.*

*Why did I go into PSYCH-K training?*

*Because two people, independently of one another, said that it might be meaningful. Although I was careful not to start yet another training, I attended the Basic workshop. I came home extremely cheerful. We had done quite a number of exercises and Balances. I felt much lighter. I could feel I had to go on with this.*

*Although I kept practicing regularly (by doing balances myself), I felt the heaviness creeping up again. Experiences within the family deeply cut into my own past. I again felt as powerless and small as before. I couldn't say: "Cut, and it is gone…" This is not the way it works.*

*Still I remain active with PSYCH-K by doing my own regular balances. It always gives me the feeling that I contribute to my fate, feelings, atmosphere in which I am living. I seem to be behind the wheel, which in itself gives me a good feeling. When I am working with PSYCH-K, I feel noticeably lighter.*

*In the meantime I attended the Advanced workshop as well. When I am doing a relationship balance, I feel my body responding to it. With the usual simple balances I also feel when something "works out" or not. If something "works out" or "catches on", I immediately feel a shift inside my body. When something does not catch on, I feel nothing at all. The same happens when I am working with other people, my body seems to respond then too. Sometimes you really feel that you are thriving. Your body tells you. You feel a kind of steadiness, an assurance in your body. Some time ago I did a balance with someone who said "I cannot do anything at all". This was transformed into "I know what I can do". And my whole body told me: this is OK!*

*I would like to share a couple of very beautiful experiences. A couple of months ago I felt lousy because of a consultation that went completely wrong. Since this consultation I have felt the ground giving way beneath my feet. I felt worthless and invisible. Although I had already done quite a number of balances, the feeling of enormous powerlessness kept weighing upon me. It completely brought me down.*

*Suddenly I felt: now I have to do a balance. My intuition kicked in. I started from the belief "I feel worthless". And it tested strongly. The desired belief "I am useful" scored weakly. The body indicated that a Resolution Balance was required. During the balance you work with very old beliefs that have been there for a great part of your life. You bring the new belief into the body through an exercise in which both the left and the right hemispheres are being activated. The exercise can take a long time or be very quick. In this I follow the impulses of the body. I prefer going too slowly to going too fast.*

*Totally unexpectedly I saw the consultation appearing in front of my eyes with the three people who were present. I again felt the utter powerlessness, littleness, and humiliation. I felt myself standing there alone. In reality I had left the room a very small person.*

*In this PSYCH-K exercise other images came up now: images of how things could have been. We were still there, the four of us. But I felt strong, answered their questions and reported facts. I told them that I understood them, but that the facts were different anyhow. During the consultation that took place in front of my eyes, I felt strong. I knew what I was saying. There was no struggle for power. I did not have to defend myself. I stood firm and told them quietly what needed to be told. And they listened to me. What I told them also got through to them.*

*This felt so fine! While the exercise was going on, I felt how important it was at that moment. In Pesso therapy this is called a corrective experience, "making a new memory". I also know in reality the consultation went totally differently. But it could have happened in this way. By seeing it in front of my eyes and by experiencing the strength in my body, I did not let myself be blown away, I again felt ground under my feet. At last I felt the power returning into my body. I had not felt it for months. I had felt beaten up till now.*

*This is one of the strongest experiences I have had with PSYCH-K. The discouragement and powerlessness of three months now gave way to power and self-respect.*

*I am convinced that taking enough time is very important in PSYCH-K. You have to feel what is to be felt. Sensitively feeling whether something "works out" or "does not work out".*

In the past I have at least done ten balances concerning "I am able to love..." I may have done the balances, but in reality I felt that little had changed. And I also felt the need to do the balance over and over and over again. But nothing happened in my perception. It was just not convenient at that moment. The following belief fit: "I give the relationship with ... one more chance". This belief completely matched what I felt then: the relationship is bad, but I want to give it one more chance. When I did this balance, I saw a horizontal line in the distance: 5/6 of that line was dark. 1/6 of the line, to the right-hand side was light. OK, this is a point of light I want to hold unto. In my body I felt hope. There was one last chance and I should take it. I could feel it quite strongly in my body.

What do I appreciate about this training?

Every step of the training you learn processes that you have to practice with each other. At a workshop weekend there are always newcomers and also people who have already completed the course. They can assist you. You can also ask lots of questions while practicing the balances. A lot of questions will be asked! Sometimes things were going too fast for me. By practicing, a number of questions will be answered. Still a lot of questions remain. What if... and suppose that... These questions are answered during the course as much as possible.

Attending practice days is always possible. These are moments when facilitators gather in order to practice balances with each other. Everyone attends the workshops, Basic or Advanced training. You practice with each other. At these sessions you can ask questions and exchange experiences.

I feel that PSYCH-K is an effective method. The events in my life require me to work with it regularly.'
K.V.O.

# 1. Beliefs Determine our Lives

*'Why doesn't your life always look like the wisdom you possess? Because your wisdom needs to become a part of your 'subconscious' beliefs.'* – Robert M. Williams

*'PSYCH-K made me realize that beliefs shape your life. We can and are allowed to be responsible for our own beliefs. In that sense PYSCH-K was a real eye opener for me. Once you are in the dynamics, a range of possibilities opens up. PSYCH-K offers perspective. It gives meaning to life and in life.'*
S.S.

## A belief is a conclusion drawn from an experience

A belief is a conclusion, a short summary of an experience. For instance, you drive to the seaside for the first time on a weekend and you are trapped in a traffic jam. The belief that you would hang on to would be 'at the weekend there is always traffic going to the seaside'. Isn't this logical? We even call this belief a fact, something that is fixed. But is this a reality?

As soon as a belief is part of our data, it is automatically applied to other situations. We are inclined and used to generalize the conclusions of one experience to all similar situations, both within ourselves and towards other people. In logic this is called *the fallacy of generalization*, a common mistake in reasoning. We make the mistake that something that happened (past tense) will also repeat it in the future. If it repeats itself, this might happen because in our 'system' a button – a belief – is switched on by which we 'make' things repeat them.

Last year I was washing up at my daughter's place and I cut myself deeply on the knife of the blender. Later at night I tried to find out how safe I am with knives. Not so! In my repertoire of beliefs there was no support for 'I am safe with knives'. So I immediately changed this belief in my system, because I wanted to be safe. But then I forgot to transform the stress of the situation in which I had cut myself. And indeed, last week I was standing on the same spot, with the same people around me, I felt the insecurity and I cut myself again. Most likely, I could have prevented this by doing one short balance. What happened?

**Beliefs are the "glasses" through which we see reality**

Every belief we have shapes the glasses with which we look at reality. This is because it is stored in the long-term memory in our subconscious mind. The subconscious mind controls our automatic behaviour. As soon as we do not take care, or do not pay conscious attention, our automatic impulses take over.

*Through rosy glasses I see the world as a good place, through dark glasses I see the same world as hostile.*

'But that is the past?' I hear you objecting. 'Something that is past, remains past?!' Not in the subconscious mind: In there it is always here and now. For the subconscious mind there is no past and no future. The understanding of time belongs to our conscious mind; being conscious means giving attention, putting our focus through paying attention[1]. Cutting myself last year and standing in the kitchen again now, is both 'now' for the subconscious mind. The belief 'I cut myself in my daughter's kitchen' is still embedded in my subconscious mind and is therefore active, here and now. That is why a belief 'makes' the situation repeat itself. While writing this, I have transformed the situation into 'In my daughter's kitchen I am safe (with knives)'.

## Our beliefs create our current reality

*'"Being able to be myself at all times", that was the objective with which I did my first PSYCH-K session. Now, two years later, I experience that feeling more and more and people tell me regularly. Recently I have put a new profile picture on Facebook and in some reactions I literally read: "So completely yourself". Isn't this wonderful? I would wish that feeling to everyone.'*
*Y.V.D.W.*

The understanding that every belief creates the experience of my next reality is disconcerting. Let us allow this understanding to permeate our thinking and our comings and goings.

Beliefs do not only determine our view, they also make us reproduce this reality[2]. This is because our subconscious mind is continuously looking for similarities between what we perceive and our beliefs about it. If whatever is happening around us, matches what is inside ourselves, we feel safe. It matches; it is predictable even when whatever is happening around us, can be quite unpleasant.

Our brain is continuously looking for congruency between the inner world and the outer world. This is in fact quite an ingenious system. Looking for similarities is one of the primary functions of our subconscious mind. It makes us orientate ourselves in the world; it makes us able to build relationships and to create a feeling of familiarity. At the same time our brain is continuously scanning the environment for possible dangers. Beliefs help us detect these dangers beforehand. Every danger – verbally encoded as a belief – is being signalled until we realize that the real danger is inside ourselves, in these limiting visions of reality.

As soon as we change a belief, the result is that we create another reality[3]. Every fear creates fear, every pain creates pain, every love and peace creates more love and peace, … This age-old wisdom is much more concrete and has a lot more impact than we realize daily.

Imagine that a little boy is unexpectedly slapped in the face. What is the belief he will keep from this? Dependent on how it gets to him, it can be processed as 'Life is dangerous', 'I am not OK', 'I can be beaten up anytime', 'They do not like me', 'I am someone who is being beaten', 'It is normal to be beaten', …
The first time the little boy will be very scared. Being scared undermines the feeling of safety. In order to create safety, the little boy will try to control the moments when he is beaten. He can foresee the beating when he provokes the beating by a defiant attitude. He shows 'You cannot do anything to me', 'Come on if you dare', 'I do not feel anything when you beat me', 'I dare you to hit me', 'I despise you', … All these beliefs will also be embedded in the subconscious mind.
Then this child will go to school. There, dependent on the situations that occur, these beliefs will be activated. It can result in him being beaten by his friends and/or that he himself will beat up other kids. If that little boy comes home and tells his mother, at an opportune moment, that he is being beaten up at school, things can go either way. The mother can accuse him 'What is it you do to be beaten up by others?' or she can try to stand by the child by saying 'If they hit you, you have to hit back' or she can deal with the parents of the other kids or she could say 'You had better be brave, don't show that it hurts', all dependent on her own experiences and beliefs. All this behaviour and the corresponding beliefs are also stored in the child's subconscious mind.

What do you think will happen in this person's life when he is a grown-up? What will his future look like when his subconscious impulses take over?

Just like the boy, we have at least three different kinds of beliefs stored in our subconscious mind: those that are connected to us being victims, those that provoke a reaction and those that legitimize our acting as a perpetrator. For our own well-being we especially pay attention to the victimization beliefs. We prefer to keep the fact that we ourselves could harm or hamper other people out of the equation. In the testimonies it is stressed that with PSYCH-K we can take responsibility for our life and ourselves. This means that we are capable of changing the limiting beliefs we have.

Take a look at your own education, your own beliefs, look at the feedback you get from others about how you come across... Our conscious beliefs do not necessarily match our subconscious beliefs. The latter are driving our subconscious beliefs[4].


**Beyond guilt and shame**

This wisdom leads us beyond guilt and shame. The experiences with the greatest impact have been stored between our conception and our seventh year of life. This is the time in which our brain functions like a sponge[5]. During these years of formation we soak up everything that is happening around us. Experiences and statements are verbally encoded and stored as subconscious beliefs. As soon as our attention weakens, the automatic pilot takes over. Our automatically controlled behaviour dominates[6]. On a daily basis the proportion of conscious to subconscious behaviour is 5 to 95 percent[7].

We are not responsible for what has been stored before our seventh year of life. Guilt only originates when we knowingly do something that causes harm to another or to ourselves. As long as we cannot control or transform our automatic impulses, our guilt is quite limited[8]. We do not have to be ashamed of it. Sometimes things turn out badly, there is a lot of work to be done; more than often everything goes quite smoothly.

The good news is that with PSYCH-K we can quickly and easily change our subconscious beliefs. I am not responsible for my past; I can take responsibility for what I am making out of my life now. At least, because I am using PSYCH-K, I can change and take this responsibility[9].

My great enthusiasm for PSYCH-K has to do with this: it is a great joy to be responsible for my own life. I am no longer ashamed of my past. I will not tell much about it, because other people are involved. However I am glad and proud of what I have done with it. I am focusing on what is fair when in contact with other people and I can realize this automatically. If I am not true to myself, I can still transform the limiting beliefs and adjust my unfair behaviour. Meanwhile I know the signals of limiting beliefs, both in myself and in contact with others. It gives me the feeling of being reliable and kind to others. Being able to do this gives me – just like S.S. at the beginning of this chapter – the joy to be alive.


**Opposite beliefs: inner conflict**

We all have conflicting beliefs: 'I am smart' and 'I am stupid', for instance. Getting my PhD has been an experience that has led to the conclusion 'I am smart'. The fact that I have just forgotten the neighbour's name makes me think 'I am stupid'. Two opposite experiences and resulting beliefs dominate my automatic behaviour. If 'I am smart' is switched on, I can under-stand the most difficult things; if 'I am stupid' is switched on, I forget what I have just written. This is not practical. It gives me the feeling of not being stable, of playing hopscotch. I seem to be wavering on the spot, not being able to go forward. We call this situation a subconscious inner conflict. This is quite tiring. One day I get up as a smart person, the next day as a stupid one. One moment you can ask me anything and I know the answers, the other moment my head seems empty and I do not understand what you are asking for.
If this inner conflict is also true for fundamental beliefs like 'I want to live' versus 'I want to die', 'I can' versus 'I can't', 'I expect the best to happen' versus 'I expect the worst to happen' or 'I love myself' versus

'I hate myself', I remain wavering on the spot in my life as well. As soon as I build something, I also undermine it. I will find the courage to start again, but failing has already been taken into account. If there is an inner conflict, I want to shake myself up and push myself forward. Choose and go for it! But a little later I give up again.

Fortunately opposing beliefs can be transformed as well. I ask myself: 'What do I really want, what am I longing for?' and I can feel the joy of abundance enter my being: 'I am *very* smart'. We store this new belief into the subconscious mind and the conflict is gone. This means that from now on my brain will only be looking for similarities with 'I am very smart', both in the inner world and in the outer world. My brain is peaceful, when there is congruency between the inner and the outer world.

There is a special balance for the fundamental beliefs. It is the Core Belief Balance, by which, like I have indicated before[10], a foundation has been put underneath our existence. Clients, who have experienced this particular balance, are quite often very pleased with its results. When I ask for feedback in the next session, I can hear various comments like 'I caught myself expecting something good', 'I have been sleeping much better since then', 'My eczema has diminished a lot', 'I do not know what you have done to me in that one session. My life is flowing and, now that I am 35, I am going to live on my own, loose from my mother's apron strings'.


**Our beliefs determine who we are**

*'I have only recently discovered PSYCH-K but I would advise it to everyone. For the first time I dare to believe in miracles. I am convinced that it can correct persistent problems or even make them disappear. The theory behind PSYCH-K and its scientific evidence are quite understandable and real. For me this was a very important factor, because I do not like woolly theories. A second important aspect for me is that the therapist, or in the case of PSYCH-K the facilitator, exudes*

*what he or she stands for (PSYCH-K brings peace) and this was certainly the case with M.R.*

*I myself am also working in mental health care and I have always considered the therapy of counselling, in which people are brought to insights, to be the big solution. Until I noticed from my own experience that insights are not always enough. For instance, I had sufficient insight into my destructive pattern of relationships and wrong choice of partners, but each time I got trapped in the same pitfall again, no matter how conscious I was of this. I realized that there was something down there that I could not reach. This has led me to PSYCH-K and the result is that I have a new relationship now with a reliable, balanced and emotionally ripe partner. I am hopeful for the future and very grateful.'*
M.L.

The beliefs we gathered from the day of our conception until this day shape us into who we are now. All impressions, observations, experiences, interpretations are stored in our subconscious mind, our personal database. This whole is 'ME'. All beliefs together determine our values; they consist of our vision of life.

*Your beliefs become your thoughts*
*Your thoughts become your words*
*Your words become your actions*
*Your actions become your habits*
*Your habits become your values*
*Your values become your destiny*

Mahatma Gandhi

Changing beliefs has a direct impact on our thoughts and on our well-being, on how we relate to others, on our way of life, the value that we attribute to ourselves as part of the whole and as such on our fate, our destiny. Just as F.T. describes in the introduction, we can evolve from a depressed person to someone who is brimming over with life.

How do you transform yourself? By accepting everything that occurs as a useful opportunity. 'But we have so many limiting beliefs', I hear you objecting. That is right, we believe a number of so-called facts, which only limit us. It is quite a mess. And it is our choice to see it as an insurmountable mess or as a mountain of honey, from which we can manage to eat bit by bit, like Baloo the Bear in Jungle Book. With every transformation of a self-limiting belief into a self-enhancing one, we tend to become lighter. We leave our own weight (and important ego) behind and just start shining.

## "I am a believer because this option offers most possibilities"

Some people have had one or more religious experiences in their lifetime. They believe on the basis of experience. It is a belief based on experience. Others choose to believe; they see it as the most profitable option in order to further develop. I once heard a catholic priest say: "I believe because this option offers most possibilities of development." I was shocked, but could understand the logic as well. Believing that we are carried by Love brings about far more good things than just assuming that the world is based on coincidence and chaos. Believing in the immense power and the incredible possibilities of people has lifted them to a level that would not have been considered possible. This priest believed that 'if he believed in the possibilities of someone, it would become a reality for that person'.

What we believe – our beliefs – become our truth, and our reality. This is not *wishful thinking* but *self-fulfilling prophecy*. As I have explained before, our beliefs create the things we are convinced of. Believing and being convinced are the same. One person is convinced by logic, another one by feelings. No matter how the belief comes into being, as soon as it is there, it does its job. The only question we have to ask ourselves is: 'Is this belief helpful or is it undermining us?'

We can, against all experiences or facts, accept beliefs that are at odds with our present life. This is just because these beliefs suit us better. By embedding them into our subconscious mind, we create a new life. As soon as we have embedded a belief into our subconscious mind, our mind is trying to find similarities. As a result we will gain experiences that match this new belief.

Let me illustrate this with an example. As a pastor I did not believe in former or parallel lives. I was convinced of the fact that we have one life and that was it. Not only during my work at the hospital, but also in private counselling did I meet with people who told me experiences of other lives. Apparently I accepted this possibility, because after some time I also gained experiences that brought the reality of other lives a lot closer. A belief as such is not just the conclusion of an experience. It also creates openness to experiences and further experiences where the belief is embedded even more strongly.


**Beliefs can affect our health**

In *The Biology of Belief*, cell biologist Bruce Lipton describes how beliefs determine our bodily functions[11]. Although the book has a firm scientific basis and elaboration, it is the most exciting book I have ever read. Lipton describes how our cells react to beliefs. Either the cells are open, so that all nutrients can flow into the cell through the cell membrane, as cells flourish when they are open. Or the cells are closed, the cell membrane remains closed and they go into survival mode. Lipton discovered that the cell membrane is being opened or closed according to beliefs[12]. Beliefs are the keys. Physically, beliefs determine whether we function in a healthy way or in survival mode. There is nothing in between. Either we flourish or we barely survive. Our whole system functions in a binary way. We are light or heavy. With supporting beliefs we become light, with self-limiting beliefs we become dark and heavy.

The consequences of the reality of our cells functioning on the basis of beliefs are hardly comprehensible. One example: in our Western society we have the idea that getting a diagnosis about an inconvenience or a disease is the only possible way of effectively treating and healing it. Whereas, according to this 'new biology' every diagnosis and the corresponding prognosis just create the result of the disease. The more definitely the doctor claims that you are dying and the larger your confidence is in that doctor, the more chances you will get of actually dying from the disease. Unless you deliberately choose to change your beliefs[13]. As conscious beings, we can change our beliefs we can choose how to act and react[14].

Does this mean that PSYCH-K can cure all diseases? No, but it can help to trigger the self-healing response in the body by tracing and transforming the underlying limiting beliefs that may be creating an environment suitable for the proliferation of disease. Such beliefs may include, 'This disease is incurable', or 'There is nothing I can do to heal myself'. Whether the body is able to restore itself, depends on several factors like healthy food, a nice environment, relaxation instead of stress, ...

I felt an enormous change inside my body twice myself. My father was crippled on one side when he was only 60 years old. 'You are like your father', was told me time and time again. For years I have lived with the belief that 'Life will be over at 60. I have to do everything now'. It gave my life an enormous drive. It was now or never. Until one day I paid a visit to my 93-year-old grandmother. Afterwards I got into the car and thought 'I might as well take after my grandmother'. An enormous weight lifted from my shoulders. I felt light and happy. Although, ... getting old with all emotional ups and downs that I was experiencing, still would be a tough job. I did not know in fact if I really wanted that. Later, when I returned home after my first Advanced workshop, it happened again. I realized that, with the help of PSYCH-K, I could easily become 112. My cells were shouting with joy! With PSYCH-K I could handle every situation in my life. Now I am just taking after myself. I will gratefully celebrate life until the very end. After the Balance of Optimal Health I will take full responsibility for wanting to get old. I have readjusted the way in which I want to live: I am taking much more care of my body. It is the temple in which I am living. I take care of my teeth, I have lost the extra weight, I eat healthily, ... Because I am living with a new perspective!

In Chapter 9 we will go further into the beliefs in connection to our health. On www.freefullliving.com you will find a link to a TED Talk about the effect of our thinking about stress on the quality of our health[15].

Let us have a broader look at how beliefs are ingrained in our culture. There are cultures in which people are cured by the laying on of hands and cultures in which people have to drink poison or get it injected, in order to be cured. As soon as your system is embedded with the belief that healing occurs in this way, the experience and also the evidence will show. In medical science this is called 'the placebo effect'. Quite a lot of healing is due to this. With PSYCH-K we can effectively activate the placebo effect, which in fact corresponds to the self-healing capacity of the body. The fact that we are able to activate our self-healing capacity by means of beliefs has been confirmed by the research. More about that in Chapter 9 'A healthy mind in a healthy body'. Maybe we should mention that PSYCH-K is a process by which the subconscious mind of the person again accepts its real power to create a healthy environment. We just need to follow the inner logic of our subconscious mind. Based on experience, as soon as the subconscious is convinced, that PSYCH-K transforms, the processes will be set in motion automatically.

The different stories in this book will make it clear what the impact of beliefs is on our daily life. Now we have a good foundation to start with. We referred to stress before. In the next chapter we will pay attention to trauma and in the one after that to stress and total exhaustion.

# 2. PSYCH-K® Works Quickly and Effectively

'Albert Einstein said,
"Everything should be made as simple as possible, but not simpler."
That is the essential structure of PSYCH-K.' – Robert Williams

**PSYCH-K works quickly and effectively**

In the introduction to this book I have stressed that the objective of PSYCH-K is peace. Peace is a choice of our conscious mind to transform all disturbances of the subconscious mind in order to realize our highest objectives (superconscious mind). Every aspect is honoured: the skills of choice of the conscious mind, our experiences that are stored verbally and non-verbally and that automatically steer our behaviour (subconscious database) and our connection with each other and the higher entity (superconscious mind). It is in the free choice we have to connect ourselves to the highest energy and the assignment to the subconscious mind to clear the job itself, where the power and the speed of PSYCH-K lie. In doing so all levels of consciousness are honoured. When the conscious mind, the subconscious mind and the superconscious mind are in line with each other, we realize our highest potential. Our focus shifts from sticking to the past to creating a new future.

It is clear now that PSYCH-K is a process with fixed and flexible parts. It is like a sandwich with a new filling every day. The sandwich comprises the same basic ingredients with changing additions and variations. This keeps the application fascinating and working with PSYCH-K creative. In what follows both the fixed and the flexible elements will be dealt with. Fixed elements are making contact with the subconscious mind, choosing and testing what you want to change and checking if this change is in your highest interest. The subconscious mind is then checked to see whether it understands what has to take place, then engaging with the subconscious mind to do the job properly in its own way, checking if what you wanted to change was really achieved, and celebrating. Finally there is a first step of action. As indicated before, the flexible parts can vary. Sometimes it involves movements of the body that make the brain function as a whole, but it may also be an addition of energy or breathing exercises.

## Aiming directly at a new future

A process of transformation usually begins in the place where we are right now, with the assumption that the things that are happening do not make us happy. Our first step is becoming aware of what there is. A lot of techniques mainly focus on seeing what is there and staying put, accepting it as it is. PSYCH-K takes it to the next level: we consciously examine what is going on right now. We then formulate our wish and next we engage our subconscious mind in realizing this wish.

This morning my husband did not feel well when he woke up. We acknowledged this and according to habit he would have left it at that. Perhaps he would have laid down a little longer or he could have taken the day somewhat more quietly in order to avoid the queasiness. He chose to examine his system for stress elements, and yes he found some. To begin with he did a Stress Balance for three minutes so that at least he could decide with a clear head what he wanted to do about it. He still did not feel well after this. Next I asked him the magical PSYCH-K question[1]: 'What do you want instead?' In this case I formulated the question slightly differently: 'How would you like to feel?' His first reaction was predictable: 'I would like to feel less tired and washed-out'. I rephrased the question: 'Less tired and washed-out, but what is it you really want?' The answer was: 'Feeling fit'. The test, of which I will tell more, indicated that he did not feel fit at the moment. We did a Balance for 'I feel fit' and a few minutes later he again took pleasure in this new day. He was able to function normally and brightly throughout the whole day.

The subconscious mind cannot create something you do not want. You can leave something out, but not create it. It is like being in a restaurant. Imagine that you would like to eat in a nice restaurant and the waiter comes to you and asks you what you want to eat. You answer: 'No chicken today'. Then this waiter goes into the kitchen and tells the chef: 'No chicken for this person'. The chef asks politely: 'Please ask her what she would like to eat, then I can cook it'. The waiter returns: 'What do you want to eat? The chef will prepare it for you with pleasure'. If you say now: 'No fish today', you will irritate the waiter and the chef. They will not bring you anything; the waiter will probably even ignore you. If you had one more chance to decide what you wanted to eat, it would be wise to take it. Otherwise you will get stuck with what you do not want.

This is what happens with our subconscious mind. It can prepare everything we wish, we only have to know what we want. Most energy is lost by focusing on what we do not want although it is a good starting point in order to focus next on our wishes: 'What is it I do want?' Quite often we are so focused on what we do not want, that we no longer give the order to fulfil our wishes.

*'What do you want instead?'*

## Establish communication with the subconscious mind: testing

In order to test if there is stress in our subconscious mind, whether something is true or not or just between a 'yes' and a 'no', we use muscle testing[2]. A muscle test is a kinesiology test[3], it measures if there is little or a lot of electromagnetic flow between both hemispheres. If there is a good circulation it is a sign that the whole brain is being used. Then we are at our best, we have access to our whole potential. As indicated in the previous chapter, we need our whole brain in order to realize what we want. If there is a good electromagnetic circulation, it will be felt in all our muscles.

Muscle testing does not change subconscious beliefs; rather it is used strictly as a communication tool with the subconscious and superconscious minds in order to guide a belief change process. Also, in PSYCH-K, we don't use it as a source of Ultimate Truth, but rather as an "advisor" about the safety and appropriateness of Balancing for the goals chosen by the conscious mind.

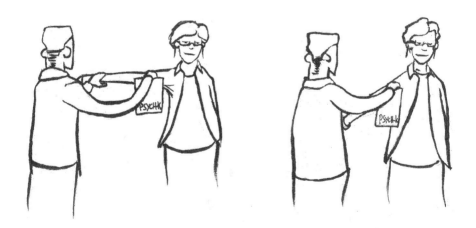

*If with a light push on the wrist, the arm stays horizontal, we call this 'Strong'. If there is little electromagnetic flow in the system, the arm goes 'Weak' and moves downwards.*

Research has shown that, when we say our own name and do a muscle test, we usually get a strong response[4]. If we say a false name, we test weakly. I invite you, the reader, to try this with me. Look down and say with full belief: 'My name is … (and then you mention your own name)'. Swallow immediately and see what happens. Now do the same with a false name. Look down and say: 'My name is (and use as a man a female name and vice versa)'. Swallow again. Do you notice the difference?

Most people feel that the false name cannot be swallowed down. In popular speech we say 'That sticks in my throat'. If you were able to swallow the false name anyway, try again with 'I am wearing red shoes' or something similar.
If this swallowing test doesn't work for you, there are a lot of other ways to self-muscle test[5].
Some people can learn muscle testing from a book; most of us need to be taught how to do it properly. For me, I learned it during a workshop and we are teaching it in the PSYCH-K Basic workshop.
Our brain cannot unambiguously support false beliefs. In these cases there is little electromagnetic flow between both hemispheres. This minimal electromagnetic flow is to be felt in our whole body. Brunhild Hofmann, a German PSYCH-K instructor wrote 'PSYCH-K im täglichen Leben. Für eine entspannte Kommunikation zwischen Bewusstsein und Unterbewusstsein'[6], a small book in which muscle tests are presented using different muscles. In the PSYCH-K Basic workshop several ways are taught to do muscles tests.

We can do muscle tests with ourselves and/or with other people. The first time muscle testing was used with me was during my first visit to a homeopath. She wanted to find out how many drops of a certain substance I had to take in and she tested it by doing a muscle test. In order to do so she used my fingers. At first I thought it a little weird that a doctor asked information from my subconscious mind by means of muscle testing. Now that I have mastered the process, it is very nice to have easy access to my subconscious mind.

Actually muscle testing is a very rational method. Our subconscious mind is, just like a computer, binary: the light is on or the light is off. However there are some items we have to pay attention to while muscle testing. We get the most reliable results when looking down[7]. Then our focus is in the kinaesthetic field of feelings. It is best to relax our body and to keep our chin horizontal. We are sitting upright and the electromagnetic energy can flow freely through our body.

Muscle testing is infallible, at least if your subconscious beliefs support muscle testing clearly and faultlessly. That is why in the Basic workshop we make sure that the subconscious mind is unambiguous about the results of muscle testing. When in doubt about the muscle tests, this doubtful reality is created in order to create conformity between my beliefs and my actions. Doubting is not the purpose. Therefore we embed the beliefs '(self-)muscle testing works for me' and 'my muscle tests give me reliable information' in the subconscious mind. Then the corresponding reality can be created.

Correct muscle testing is of the utmost importance for the use of PSYCH-K. It ensures an easy access to the subconscious mind. As soon as fluent communication is established with our subconscious mind, we can test if there is stress in our system and which beliefs are stored in our database. This is our choice.

## A straightforward choice: a conscious mind

The function of the conscious mind is to choose from the many possibilities available. The conscious mind makes choices by paying attention. We evaluate and choose from several options.

L.G. has attended the Basic, Advanced and Divine Workshops.

*'What does PSYCH-K mean to me? It is so incredibly beautiful to find out how much influence you have on your life. Due to small and big traumas your life can be completely upside down. Everything you have ever known or thought you knew about life has then suddenly*

*disappeared and you have to start all over again. This happened to me. I could only take small steps quite slowly and carefully. With PSYCH-K I now take big, important and powerful steps. What a wonderful feeling it is to have such vast control. This will be forever! For the rest of my life. The most beautiful thing is that everything feels so normal. It is a kind of coming home, remembering. I acknowledge that this is the way I am and I can transform things myself. And apart from that I can share it and apply it to others. I can offer them the same feeling.*
*Once I described PSYCH-K to someone with the words: with PSYCH-K you build on stone and no longer on quicksand. You can move on. And so much more.'*
*L.G.*

This morning my husband could have chosen other beliefs, like 'I am healthy', 'It is OK for me to have an off-day', 'I enjoy my breakfast', ... I also made a suggestion to him: 'I feel energetic'. These were my words, not his. The best choice is the one you make yourself. When they are your words, it is your energy; it is your vibration. The highest frequency you will achieve is by expressing the text that has the most importance to you now. The beliefs we 'install' in the subconscious mind of the partner should fit the partner's belief. If I impose beliefs as a facilitator, it won't work at all.

*'I had only just started working with someone who had followed a good deal of therapies in order to be less troubled by her traumatic youth experiences.*
*She had been very sceptical before, but she was quite pleased to find out that this is a method containing no judgment!'*
*M.C.*

This is what is so special about PSYCH-K: we can only create in the subconscious mind what is of great importance to the partner. The priority is what the system of the person chooses. The behaviour of 'I know what is good for you' is not appropriate; brainwashing is impossible.

A young lady aged15 came to me for a session. She came accompanied by her mother. Her school results were not satisfying and they wanted to do something about that. At a certain point I asked her: 'Do you want to test "studying is nice"?' She agreed. It turned out to be a weak response. As I had expected, her whole brain did not support this belief. When I asked her: 'Do you want to change this?' she did not. She said: 'I will never like studying'. Her mother insisted, but without any result. It was her choice to not like studying. In the past she had had a lot of experiences with how tiresome studying was, so the belief 'studying is no fun' was in her system. On the spot she decided she did not want to like studying. Period. That is a pity as choosing another way of seeing things could have brought her a lot of joy. I have advised her to attend a workshop, so that she could personally choose what she would like to realize. If she does, she can find out for herself what she wants and she could incorporate that into her system as an automatic operation.

Our conscious mind makes the choice about what we want to introduce into our subconscious mind as an automatic response. This is the objective we want to go for by following the further procedure. I will describe this process in what follows. You can see how it works. In order to try it out yourself or to apply it to others, it is imperative to attend a workshop. We train our skills when we practise together with others. Whilst practising you will discover the pitfalls.

**The whole universe works together in order to help us: the super-consciousness**

As soon as we know what we desire, we submit this wish to the super-consciousness. That is the place that knows what is good for us as a unique human being in relationship to others. Most of the time our wishes match what is good for us, but sometimes we cannot see the greater whole. At this point we use the muscle test with the intention of knowing what will be the best for us now and in the long run. And we know that we can do Balances at all times to readjust the effects. When I was preparing my third PSYCH-K workshop, I left my house when no one else was home. While packing I realized the projector was missing. Apparently we had lent it out. To make matters worse, I could not reach the people who had it. I made the decision to buy a projector, I phoned a company and was able to borrow a projector for the next few days. We agreed that we would call each other to determine how this projector would be delivered on Sunday evening. At the location where the workshop took place, I looked at my mobile phone. The screen said: PUK code needed. Apparently I had pressed some keys a number of times and the phone had been blocked. Was this an unlucky day or a sign?

The first thing you can do in such a situation is a Stress Balance. During this Balance it went through my mind: 'You can do nothing on your own', the words that my mother had told me hundreds of times during my puberty. They were fixed in my repertoire of beliefs. I was alone, so I created my 'being unable to'. At the same time it was quite a personal delusion. I have always been proud to be someone who likes working together with other people. Was this somehow unconscious evasive behaviour?!

When I asked myself: 'What is it that I want?' there came only one answer: I want to do it on my own! I submitted my 'I can do it alone' to my superconscious mind and I did not receive permission to embed this belief in my subconscious automatic system. At first I was upset. It is good to do things on your own isn't it? See how difficult I made life for myself now? Then I realised that doing everything alone straight away would alienate me from my social context. It would stop the dynamics of giving and receiving between me and them. I readjusted the belief to 'When necessary I can do things on my own' and this time the superconscious mind agreed. A couple of minutes later the Balance was finished and ever since then this belief belongs to my automatic behaviour. Everything has gone smoothly since, even when I am alone.

Language is creation, creating the right word or the right sentence is the highest reality. By directing attention to the superconscious mind during a Balance we are certain to participate in creating what is the best for ourselves and for others.


H.V. more than once attended the Basic, the Advanced and the Divine Workshops.

*'What do you do when you do not get "safe and appropriate" result? Take heed. Accept that such a moment may contain special wisdom. This could be the breakthrough in your life. You will find an example here.*

*In 2008 I worked with P. (a friend of mine) with a belief (I do not remember exactly which). We did not get a "safe and appropriate" for it. In such a situation the question that often helps is "Why is this balance not safe and appropriate?"*

*Together we examined it. Through muscle testing you can communicate with the Higher Self; intuition and conversation will do the rest. In this way we found out that doing this balance would only be safe and appropriate, if I left the room during the process of change.*

*This fact surprised my friend. For him I was just one of the people with whom he thought he felt at ease. He discovered that in fact he had no idea at all of what "I feel at ease" could be. For him this was the eye-opener of the evening. He learned that he in fact had never before felt how it was to be relaxed together with people. He changed the belief to "I feel safe and relaxed in the presence of people." He did his balance, while I was out of the room.*

*That evening P. had a date with a woman. At 2am in the morning he sent me an SMS saying he had never before experienced such a beautiful presence...'*
*H.V.*

By contacting the superconscious mind and asking its permission whether embedding something in our subconscious mind is in our highest interest within PSYCH-K, we make use of the greatest power as it is known in world traditions. It is the power, which people focus on when they meditate, when they practice mindfulness and the power that is addressed in several religions.

I myself have a catholic background and so I am trained in analyzing, understanding and commenting on the Bible stories. I made the discovery while using PSYCH-K that the healing stories in the Bible show the same structure as a PSYCH-K balance. Just like we ask permission, Jesus looks up, before someone is healed and asks permission to the powers that surround us to be directed in this person's favour. With a pure intention we have this power at our disposal even today. In principle we do not need anyone else to use it, we ourselves have access to it, and we are part of it.

The superconscious mind is in and around us; it is comparable to the water in which fish are swimming. It is the greatest power that exists, it is responsible for the beginning of life, and when it is concentrated, it is capable of definitively lifting blockages. Is PSYCH-K a kind of faith healing? I do not see it as such. The greatest difference is that the person himself mobilizes this power in favour of himself or of the partner with whom he or she is working. Neither a facilitator, nor any other outsider can use this power for us. It is the system of the person you work with that makes the connection. We do not need priests or intermediaries. By connecting with the superconscious mind the person himself checks what is best for him or her. He or she is then enabled to realize what has always been potentially there. A Balance therefore is directed at creation, not so much at keeping off a so-called disaster.

How can we imagine these powers? It is the field we live in[8]. I think of these powers as the empty space within an atom.

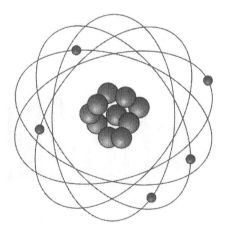

As a student I learned that I myself and everything around me consists of atoms. Every atom consists of positively loaded protons and negatively loaded electrons. In my younger years importance was only given to the matter of the proton and the electrons. In the meantime we have learned that, if we joined together only the matter of for example Mount Everest, without the empty space between protons and electrons, this mountain would fit in an ordinary room. However, this compact block would keep the same weight. Even we ourselves, and all the matter we know of, consists of an immense amount of empty space.

This empty space has to do with the reality in which we live. Particles however big or small are connected with each other and thus exchange information directly. When I realized this the phenomena of telepathy, simultaneous discoveries in different places of the world, family constellations, influencing at a distance, etc. became obvious events.

In our quantum universe the information flow is determined by intention more than through matter. Energy flows where intention goes. Since the discovery of the Higgs particle we know how space 'sticks' together. We look like separate entities because the different substances we are made of stick together because of this Higgs particle. This is what I understand from physics as an absolute layman.

Within PSYCH-K the superconscious mind is not only contacted in order to get permission. It works in very different ways. Through the super-conscious mind we have access to messages that are hidden in the situations in which we find ourselves. We can make the whole of the universe work together in order to make our wishes come true, we can work with people who are not physically available at that moment, … There are lots of possibilities that can only be applied in the highest interest of all participants[9]. This is quite important to me as an ethicist. We even have an entire workshop, the Divine Integration Retreat, which is devoted to realizing a flowing contact with the superconscious mind.

PSYCH-K differs from most spiritual techniques, because it does not only work with the superconscious mind, but also explicitly with the subconscious mind. The subconscious mind can be channelled in a safe and appropriate way to our own and our environments' highest good. That is why we communicate openly with it, in the language of the subconscious mind.

## Respecting the language of the subconscious mind

The language we speak to one another differs from the language of the subconscious mind. Generally we use quite a number of abstract words, whereas the language of the subconscious mind is literal and simple. In order for the subconscious mind to understand what we mean, it may be necessary to translate a rather abstract wish into concrete sensory reality.

If I have the objective to 'write a book about PSYCH-K' it will be necessary for me to imagine what that book will look like. How, where and when am I going to write? Who is going to publish and distribute it? What kind of reading public do I consider? Will it only be printed in Dutch or also in other languages? How much time will I have to allocate to write it? Which name will I have under the preface? The better I can visually imagine what it will look like, the more energy will be centralized around this project. We call this the visual preparation. In order to make it as sensory as possible and therefore to be fitting for the subconscious mind, we also need an auditory and kinaesthetic (sensitive) preparation. What do I hear people saying about me if I write this book? What am I saying to myself?
How do I feel in this respect? In order to fully absorb the writing process, I close my eyes and try to physically experience where in my body I feel it the most. It is wonderful to feel this writing process completely developing in all my cells. In the end I know perfectly well what I want to reach with this book: making PSYCH-K accessible to everybody.

Each belief, which could be too abstract for the subconscious mind, has to be checked in order to see if this threefold design: Visual, Auditory and Kinaesthetic – we call this a 'VAK to the Future' – will be necessary. If a wish or desire remains too abstract, our system cannot imagine anything at all and so, like the chef in the kitchen of the restaurant, we cannot create what we don't choose.

Subconscious language still has another characteristic: it is leading. Just as we do not ask a three- or four-year-old child 'Would you put on your slippers?' because such a question offers too many possible answers (yes, no, perhaps, later, not now...), we do not question the subconscious mind. Just as we address a four-year-old child with 'It is time to put on your slippers', we do give the subconscious mind clear directives. If the subconscious mind is approached leadingly, it will carry out this order directly and unambiguously.

Leading language is also used in other assistance techniques like hypnosis. PSYCH-K differs from hypnosis because the person remains conscious during the entire process. He or she can choose to stop the Balance at any moment.

If we respect the language of the subconscious mind, an abstract wish or desire, expressed by the conscious mind can automatically be carried out. What is more, the synchronicity in the universe takes care of the simple materialization of our wishes[10].

As soon as we send an unambiguous signal into space, like for instance 'I have self-confidence', we immediately have the chance to enact the newly required possibilities.

*'I., 10 years old, came to me with her parents in order to Balance to get more self-confidence in all aspects of her life. It was just before Christmas.*
*When she returned home, a schoolteacher called her to ask if she could read a little text in a Church service a week later.*
*Normally I. would have become stressed and certainly refused, she said, but now she told the teacher quite gently that she would love to do it and stunned her parents with that.'*
*R.M.*

## We leave the job to the subconscious mind

One of the big trumps of PSYCH-K is that we leave the job to be done by the subconscious mind itself. In chapter about trauma we become aware that our most disturbing behaviour finds it origin in situations of loss of control. During loss of control no memories are being stored. Separate sensory signals are laden with the signal 'Help. I am dying'. These sensory signals are not consciously accessible. The fact that our body works in this way, makes it impossible for us to find out with our conscious mind where the origin of the present defensive or reactive behaviour lies. Without memory the conscious mind cannot trace these alarm signals. As an escape route it tells a fantasy story about this.

My whole environment knew that, if you were walking alongside me, you had better walk to my right. I could not bear walking to the right of someone. I had an explanation for this. I don't see so well from my left eye and before I wore glasses (before my twelfth year!) it was necessary for people to walk to my right in order for me to see them. This had turned into a habit. This is the story that my conscious mind had made up to explain why it was absolutely unbearable for me to have someone walking to my left. During a workshop I did a Balance for this. It is over. You can walk to either side of me now. My subconscious mind has found the stress and transformed it. I do not know what ever was the matter. That has never reached my conscious mind. And I don't need to go searching for it.

It has been a serious handicap – when aiding and assisting ourselves or one another – that we do not have a memory of the most traumatic moments in our life, but still have kept sensory alarm signals. That is why people continue to experience stress and panic without it being possible to be solved. We also know that people 'tell little stories' in order to explain why they behave as they do and we challenge their value, but because of the lack of an effective technique we keep on looking for methods in order to get on with ourselves, to distract ourselves or to channel the ways in which we try to let off steam. Fortunately the PSYCH-K procedure does offer access to these sensory signals and so we can weaken the alarm in no time.

The only thing we have to do is to engage the subconscious mind in tracing and transforming the stress that is in our system in connection with a belief, a relationship or a situation itself. Is our body ready to transform the stress? Does it want to do so? And is it able to do so? If we have a positive answer to these three conditions of possibility, we only have to give the order to execute the transformation.

At the same time we test if the subconscious mind at this moment physically gives priority to realizing the transformation. In order to balance the core beliefs, which correct the foundation of our life, the subconscious mind generally needs an hour. If at that moment there are other physical needs that have to be met, they will take priority.
Sometimes just before going to sleep I have a clear idea about what troubles me. Then I want to work on it immediately. But at the same time I am tired and want to sleep. In these moments my subconscious mind 'passes'. 'It' doesn't want to do it then.
The same can happen when a partner is hungry or thirsty or has to go to the toilet. Physical needs take precedence over doing a Balance.


**The subconscious mind chooses the procedure to do the job**

The subconscious mind also chooses the way in which it wants to realize the transformation. This can be whole-brain movements, it may be the addition of energy or a goal-oriented way of breathing. There are short, even very short and longer Balances.

To realize that the subconscious mind is doing the job is to be experienced during a Resolution Balance. The subconscious mind receives the task to bring the arms in motion from an open to a closed position. This is a testimony of V.V.D., when she experienced this for the first time during the Basic workshop.

*'What it boils down to is that I was stunned by the fact that my arms automatically came together without myself having to do anything at all. I thought this would not work without any self-manipulation, but I gave it a chance and just waited. It was a wonderful feeling that "something" brought my arms back together! It created a real wow effect.'*
*V.V.D.*

According to what there is to be transformed in the subconscious mind, the same Balance can last a shorter or longer time. The subconscious mind decides. For a Core Belief Balance I usually plan one hour and a half in my agenda. However, I do not know how much time the subconscious mind needs to finish the job.

The spectacular testimony at the beginning of the third chapter about trauma, deals with results after one Balance. But this one Balance, that changed the woman's whole life, took at least five hours of work – and this is very exceptional. Fortunately I had some unscheduled time in my agenda that day; otherwise we would have had to make an appointment at a later date to continue the process. The limitation is not in the subconscious mind of the partner, but in the limited possibilities of the facilitator.

The subconscious mind knows what the problem is and as soon as it has committed itself to the transformation, it starts working. Time does not exist in the subconscious mind, as it is always NOW. So, it is carrying out now what the conscious mind has ordered.

Some people dislike certain movements like for instance cross-crawls[11]. It is remarkable that the subconscious mind will then not choose this process. If working with energy is not your cup of tea, then your subconscious mind will probably choose balances that do not need this process of transformation unless the time is ripe in order to let go of the limiting beliefs or stress connected with energy. When using PSYCH-K we learn to trust whatever shows up and we consider whatever happens as a gift in order to grow.

At the end of the Advanced workshop we teach a high-speed way of transformation. At that time the subconscious mind is so used to the Balances that it can – so to speak with a snap of the fingers – transform whatever the conscious mind asks for.
As for myself there really is life before and after the Advanced workshop. Not only have I since used the speedy way in order to appease whatever comes up in my life – and it takes less than one minute – but since that

workshop I also know that I can handle all situations in my life. I have the tools. And that gives me quite a profound feeling of peace.

According to the procedure, the position of the body also changes during the process. There are balances that take place in a sitting position, others in a standing or lying position. The high-speed Balance can be applied always and everywhere, even during driving the car. Do you feel stress in a traffic jam? Time for a new Balance. This time imposed on you to stay in the car is given to you in order to further shape the future. That is how simple life can be.


## Checking if the transformation has taken place

If you have completed the procedure that the subconscious mind has chosen in order to carry out the transformation, you will also want to check if it really took place.

This I what I love about PSYCH-K: you can check if your efforts have achieved the intended result. In contrast to most other techniques it is possible to determine the results of a Balance through muscle testing. Muscle testing works in a binary way, it is 'yes' or 'no'. In fact it is always 'yes'. The subconscious mind has initially committed itself to deliver the intended result. As soon as the contract is confirmed, the result will be there. The subconscious mind is a machine that infallibly carries out what has been asked, just like for instance a coffee machine does. We press the button and we know the result.

Our conscious mind, which likes to keep the impression of having everything under control, is often amazed at the speed with which the job has been carried out. Because the subconscious mind does the job, the speed is determined by the subconscious mind and not by the conscious mind. The subconscious mind is more than a million times faster than the conscious mind, which explains the astonishment we feel. We do a muscle test in order to give the conscious mind the necessary information: the belief required is in the system, the alarm signals have been disconnected from the situation, the relationship with the person peaceful. Whatever it is, it will be tested in binary mode and the result is crystal clear.

The conscious mind enjoys the control. You do not only consciously determine what you want to realize, you also double-check if what you desired has happened[12]. This occurs with all mechanical processes in industry and in healthcare. So far it was only in mental care where this feedback was lacking. Through PSYCH-K the mind has become transparent. We do not only test whatever we desire, we transform whatever stops us into something that will support us and then think of what the next step could be. The first one is 'celebrating'.

## Celebrate!

Every balance ends with 'Celebrate!' The partner is asked to do something, which shows that he or she accepts the result. By celebrating, we both honour the subconscious and the superconscious mind of the person.

The subconscious mind has committed itself to carrying out the job. The fact that less stress is present in the system after a balance is in itself already a celebration for the body. Should we add anything else? Well, the subconscious mind automatically carries out the same patterns. A PSYCH-K balance has a fixed pattern. Both at the beginning and at the end always the same steps are being followed. This is quite useful for the subconscious mind, because it is programmed in such a way that it plays the same scenarios over and over again. By ending every PSYCH-K balance in the same way, we support the way in which the subconscious mind is structured. By 'Celebrating!' we give the explicit signal that we are grateful because of a job well done. By thanking the subconscious mind for doing the job at the end of a balance, we build extra confidence. This will lead to more trust when performing PSYCH-K balances.
This Celebrate! action puts PSYCH-K in line with the world traditions. We are thankful for the renewed life, for the extra possibilities, for the stress that will never return in combination with that particular

situation. By celebrating we recognize that we live 'in grace', that everything we wish is accessible. Our human possibilities are unique and so much more extensive than we ever thought possible.

'Celebrating!' is thanking in joy. The person, who goes through the transformation, determines the way in which it should happen. In my practice I have observed a number of celebrations. There are people who keep quiet for one minute, drink some water, make the movement of Namaste, hug themselves or hug me, do a little dance, stand on their hands, give a high five, … According to the principles underlying PSYCH-K it is the person himself who determines the way it should be done.

As soon as the system is in peace with the new perspective, the Balance is over. Life can engage itself into the new direction. Renewed? The last step of a Balance is action, in order to realize in the inner or outer world what has been installed in the automatic system.


**Living freely and fully: taking action**

As soon as a new belief has been installed in the subconscious mind, the subconscious mind scans reality for similarities. I have once experienced this 'scanning of reality' in a very real way.

I am a curious person, so I try to get insight into the limits of what we can reach with PSYCH-K. The next testimony is one of the experiments to which I have surrendered myself.

A lot of people in our Western society struggle with their weight. I myself am 1.70m tall and a few years ago I weighed 85kg, so I know what I am talking about. I followed a protein diet once and after promising myself that I would never follow that same diet again, I reached 72kg. I was quite pleased with the result. When I got married I used to weigh 68kg, so this seemed a sensible weight to me. I had always been told that I was 'well built' and as I have a trusting disposition, I was happy with this.

I chose to do a balance with the belief 'I weigh 60kg'. What a challenge! The first step of action was leaving out the butter on my thickly covered sandwich.

As soon as I had done this Balance, I tested 'strongly' – which means that 'I weigh 60kg' was OK for my subconscious mind. While the muscle test indicated this, the next two months the result on the scales was 72kg. The Balance had worked, but without any tangible result.

Then I had a client who happened to follow a diet against Candida. Candida is a mould that can be present in the whole body, especially in the intestine, under the nails and between the toes. Candida mostly exists as a side effect of antibiotics and causes several complaints. Understanding the description given by this man, I suspected that this mould had also lodged itself into my system.

As soon as he talked about his diet, I knew that this was something for me. Exactly at that moment I experienced in my body what it means that our subconscious mind 'scans reality for similarities'. It spontaneously discovers what is in line with the beliefs that are stored in you. I knew that if I followed the diet, the 60kg would be reality.

But consciously I did not like this diet, so I did not choose it!

The week after I met a friend who also followed this cure. The fact that he could continue seemed to lower the threshold for me. But still, I did not want to choose it!

On a PSYCH-K Introduction and Practice Day, which I organized a week later, two interested people showed up who also followed this cure – remark that I am now talking about a 'cure' which made the step even a lot easier.

A couple of weeks later I had a health scan taken. From the results it appeared that my intestine contained a large quantity of Candida mould. This result finally made me make up my mind. I consequently decided to follow this cure against Candida and eight months later I got the confirmation that all Candida had left my system. I felt a lot fitter!

At the end of this cure I weighed 57kg, now it is back up to a comfortable 60kg. As an extra I also got strong white healthy nails. The belief 'I am well-built' was replaced with 'I have a slim and powerful body'.

Something important from this experience became obvious to me about PSYCH-K. It is not, because something tests quite strongly in our subconscious mind that it will immediately be realized in reality. We need certain action steps in order to bring a belief into practice. The beliefs in my subconscious mind therefore anticipated reality. The beliefs have found a place in my system, which means that the subconscious mind scans the environment, both inside my thinking and in the outer world, for correspondences. So it becomes quite easy to automatically realize these beliefs. But action is required.

In fact the realization of this one belief corresponds with the beliefs about optimal health, for which I also did a Balance. The Balance for optimal health is a separate Balance, which, just like the Core Belief Balance, installs a cluster of 22 double beliefs in the subconscious mind. People who get old in a healthy way, have these beliefs in their system; 'I am in perfect health' and being free from destructive intestine mould of course go together. My subconscious mind has realized everything simultaneously.

As a matter of fact I can still decide for myself to oppose my automatic impulses. It is not because I feel what I have to do, that I do not have the free will to oppose this. I have tried this for a very long time, but 'it summoned' me to follow. My subconscious mind sent me in the direction of the beliefs that are to be found in my database. If these beliefs are destructive, then I will be inclined to show destructive behaviour. If the beliefs are constructive, then it will be easy for me to carry out what is healthy for me. The past for me is over. I am no longer doomed to just repeat the same destructive behaviour. I choose to live a healthy life and it is easy for me to act accordingly.

Not all beliefs need eight months in order to be realized. Most of them are directly put into action from the inside, although it might be necessary to take a first step of action. A Balance changes our potential; a first action step changes the reality. To take action in our inner and outer world is a merit to us.[13] We effectively build a world we love to live in. As soon as we take action, the ball starts rolling.

For example once I did a Core Belief Balance with a young woman. When she came for a session the second time, I asked her if she had noticed that anything had changed. She said not, but she had caught herself anticipating good. In herself the belief 'I expect the best to happen' was put in action. She had never before in her life experienced the feeling to expect the best.

This leads us to one of the difficulties PSYCH-K has to fight in order to break through in all domains of life and on all scopes: all changes happen from the subconscious mind of the person. He or she feels his or her behaviour as something that belongs to him/herself. Therefore he or she will not attribute the possible changes to one Balance or other. Whoever applies PSYCH-K regularly, will look different in a short time: more vital, healthier, with a lot more joy of life and energy. Living freely and fully is not only possible; it realizes itself.

As a conclusion the power and the speed of PSYCH-K are to be ascribed to the following factors.

- It is radically directed at a joyful future for oneself and the whole, and it effectively will create it.
- It allows us to test what kinds of beliefs are stored in the subconscious mind and it transforms subconscious stress.
- It makes free choice really free: undisturbed by awkward sub-conscious disturbances. That is why we can take true responsibility for our own life.
- It is only possible to transform what the person him/herself wishes.
- Only what is in the highest interest of the person-in-relationship can be added to the subconscious mind.
- Open communication is possible, both with the subconscious mind and with the superconscious mind (although the latter will not easily be caught, our conscious mind remaining responsible for the choices we make).
- With PSYCH-K the subconscious mind is addressed directly. It follows the orders to transform whatever the person wants.
- We do not need an effort to realize the good: the subconscious mind automatically carries out whatever we choose.
- By allowing the subconscious mind to do the job itself, the hidden disturbances in the subconscious mind are transformed, the parts of the subconscious mind of which there doesn't exist any memories (generally called the 'unconscious').

- The subconscious mind itself determines the time it needs to realize the transformation. Once the subconscious has accepted to remove the stress factors, the job will be done to the very end.
- The results of PSYCH-K are to be checked through muscle testing. We do not have to remain in doubt about whether the process has worked out.
- Because the subconscious mind does the job, this process works more than a million times faster than techniques in which the results depend on the concentration or the effort of the person involved.
- The result is peace, conformity between the database of the person, whatever he or she chooses him/herself and the superconscious mind.
- Every Balance ends in celebration! This last step in the protocol does not only make PSYCH-K effective, but also a fine occupation.
- The subconscious mind scans reality so that in the inner and outer world, whatever the person chose is automatically realized through actions.

# 3. Trauma

*"Trauma is a set of perceptions associated with a painful emotional, or physical event. When you change the perception of the event at the subconscious level of the mind, you can often change the effect of the trauma, emotionally and physically." – Robert M. Williams*

Trauma, stress and total exhaustion physically seem to comprise three different processes. In this chapter we will treat the first one.

Trauma starts with loss of control. Trauma-related behaviour is triggered by the amygdala, the centre of fear in our brain[1]. I suppose it is a possibility that trauma, stress and total exhaustion are similar as their origin could be the same but with the knowledge that I have at this very moment, I cannot verify this hypothesis, nor exclude it. However, it does not matter that much: trauma, stress and total exhaustion can be transformed by means of PSYCH-K.

In this chapter I will closely examine how trauma comes into being and it works on us. In the next chapter I will focus on stress and total exhaustion.

Before diving into this heavy matter we have to remind ourselves that we humans like to be open and curious[2]. Our whole bodily system works optimally in open, free and relaxed conditions. This is what we are aiming at, so as to be the best we can be. If there is peace, we are relaxed.
Throughout this chapter you will find out how hard our body tries to reach this objective. We are 'hedonistic animals' who grow to the highest level of humanity when growing up happens in safe and loving conditions[3]. That is our objective.

**Trauma**

Case history. This person was sexually abused as a child. She took part in two PSYCH-K sessions and then attended the Basic workshop. According to her, the effects she describes are due to the first session.

*'How it used to be and how it is now*

*For about 25 years I dragged myself through life. Not a day passed by when I did not think of wanting to be dead (suicidal tendencies). Now I want to live! Imagine! Even when there are a lot of worries and problems in my life, I still want to live!*

*Formerly I fried a steak in a pan and in the meantime I was vomiting in the sink next to it. For years I could not eat meat, rice pudding (the feeling of lumps in my mouth), a flan dish, pudding, yoghurt, whipped cream... Now I have already eaten some little pieces of steak without queasiness. It was delicious actually. I have also tasted lamb (which I had never done before) without retching and in fact it was delicious (freedom!).*
*I am more forgiving, I do not take myself nor my painful feelings so seriously anymore, I am more assertive, I dare to be myself. Although I still take the feelings of others into account, I am quietly able to express my preferences, ways of thinking and more. I used to be convinced that I could never do anything well enough for other people. Now I am the one proposing to help them. I care much more about, and am more interested, in them. I can put things into perspective; I can think and evaluate things (weigh up the pros and cons) before I decide. I have a new sense of dignity and self-respect; I have more self-confidence and take care of myself in a more loving way (I love myself).*

*I am neither dirty, nor worthless nor defiled nor lost forever. Thanks to PSYCH-K I have won instead of lost and that cannot be taken away from me ever! Lots of things can be done to me in life, but with the balance of stress and the "implantation" of beliefs I can get rid of all pain. That provides certainty.*

[The Core Belief Balance][4] has turned me completely upside down, has shaken me up. I had lost sight of everything, but eventually I was allowed to fill up the "empty spaces" myself. The "little voice" inside my head does no longer determine my comings and goings. Instead of having to do everything compulsively, I can now just choose from which mug or glass I drink. I now am free to choose for myself.

That one flashback, which ravaged my life from the time I still was a tiny little girl, is now just a memory without everything that it did to me. (In fact from that moment I wanted to be dead.)

The people who are closest to me (husband, mother, friends) tell me that I have changed a lot. I am no longer as emotional as I was and I like that! I like the rational hemisphere (I wish I could have used it earlier). Crying over the smallest foolishness, the role of the victim, the depressions, it is all gone. Our family life has improved a lot because I am more rational now and do not start crying immediately or take up the victim's role. I used to want a divorce every month when my periods came.
I tend to live much more consciously than before. The world around me seems more genuine (more real). The haziness inside my head is gone (dissociation). I often felt like Shrek, with his many layers, like an onion... the layers are gone... and I am very grateful for this. At last I dare to be myself!!!

There are no more sharks that frighten me in the swimming pool. Counting from 1 to 4 and at the same time stamping my feet, it is all gone. Repeating some words in my head and so on... the obsessive compulsory eccentricities – or whatever one might call them – they are all gone.
The things I have noted down here (and that is not all of it) are what I experienced after just one Balance (the Core Belief Balance) (the sheet with "I want to live", "I can..."). There is still a lot of work to be done, but I do not want to be perfect anymore. My life has become liveable and that is what I have pursued for years and that is my wish for everyone.

Thank you for that.'
A.X.

## Research and story of a trauma

At the end of a five-year research into how and why professionals behave incorrectly, I have rather unexpectedly discovered how trauma comes into being and how it progresses in our life. In 2011 I wrote down my findings in my PhD dissertation and presented them to a large audience[5]. What I had discovered, was so logical that I did not get any fundamental criticism from the jury. The report of this process of discovery, situated in contextual thinking, was published by Acco in 2012 as *'Constructive counselling, Destructive right in professional consultation'*[6]. The academic world has hardly done anything with my findings. No workshop, no lectures, no interviews. The discoveries may have been so innovative that the time is not yet ripe for them. You, reader, may determine whether the times have changed …

I want to report my findings as simply as possible, on the basis of a fictitious story with a true beginning. I will explain the consequences of what I discovered about trauma and describe how often traumatic behaviour takes place[7]. After that I will connect these elements with the testimony of A.X., as they spring from her story. First I will give the commented story.

At the end of 2010, our daughter's car overturned due to of a layer of ice on the road. All in all she was safe and sound. But imagine that she would have died in the accident. In Belgium a police officer would ring your doorbell and convey this painful message.

Imagine, that I am in the kitchen doing the washing up at that moment. I feel and smell the warm soapy water, I hear the Beatles in the background, I have a peppermint in my mouth, I am looking at my hands cleaning the pots and pans. Five sensory signals that in normal conditions – normal means 'safe' – are clustered into a memory. A memory therefore consists of all momentary sensory signals, tied together with the code 'everything is OK, I am safe'. This memory is permanently stored in the subconscious mind, in that big database with all our experiences.

In fact doing the washing-up is an event that evokes little emotion. Therefore the chance that I will remember it later is not so big. Unless something happens that causes more emotion. From educational science we know that we learn things more easily – observe, store and recall – when different senses are stimulated and when they are linked to an emotional content. The more negative the content, the sooner we will remember it. This has to do with our survival: we want to avoid painful things, so they are floating on top and our subconscious mind will call them up more quickly. So let me return to my story.

I hear the doorbell, throw the towel over my shoulder and walk to the front door. Up to this very moment all sensory signals are clustered in a normal way and stored in my recollection as memories.

I open the front door, I see the neighbour passing by, I wave and then I see the police officer. As soon as I notice him, I feel that something is not right. At that moment I become alert, all my attention is focused on the policeman. Focusing means that all sensory signals are now being clustered with high emotional value and stored in my brain with high priority[8]. The light blue colour of his shirt, the heavy frame of his glasses the movement of his hand, while saying 'it is always the same with such weather', his smoker's breath, the position we have towards one another, his uniform... everything is loaded with high emotion. All these sensory signals are then being stored in me with high alertness and so later I will be able to tell again and again how things went. These are of course memories that will come back over and over again. At the moment that the police officer tells me that my daughter has died, the clustering of sensory signals falters. My conscious mind breaks down. This is what we call a blackout. I do not store memories of this situation. This is because this situation is too painful and life threatening for me. My conscious mind has lost all control, so we call this loss of control a blackout. My subconscious mind completely takes over. I am on automatic pilot.

What is happening in the brain in the meantime? During a blackout all sensory signals are being coded with the addition 'help, I am dying!' (Red Alert). Instead of being clustered they are stored separately in the sensory centres. The light blue colour of the shirt and the heavy glasses' frame in the sensory centre, the voice of the policeman and the words in the auditive centre, his smoker's breath in the olfactory centre, the peppermint in my mouth in the gustative centre, his movement and position towards me in the centre where movements and positions are being stored. Every signal separately bears the code of 'red alarm' – freely translated as – 'help, I am dying'.

Through this bodily mechanism I have a straightforward advantage: I survive the situation. In fact my body has brought me into a state of narcosis, in auto-anaesthesia. I don't feel anything and cannot remember anything of the worst moments afterwards[9]. In this painful situation of panic this is the best thing that can happen, but the long-term effects are pernicious and burden our further life. This will immediately become clear in the rest of the story.

The blackout lasts as long as my conscious mind is unable to grasp the situation. Imagine this will last until the night, when I am in bed. With my husband's arm around me my conscious mind will come back. The sensory signals are again being clustered, first with great alertness, later again with the code 'everything is OK, I am safe'. The first clustering goes with a high emotional release. The disconnection of conscious and subconscious mind is over, I see the dark bedroom, I feel the arm around me, I smell my husband and the sheets and I taste again what I have eaten and drunk before. All these sensory signals are again being stored in my brain with high alertness.

I will be able to remember what has been stored with high emotional value. I will tell this story again and again, because it is so emotionally loaded. But the intermediate sensory signals, those that were stored with an alarm code during the blackout, I cannot retrieve because there is no memory of them. In order to fill the gaps, the conscious mind does create a story[10].

**How trauma works on**

Let me take the story a little further. What does my life look like some weeks later? During a meeting I see a woman, dressed in a light blue dress, she has a cigarette in her hand and says in a high voice 'it is always the same with such weather'. I react as if a snake bit me and whisper to the person next to me: 'This woman is not reliable, I can feel this intuitively'. So when meeting the woman with the high voice I react in an unfavourable way, to which the woman reacts quite sharply. The drama has started, the dynamics in which the one reactive behaviour calls up the next[11].

In fact my brain has discovered three alarm signals in this woman and my body as a result has taken the reaction of fighting, fleeing or freezing[12]. Because this woman embodies these sensory signals, my perception tells me she is the object that causes this alarm. She should be avoided at all costs. My brain wrongly connects the sensory signals, which are effectively transmitted by this woman, with the stored reaction 'help, I am dying' in connection with the death of our daughter. This is logical for the amygdala, which continuously scans the environment for danger, but is illogical for our conscious mind. With regard to this woman I behave incorrectly and this has nothing to do with her, but has everything to do with the reference material in my brain.

A couple of weeks later, after I recovered from the blackout, my husband and I start having marital problems. Every night when I am in bed, I have an anxiety attack. I attribute this to my husband and tell him that I have become afraid of him. I find he has changed so much ever since our daughter has died. He does not understand this and as a result I rebuke him for not understanding me. The same dynamics loaded with incomprehension leads to drama and an immense amount of pain. In fact I react to the sensory signals. Every night in bed I have the same stimuli as I had at the moment when I recovered from my blackout. My amygdala has been alarmed and gives my body the signal that I am in danger. My husband gets the blame. He calls up the signals and I blame him for frightening me. In fact the cause of the problem lies with me.

The causes of all this reactive behaviour are hidden in my own brain. They are in the separate sensory centres in which colours, forms, smells, words, tones, gestures, tastes, positions, ... are loaded with the code of red alert 'help, I am dying!' The amygdala continuously scans our environment for these alarm signals. And as soon as three – just three – of these signals are being activated, it is as if someone inside our body presses an alarm button. And so we react with one or another panic reaction. In the film about the function of our conscious and subconscious minds Bruce Lipton calls 'pressing the button' being catapulted into a previous moment in our life[13]. This is how it really works. If the buttons are hit, we show exactly the same impulsive behaviour as when we experienced the trauma. If we wanted to flee then we will do this again now; if we fought, our hands hit again; if we froze, we show the same reaction as then. It is typical that we do not feel what we cause to others. Because we are in our brain of fear, we do not have access to our brain cortex. This means that we miss our most human capacities like empathy and openness...[14] Although we can stop this behaviour with our subconscious mind, the impulse and the state of defence in which our body finds itself with all the accompanying consequences, remain[15].

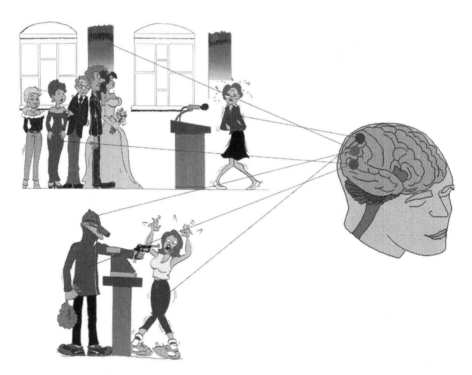

*Our reaction is connected to what happens in our own brain*

In my research I have discovered the following. Activation of alarm signals changes our perception of the environment. As soon as the amygdala finds three similar alarm signals between the outer world and the inner world, we perceive our environment as threatening. Our body immediately finds itself in a state of alarm (reaction of fighting, fleeing or freezing). We see the others as enemies against whom we have to defend ourselves. Our reaction of defence is perceived by the other as an attack. War has started. We ourselves definitely believe that the cause is the other person[16].

This is the end of the story. It has become clear that our amygdala wrongly experiences the sensory signals as actually threatening and that our body as a result of this finds itself in a state of alarm. It is important to recognize that, as soon as we react from this centre of fear, we see and experience ourselves as the victim of a threatening other party. However the problem is located in our own system. If we react from our centre of fear, we wrong the other party, and this is only because we no longer see them as a sympathetic fellow being, but as an assailant.

Indeed, the biggest problem is that the subconscious mind perceives the environment as threatening straightaway. In all literature that I have gone through in connection with this matter, I have read nowhere that the post-traumatic stress reactions of the person go together with sensory signals[17]. It is normal that this cannot be found. We are not conscious of what is happening. As soon as our body goes into alarm, we experience the other as an attacker and this is what we store. So, afterwards we only remember the attack of the other, but not that our changed bodily situation came before that.

One of the difficulties in the whole research is seeing the connections. Accidentally, my research material and the literature I had to go through for my research hit it off. That is why purely on the basis of research data it became clear how trauma works on.[18] Trauma creates what, within the psychological literature, is called 'blind spots': we cannot see and feel what we ourselves do as a result of these.

## There is no memory of sensory signals

The fact that during the blackout no memories are being formed, has vast consequences. The big advantage is of course that we can remain psychically standing in the most gruesome conditions. The effects in the long run can, according to the activation of the sensory signals, go from not happening to engulfing our whole lives. If I get a trauma high up in the mountains, while I myself live in a flat country, the consequences may be limited. If I am confronted with the same sensory signals every day, because the trauma took place at home or in the office, then I have a serious problem. Everlasting stress can lead to extreme exhaustion. I will talk more about this in the next chapter. The fact that we do not have memories of the most painful moments in our life has, among other things, meant that the effects of 'discussion therapy' are minimal.

The power of this counselling is that the person gets recognition for what he or she has experienced. Misery is shared and that reduces the feeling of loneliness and incomprehension. Experiences get labelled, a diagnosis is made and that gives a grip in difficult times. Possibly the symptoms can also be suppressed so that fear or irritations become bearable.

The big disadvantage is that talking does not dismantle the alarms because the gap between realization, knowledge or feeling will not be bridged.[19] Sometimes the symptoms even get bigger. A female psychologist asked to come for counselling together with a client who had come to her because she was afraid of injections. During the therapy a history of abuse appeared. Although the client was able to function quite reasonably before the therapy, it became much worse throughout the counselling as talking activated the signals and so the body went into alarm. The more often the body is in alarm because of different sensory signals, the more diverse the symptoms become. The reactions of fear will expand and so will the reactions in order to avoid the fear. It tends to become a big mess without beginning or end. Only the pain, the inconvenience and the discomfort prevail. I have experienced this both with myself and with my counselling partners.

Because our conscious mind has no memory, it is looking for a logical story to fit what is happening. Therefore Victor Lamme calls our conscious mind the 'big storyteller'[20]. In order to give ourselves a safe feeling, we tell a story. The story that goes with the picture on page 64 is 'I dare not speak in public'. The illustration shows the origin of this is to be found in an incident from that person's youth. Just like the little girl lying in bed in the next image, the people around her do not know what alarm signals will be triggered later. The more black-outs and limiting stories unfold, the higher the pile of stress and beliefs that stop us from living to the full.

*In moments of loss of control, no memories are stored, we have a black out.*

With our conscious mind – our attention and focus – it is almost impossible[21] to find a connection between the stored sensory signals and the present situation. Even if we knew the connection we wouldn't be able to break through the subconscious pattern because they are stored as beliefs and automatic behaviour of avoidance in the subconscious mind. As mentioned before, our state of defence troubles our perception and memories. As soon as our system raises alarm – and that happens one million times faster than we consciously perceive – our perception changes[22]. When we see the situation before as safe and the persons as benevolent, as soon as the alarm goes off, we perceive the situation as hostile, and include the persons involved. We localize the sensory signals and we immediately try to repel them. We immediately perceive the other(s) as attackers. And, of course, we have to defend ourselves against someone who attacks us.

The function of the conscious mind is 'to make up a story'. Negative feelings (fear reactions), of which we do not understand the origin, give us an uncomfortable and limiting feeling of loss of control. Because this uncertain feeling is unacceptable, we are diligently looking for a logical explanation for this feeling. The beliefs (systems of belief), which we develop as a result of this, are incorrect, do not serve us (nor others), but they calm us down. They give us the impression that they are the only logical explanation for what we feel.

The stories we construct serve us in order to justify our defence, which in the eyes of the opponents is an attack. They give us a safe feeling and locate the problem outside ourselves.

As a consequence we tend not to sleep well afterwards: during sleep the subconscious mind synchronizes the data and it keeps on finding sensory signals with a story that does not match. I can describe this so clearly, because I have had more than 50 years of experience with this phenomenon. I kept telling myself that I lay awake, because I was so out-raged about the injustice that was done to me. But now I have to recognize that it was a purely a bodily reaction. The data of my thoughts about a situation and the registration in my subconscious do not correspond which means my brain computer gets stuck. Deeply ashamed I often realized deep into the night that I interpreted the behaviour of someone as offensive whereas it was all about my wrong interpretation of the situation.

At first this discovery may seem shocking, but as soon as you realize its value of reality, it is really liberating. Because this fault is really inside *myself*, I can change it. In that sense I have had to readjust my view of the function of memories. I now realize that again and again I am being drawn to nasty memories, because my subconscious mind asks me to transform the stress that goes with them. After all I am a 'little hedonist animal'; everything that stops me from enjoying life, comes to my attention in order to work on it. So that life can be joy!

How can we realize this? Yes, through PSYCH-K. I have not yet found a better method to get this sorted more rapidly and effectively[23]. Why PSYCH-K works so fundamentally will be discussed in Chapter 4. First let me dwell on the frequency of trauma-related behaviour.

## Trauma-related behaviour

In my research 12 participants took part[24]. 9 of them recorded 10 counselling sessions each. The recordings happened randomly. Every person whom the social workers wanted to interview, was asked permission to record the conversation. From these conversations they chose the best and the worst session and in a next interview they determined the evaluation criteria themselves. The best and the worst conversations, together with the interview, were written out and analyzed. The result was saddening. Although these professionals kept high ethical norms themselves and used the best of their abilities for the well-being of their counselling partners, the results were disappointing. From this work I have kept a list of all possible evasive and aggressive behaviour among professional counselling: Each professional therapist should look in the mirror[25].
The participants in this research got together to discuss the first results of the research. They were disappointed by what they had read and some even showed a lot of shame. They never expected this defensive behaviour and especially its frequency in themselves. How was this possible?

The first and the last result of the research clearly indicated that we are either open or in defence. There is nothing in between, just as Bruce Lipton describes cells: they are open or closed. The level of 'being in defence' varies and the expression the person gives it does so too. But whether someone is open mode or in defence mode is very clear. We appear to be much more defensive – or reactive[26] – than we perceive ourselves to be. Every irritation, displeasure, every unpleasant feeling, all behaviour that springs from fear of being rejected, every judgment, every time we stick to our opinion,... no matter how subtly, as soon as it occurs, our system goes into defence.

The research material showed that as soon as we go into defence, it is very difficult to return to an open attitude. The smallest irritation may upset us and cause us to no longer function optimally. Through our coping ability we divert our frustration through eating, slamming the door, smoking, sleep, rest, or even gossip but we remain closed up from one situation to another.

The material showed that without a specially adapted technique it is difficult to get into safe shape again. That is why the ethical quality of the recordings was so disappointing. Social workers, who started the counselling in an open way, could get out of sorts triggered by the smallest irritation, so that the quality of the counselling deteriorated. Partly they could start all over again, but the flow was gone.

What applies to social workers, applies to each of us. Social workers tend to concentrate, so that they can control their reactive behaviour even better. In our daily contact with each other, especially during moments when we are quite focused on something or tired or feel some irritation, we react from our (subconscious) automatic pilot. In other words, we are completely at the mercy of the automatic reactions to the sensory signals that occur[27].

From the research we learned that we show much more trauma-related behaviour than we think. We lose control more often than we realize. This reactive behaviour manifests itself in a very subtle way: in irritations, feelings of displeasure, being tired, not feeling like it,... whereas being open is quite normal: safe, free and curious, pleasant to each other.

## More trauma than we think

Some traumas in our life have a generally recognized impact. Being beaten, (sexually) abused, humiliated, pain, social shame, falling and being frightened, … But there are many more traumas than those we find it normal to consider or suffer from. For every time we lose control, we are having a blackout for a few seconds or minutes[28]. If you ever had a fall from your bike, you know the phenomenon. You are cycling and suddenly you are on the ground. Floating through the air and touching the ground is an event that most people cannot recall. This means that we were 'absent' for some time and that the last focus before we fell and the first moment when we are back, left some sensory alarm signals. In the nineties my car overturned. As I was driving and my speed slowed down a bit, the trailer at the back started swaying. The trailer was very heavy and it overturned our car. I still remember that my body went into alarm after I released the gas pedal. That was obviously the moment when the blackout started.

Every loss of control situation has sensory alarm signals. Of course as a child we have more loss of control than as a grown-up. But also as grown-ups we experience traumatic situations. In our brain more and more sensory signals are stored with the code 'help, I am dying!' In our surroundings the amygdala tends to find more and more similar signals, by which we are burdened more and more. Imagine all these sensory alarms, from our conception until now. They burden our body and our mind. They create a life set on automatic pilot, which is a surviving mode rather than living to the fullest. In fact the remains of the loss of control determine the quality of our present life.

From my research material it becomes clear that our body gets into alarm mode more often than we realize. Lately I have been paying attention to this. Every time I notice an unpleasant feeling, I test myself in order to evaluate whether I am still functioning optimally or not. This test lasts exactly four seconds. If my body is in stress, I do the quickest PSYCH-K Balance[29]. It takes 15 seconds. After less than half a minute I am functioning optimally again. By doing this exercise every time when I do not feel right, I prevent myself from throwing the noise in my system – my destructive reactive signals – onto others. At the same time I also transform signals, so that fewer and fewer remain.

That makes me lighter and lighter until I am shining. By these short balances I can also work quickly and effectively. I can concentrate fully on where I am. You found out more about this in Chapter 2 where I talked about how PSYCH-K is working.

## Trauma-related behaviour in the testimony

The testimony of A.X. at the beginning of this chapter is really striking. She describes how her life before the Core Belief Balance consisted of evasive behaviour, continuous attempts at staying out of panic or alarm mode. In order to see this I call on your power of imagination. This woman was abused orally, vaginally and perhaps also rectally, involving blood. What sensory alarm signals do you think she was daily confronted with?

- Wanting to die: when the panic or the pain is uncontrollable.
- Steak is red meat (blood). Eating meat is traumatic because of 'flesh in the mouth'.
- Vomiting: it has to be cleared from the mouth as soon as possible.
- Swallowing down (after the ejaculation) gives her a feeling of suffocation.
- Everything that is soft or weak in the mouth is charged with alarm bells.
- Has she received something with a milky taste in the mouth before or after? Maybe a bottle?
- 'Not being able to do something well': who told her she had to do it well and that she hadn't?
- Because she is no longer emotionally controlled by the impulses, she now has space to think, to consider, to evaluate and choose freely.
- She used to feel dirty, worthless, defiled. As soon as the alarm is neutralized, these feelings are gone.
- The little voice in her head helped her control the situation in advance: for example by counting, by drinking compulsively from a certain mug or glass. While doing the things she could

control herself, she did not have to concentrate on all the other stuff.

- By not losing herself anymore in avoiding the sensory alarm signals, feelings of being at the mercy of events and being a victim are now gone.
- Monthly periods: seeing blood and touching the vagina while cleaning it, raises alarm.
- Haziness in the head and dissociation: not feeling the body is a repetition of her attempt at not feeling the pain and the humiliation during the abuse.
- Fear of water and fear of suffocation are part of oral abuse. At the moment of ejaculation the child has to swallow: while swallowing there is no supply of air.
- Counting and stamping the feet are things she concentrated on as a child in order not to feel when the sensory alarm signals went up.

The behaviour that A.X. describes has several names in psychiatric literature. I have mentioned some and so has she: PTSS, obsessive compulsive disturbances, dissociation,... They are all names for trauma-related behaviour, activities that show up to avoid or get and keep control of the alarms following sensory signals.

Does this mean that all psychiatric or all trauma-related disorders can be healed with PSYCH-K? That I can't say... What I do know is that people who consulted with, who participated in some sessions and afterwards learned to apply the process themselves, made spectacular progress by using them regularly. Their quality of life improved tremendously. I am convinced that our regular assistance will gain more quality if the professionals integrate the discoveries of my research into their way of thinking. Social workers who expand their supportive facilities with PSYCH-K have a lot more to offer their clients.

Why is PSYCH-K working so well? Because it is able to disconnect the alarms from the sensory signals. That is why it distinguishes itself from all the other methods of assistance that I have examined. In Chapter 2 we described how this process of disconnection is accomplished quickly and for ever. Let me emphasize 'the secret' again: In the procedure of PSYCH-K there is a formula through which the subconscious mind engages in tracking and relieving the alarms single-handedly, so that, by means of a Balance, it becomes possible to transform the traumas of which we do not have a memory.

More feedback from A.X after reading her testimonial:
*'While I was reading my experience, I realized that I had not shared that much yet, that there is much more to tell.*
*The nice thing I find that those beliefs still continue to work. There is not only a "temporary" liberation for a few weeks, but it continues to work. For example "I love myself" is still actively shaping my life. I can be difficult to explain in written words, but I believe that you understand me.*
*Tonight I invited people. In the past I was busy with making food and doing other preparations, for I don't know, how long. Always busy with people and doing so much for them. And now? Now I prepare something that I also like to eat (hopefully this to come across as selfish, this is not my intention). In this way I can have a nice meal with them and enjoy myself. You see, it continues to work, those beliefs. Basically I do not need to explain this to you. You know it better than I do, hey.'*
*A.X.*

M.B. has experienced some private sessions and followed the basic workshop.

*'As a child I have been repeatedly abused. Now that I am finally conscious of my abuse and looking for a road in life, that helps me to deal with it, I often feel how I let myself be used – for me this is "abuse", while it is "use" for others – to fulfil their own desires or needs. I dare not to react to this.*
*PSYCH-K makes me aware that abuse can be fixed by being present with yourself and learning to think differently. I will not disadvantage the other when stand up for myself.'*
*M.B.*

H.B. works as a health coach. He followed the Basic and Advanced workshop.

*'There came a young woman into my practice. According to herself, she was restless by nature. I saw that she carried a traumatic event in relation to her stepfather and she agreed. She was sexually abused by him and was reminded of this every day by television and the headlines in newspapers, which were reporting abuse.*
*Her relationship was under high voltage as a result. I proposed to her to apply her PSYCH – K to remove the event from the hard drive. No sooner said than done. We did PSYCH – K and since then there is no more trauma present in relation sexual abuse.*
*With the other capacities, which I have in me, I can help her well on her way. So you see, it works in an excellent way when the people are open to it.'*
*H.B.*

This chapter about trauma is somewhat more extensive because I integrated the results of my own research. The next chapters will be shorter. The following one deals with stress and total exhaustion.

# 4. Stress and Total Exhaustion

*"Stress can be dramatically transformed by being in a Whole-Brain State."* – Rob Williams

Stress is an inadequate functioning of body and mind. In situations of stress some parts of the brain are inactive[1]. In a stress situation a person misses free access to his or her whole brain. All bodily functions carry a lot of weight due to the effects of stress.

If we are continuously exposed to stress, we get exhausted. Total exhaustion can be seen as a stress pattern, a circle of stress reactions in which the bodily functions are trapped. As a result of continuous stress body and mind are overtired or ill, totally exhausted.

First we will deal with stress and then with total exhaustion.

## Stress, a testimony

This testimony comes from M.B. She has attended three PSYCH-K sessions followed by a Basic workshop.

*'First I had a treatment with PMA (a kind of regressive therapy). This took me all the way back to my birth. The feeling was quite an extraordinary experience. And this feeling had to find room in my life...*

*PSYCH-K has come my way and ever since has helped me bring my feelings more and more strongly to the foreground and not avoid them or push them away.*

*Increasingly I experience how liberating these balances are. My right shoulder had been aching for years. During one of these PSYCH-K weekends somebody said to me: "It is time for you to deal with this shoulder". "Yes, but it is an infection". I replied. "Do a balance anyway, go for it", he said. During the balance I felt the pain move from my right shoulder to my left shoulder, run across my back until it disappeared through my belly. It was quite an experience. Since that day the pain is much more tolerable. I know now that there is much more stress present in my body.*

*In my life I have been humiliated a lot. I was educated with the remarks "that is not for you. Leave that to clever people. You should keep a low profile". This stuck. I hardly dared to do anything. Until I discovered PSYCH-K and did a balance for my feeling inferior: "I matter too". And it worked: now I dare to stand up and utter an opinion, I walk towards people in order to greet them. It does not go smoothly yet, but I feel myself growing and that is very enjoyable.*

*During the holidays I felt some pain in my eye. I thought: "I have been reading too much" and also: "I know that I have too much liquid in the eyes". I did a balance and a few minutes later the pain diminished and my eye felt relaxed...*

*A balance will provide a surprising feeling time and time again... It is so liberating. You don't realize what stress can do to a human being and how long it can hide in your body.'*
*M.B.*

## The whole brain available

In order to engage completely in what we want to realize, we need our whole brain, both our logical thinking and our sensitivity. *Split brain research*, research into the different activities of both hemispheres, showed that each hemisphere separately coordinates different brain functions[2]. Broadly speaking our left hemisphere gives access to reason and the right hemisphere is responsible for our emotions.

Our left hemisphere speaks with words, rather logically and well structured. This side is specialized in analyzing, dividing into parts. It likes order and control. Time is also divided into past and future. When we look at a group of people the left hemisphere sees separate and single individuals. My left hemisphere likes filling this book with bits and pieces of theory and I have to temper myself in order not to give too many nuances. I would like to write it as precisely as possible. The left hemisphere would perhaps like to find a footnote with every little paragraph, so that everything I describe can be validated sufficiently on a scientific basis.

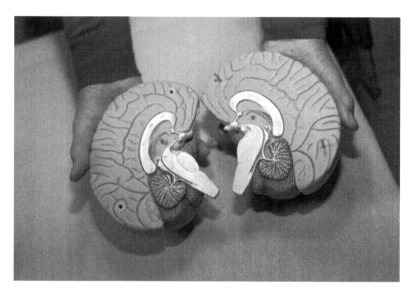

Our right hemisphere speaks in images and stories. From here everything should sound unscripted. It likes free spontaneous associations. Intuitively it wants to feel if everything is OK. This hemisphere is specialized in relationships; it is making new connections right now. In a group it sees connections between people. Time is a whole, it is now. My right hemi-sphere wants to work with stories. It does not want to explain but it wants to tell and give examples that are current. Here lies my motivation: I can already see the book in the bookstore. I feel where it threatens to become boring, where drawings should be inserted.

Whereas my left hemisphere calls up obstacles or objections, my right hemisphere tends to solve all difficulties in a playful way.

The explanation of the function of left and right hemispheres may seem like an abstract piece of theory. Let us make things somewhat more concrete. How do you quarrel? Do you use of lot of words or do you have a lot of emotions? Are you going to chatter and carp at details? Do you feel what you are doing to the other person? In this case stress grows by activating your left hemisphere only. Do you have to cry and do you feel sorrow at the lack of connection with your partner? You do not completely understand what he is saying so you wallow in self-pity? Here you grow stress while your right hemisphere is mainly in action. How does this work for the people around you? In order to get along with each other, we both need an active left and an active right hemisphere. Only then can we understand in a sensitive way and do we have words for our feelings.

*Our left brain hemisphere talks in words and likes order
whereas our right brain hemisphere thinks in images and makes
spontaneous associations*

There is much more to be said about the functioning of our brain and its effects on our behaviour. Darcia Narváez[3], a researcher at the University of Minnesota, to whose book I was given the opportunity to contribute[4], distinguishes three large parts in the brain from which different ethical behaviour springs[5]. If we are open and free, we can use our imagination. So we can create inventive solutions in which we can evaluate and sense all interests. Physiologically speaking both hemispheres are active then, we are in a 'whole-brain' state. That is what we are aiming for in PSYCH-K.

If our behaviour springs from our limbic system, we are directed towards the clan or the group. We are only committed to the people we are connected with. Only the solidarity of the group matters, 'our own people come first'.

If we act from the reptilian brain, which is activated through trauma, we act in a completely self-protective way.

Quite often stress causes us to lapse into self-protective or clan behaviour while we don't realize it. The most human part, our cerebral cortex, is optimally used when we are in a whole-brain state. This is what we need in order to live together in a peaceful society.

From this short excursion into the physiological origin of our behaviour it becomes clear that stress is a real given. It is much broader than what we in popular speech call 'being stressed'. We grow stress when our brain is not functioning at our highest possible human capacity. I will show now which forms this can take.

## Our brain does not function optimally under stress

If we function optimally with our whole brain, stress can be considered to be a dysfunction, an incongruity between different contrasting impulses. Parts of the brain do not support the feeling or the words. This is clearly seen in the testimony at the beginning of this chapter.

M.B. was raised with the words 'that is nothing for you. Leave that to smart people'. As soon as she tries to undertake something, her parents' words are still heard, because she has stored these beliefs. What she has taken away from home, does not match her highest potential, does not fit who she really is.

She hears little voices inside her like 'I also count'. These are the beautiful sounds of who she is and can be, the music of her desires. These different visions of herself do not match. She is not consistent as to what she believes about herself. There are parts inside her that support the statement 'I also count'; others do not.

This is what we call stress: parts of the brain show too much of this belief, others give some counterweight. But the latter make us feel heavy. By doing a PSYCH-K Balance, she will take care that her whole brain supports the desired statement. As soon as only this statement is embedded in her system, she will – as described in the first chapter – notice everything in herself and in her environment that matches this belief. In so doing she will create a pleasant life.
After a Balance the change is also physically noticeable. As soon as the heaviness is cleared from our system, we tend to become lighter, we start shining and we are perceived differently by our environment.

Stress reactions do not only come into being when there are contradictions within us. Also if we have other opinions or feelings other than our environment, stress develops in our system and our brain functions incompletely. Then it will depend on whether our own beliefs or our feelings are consistent. If in ourselves there is a clue for limiting thoughts or judgments from our environment, we will vibrate along with it. This was clearly shown in Narváez' research[6]. If we are not in the whole-brain state, we take over the lower frequencies of vibration from our environment. In stressed surroundings we get stressed, and if the beliefs of these surroundings contradict ours, the stress will be doubled. That is why it is so important to feel we are in a safe place. The more safety, the better our body and mind can function in a whole-brain state. In the context of dissatisfaction however our stress system is continuously activated. A chronic burden develops in our body and mind.

If we keep away from the stressed zone and remain in a whole-brain state, we can, while consistently keeping up this way of life, contribute considerably to the well-being of the group.


## In our subconscious mind it is always now

In our subconscious mind everything is stored that we have learned on our way from conception until now[7]. Irrespective of what we have learned is right or wrong, the subconscious mind reacts automatically with the behaviour that we have been taught. If at home our mother's norm was that the washing-up had to be done immediately after dinner, our system can create stress by still seeing the washing-up undone the next morning. Because the situation does not match what we have been taught.

The fact that in our subconscious mind it is always now has the effect that we experience stress both when we witness a situation and when we think about it or talk about it. In fact we do not have to see the people who we find troublesome in order to generate stress towards them. Thinking about them already suffices.

Our body reacts in a similar way when we ourselves experience something painful or are just present in a difficult situation. If someone tells a thrilling story, we can get heart palpitations because of the tension. Also when we talk about the past or experience something at present, our brain receives similar reactions[8]. As soon as we speak of something, we 'are' close to the thing being told.

This has not only to do with the fact that the subconscious mind is here and now, it is also due to our reflective neurons[9]. 'What happens to that person, also happens inside myself'. These reflective neurons have the great advantage that they can sympathize with each other[10]. Among social workers sympathizing with their clients' traumas can even lead to so-called secondary traumatisation[11]. Social workers can be traumatized by hearing about traumas. In fact we can only become 're-traumatized'. Only when the things told correspond with their own alarm material, our own sensory alarm signals become active when hearing a story. I call this 'a hook'. A hook in motion is just like calling someone with our index finger: 'Come here'. Who has 'a hook', asks someone to come. Whoever has sensory alarm signals himself concerning taking a beating, for example, calls – with a moving index finger – people towards him who have ever taken or given a beating. These people can 'hang their coats' on this hook. They can tell their story and so the social worker is deeply moved by it. His or her whole system vibrates along with it. In this sense social workers mainly attract clients with whom they can vibrate. It is my belief that the universe we are part of is well arranged: social workers seem to meet people in order to be able to transform their own stress material too.

For whoever works with PSYCH-K, this can be a blessing. On the one hand clients do not have to tell their story in detail, because the process also works without this. On the other hand these social workers attract the people who reflect things similar to their own problems. They do not have to be traumatized secondarily by this, because by just adding something to the balances they are transforming their own material as well.


**People do not have to divulge their entire soul**

It is quite fortunate for whoever works with PSYCH-K: this method does not require that the partner you are working with gives an insight into the stress or the trauma. Some people like to tell you what is the trouble, and if the person chooses to do so, that is fine. But for the person who is bothered by this, it is not necessary to tell it in order to transform the stress. After the stress has been cleared from the situation by means of a stress Balance, the partner in fact does not feel the need anymore to tell the whole story. The need to divulge disappears after the stress has been transformed. As stated previously we are primarily pleasure animals. Our brain clings to the stress in order to transform it. As soon as the nuisance has been cleared, we can focus on other things.

The disadvantage of PSYCH-K is that whatever has been transformed, is gone: the person hardly remembers it. There is a form of dissociated memory i.e., memory without the former emotional attachment, but the past stress response is gone. We have noticed before that we especially remember things with a lot of emotion, in particular negative emotion. As soon as this transformation of perception is active, the subconscious mind sees the past situation in a new way, without the stress response. Also the fact that this transformation happened by means of PSYCH-K very soon leaves our thoughts. It is like toothache. As soon as it has been resolved, we do no longer think about it, or about the dentist either.

A client has come for a session because of an infection of the hamstring. I happen to see her on another occasion and ask her how walking is now. She looks at me in a surprised way and says with a laugh: "Oh yes, I may have had some trouble with it!"

It is a disadvantage that she does not remember that her problem has been solved by using PSYCH-K, because on another occasion PSYCH-K will not be her first thought in order to deal with difficulties. Many of us have learned to go first to authorities outside ourselves for advice in connection with what is wrong with us, whereas most of the answers we need lie within ourselves. As soon as we know it starts with ourselves, the problem has taken its first step to being solved.

The fact that people do not have to bring the whole story is really an added value in this method. It is exactly the thing people are not able to face. They want to get rid of their current problems without having to tell their whole life story. And perhaps they could not tell it at all! Because in the chapter about trauma we saw that we do not remember our most painful moments. And a good thing too! The consequence is that we cannot put into words what troubles us the most. Moreover, in our story we cannot catch where most of the stress is to be found: is it for instance in humiliating words or in the fact that someone was a witness to this humiliation? For a PSYCH-K Balance this does not matter: the subconscious mind takes away the stress wherever it is found, often bypassing the need of the conscious mind to precisely know the cause of the stress.

In the testimony we see many more manifestations of stress: pain, reactions to infection, limiting beliefs, giving an explanation of what is happening, ...[12] and there are so many more. During a workshop we made a list of several stress manifestations. And also that is just the beginning. Which behaviour do you show when your brain does not function well?

## Three kinds of stress reactions: fighting, fleeing and freezing

If we perceive another person or a situation as hostile, on the whole we can show three reactions: fighting, fleeing or freezing. If we think we might win, we start fighting. If we assess whether we might be able to get out of the situation, we flee. If we do not see any possibility that we can obtain victory or run off in time, we freeze.

*Fight, flight or freeze*

Here you will find a list of behaviours that can much more efficiently be transformed by means of a Stress Balance than by working it off. A Balance works fast and efficiently. So space is made for whatever the person wants to realize. In the next chapter we will look in detail at how such a Balance works. The three well-known categories – fighting, fleeing and freezing – have not yet been explained in great detail. Let us make an attempt. I am looking forward to your specific stress reactions. Please mail them to www.freefullliving. com/contact

***Fighting reactions***

Arguing
Wanting to justify oneself
Quarrelling
Working out irritations on others
Creating tensions
Spitting out judgements
Making humiliating remarks
Showing awkwardness, madness
Taking a lot of space
Showing irritation, over-excitement
Showing complexity or perfection
Aggressiveness
Accusations
Inappropriate questions
Being tough, …


***Fleeing reactions***

Wanting to leave
Withdrawal
Wanting to run off, run off
Doing something else
Talking about something else
Procrastinating
Looking for distractions
Daydreaming
Watching television or zapping, computer games, surfing on Internet
Being bored
Taking things too easily
Using drugs, smoking, alcohol, sugar, coffee, energy drinks, sport, …
Sports
Going to the fridge, emotional eating
Feeling resistance
Doubting
Bungling (one part is present, the other is not)

Fainting
Keep putting things off
Explaining why things are the way they are, ...


***Freezing reactions***
All possible fatigue symptoms
Feeling dizzy
Feeling sick
Feeling ill with flu
Showing anxiety
Opting out
Sustaining infections
Stomach problems
Having an upset bowel
Crying
Doing nothing at all
Locked up in oneself
Ignoring, ...


I myself started to deal with my stress systematically. For instance, every time I think 'I want a cookie' or 'I feel low in energy' or 'I cannot write any-thing straightaway', I test whether I am in a Whole-Brain State and if necessary I do a stress Balance. And within a minute I can go on being creative. This is a very simple life!

Very often we do not realize that we cause stress reactions, or that we can transform them by means of a Balance. Because we have learned – and we do this automatically – to endure ourselves, to distract ourselves or to work things off. This is quite difficult for people who experience stress continuously. As soon as our stress reaction runs wild, it tends to become almost a normal way of being.

**Total exhaustion of body and/or mind: the stress reaction running wild**

M.V.D.E. has attended the Basic, Advanced and Health and Wellness workshops after 'Other Life'.

*'Two years ago I arrived at "Other Life" with serious fatigue complaints and fibromyalgia (continuous pain in my muscles). I am 58 years old and have had these complaints since my early youth. Both in regular and alternative medicine I had already tried out a lot, sometimes with some – albeit temporary – results.*

*As a preparation to "Other Life" training I had had a PSYCH-K session with H.V. I had no idea of what I could expect. Within two hours' time I felt my shoulder muscles go down and relax. On the subconscious level I seemed to be quite fighting myself and life. The spasms in myself had been transformed into spasms in my body, with all its consequences. In quite a simple way all tension flowed out of my body during the session. Until today I have felt liberated and my body and inner feelings are quite in balance.*

*PSYCH-K works in a simple and VERY effective way and is quite useful in order to discover and transform uncooperative subconscious beliefs. Using the Alexander Concept and "Other Life"'s training, I can stop and replace those uncooperative beliefs with whatever is helpful to me. This makes the combination of PSYCH-K and "Other Life" training very powerful.*

*After more than 50 years of fighting illness I now feel healthy: no more asthma, allergies or unhealthy fatigue. I feel healthy, energetic and in balance.*
*I am very fortunate now to be working as a co-trainer with "Other Life". Working with PYSCH-K during the preparatory session has given me a fantastic handle; I see people relaxing before my eyes. It is wonderful to be able to contribute to healthy life in such a way.'*
*M.D.V.E.*

C.C. has had the diagnosis of chronic fatigue syndrome and fibromyalgia for seven years. She has had a traumatic youth. At the age of 21 a piece of her small intestine was taken away due to an obstruction of the small intestine linked to stress. When she was 31 she had a breach of the large intestine due to even more stress. For more than 20 years she had to cope with digestive disorders and she became undernourished and exhausted. In the past 10 years she had experimented with lots of methods until last year she discovered PSYCH-K. She attended one private session and then the Basic workshop[13].

*'Old beliefs of self-sacrifice and self-hate have always given me heavier complaints of health. Reading the book of Bruce Lipton and learning PSYCH-K brought a turning point in my life. PSYCH-K is a simple but very powerful tool to work with my own process of consciousness myself. Little by little I break free from the straitjacket of destructive beliefs and my life becomes different and better. No one has to tell me how; I have my life in my own hands, everything becomes possible!'*
C.C.

M.D.M. has been troubled by chronic fatigue syndrome for over 10 years. She has followed training with 'Other Life', she has attended the PSYCH-K Basic workshop and after that she has had two private sessions.

*'I find it difficult to indicate concretely how the PSYCH-K sessions have influenced my daily life. I did have a boost immediately after both sessions.*
*I immediately fall asleep, I may still wake up at night, but I fall asleep again. What a pleasure!*
*This spring I have enjoyed nature enormously. Now and then I have a lot of energy, like "rolling up the sleeves". At another moment I find myself more inside, more acquiescent.*
*I am aware that now and then I remain in a "weighing up things" state and that I must do things: action. I myself find some beliefs, which I then test.*
*Furthermore I am sometimes scared out of my wits and at night I may sweat a lot. I respond to this with the stress Balance, just as you*

indicated. I have the confidence that my body and mind need time to process the new belief.'
M.D.M.

C.K. only attended the Basic workshop.

'I gladly want to express that, at the moment of my coming home after the Basic Course in the spring of 2012, I landed bang in the middle of my elaborated themes. This process is still current, but almost finished. It was very violent: a relationship of 20 years, of which 19 years married, over and out, a child that went living apart, and another circle of work. I wouldn't have missed it for the world, I have found back my roots and identity. PSYCH-K has helped me a lot, I use it every day.'
C.K.

A.O. attended two private sessions and the Basic workshop.

'After my first private session with you I did no longer feel the need to overeat. Unfortunately after some time the effect has disappeared. This may be because I do not sufficiently practice PSYCH-K. I am far too busy to live consciously and it causes a lot of trouble to come (and stay!) out of this negative spiral of habit. In the future, I want to get going.'
A.O.

R.L. has attended four private sessions in total: two before the Basic, the Advanced and the Professional workshop, and two afterwards.

'15 years of chronic fatigue syndrome with countless complaints brought me to a personal process of growth. It gradually became clear to me that "emotions" have an important share in these problems.
I experimented with everything that exists: homeopathy, osteopathy, acupuncture, Mir method, Dofna, yoga, E.F.T., Emotional Balance (E.B.), Rebirthing, Reconnective healing and Mickel therapy, etcetera. These only gave a limited improvement.
It is my objective to be completely healed, so I kept on looking. In the meantime I became more aware of my own body and mind. I realized

that I am continuously in an extreme situation of stress. So on the Internet I discovered PSYCH-K and attended some private sessions with M.R. For years I have had the feeling that there was an incredible lot of sorrow inside myself. This was also clearly revealed by PSYCH-K.

This method gives me the possibility of allowing and transforming all these emotions. My rucksack full of suppressed emotions becomes lighter every time. As a single mother with three children I have always wanted to be a strong woman and so I pushed all the emotions far away.

PSYCH-K offers me a golden handle to transform stress and sorrow completely autonomously. I do not have to go to a therapist every week, I can do it all by myself.

As a highly sensitive woman I have been hurt an awful lot. People did not consciously do so, but my interpretation of words is quite emotional because of old traumas. The result was that I avoided contact with others a lot, because this quite often resulted in a serious regression. In the past I even suffered from complex cardiac arrhythmia as a result of being hurt, and this led to hospitalisation in intensive care. No bodily causes were found, although extreme disturbances were present. The doctors thought that a heart attack was imminent. Now I know that all this was the result of emotions and bodily stress I could not cope with. I wanted to continue even further with PSYCH-K. I attended a four-day Advanced workshop. On the first day I was in a large group of participants, and they were all strangers to me. Suddenly, quite unexpectedly and without deliberate cause, sorrow came again. I did not want to show off and express my sorrow within the group?! At the end of the day I could barely walk 800 meters from the training centre to the sleeping accommodation. My energy did not flow any longer, I was completely exhausted, I felt sick and could do nothing at all.

Fortunately M.R. was in the neighbourhood. Looking for the message and a trauma Balance with PSYCH-K resulted in a spectacular revolution within half an hour! Without PSYCH-K such a regression meant at least a couple of weeks of lying down until the energy returned. Now it only took 30 minutes. I could just continue the three-day workshop and on the last day I even intuitively danced in the park.

104

*This opened my eyes for good. Every day I now make use of these Balances, because my quality of life is improving enormously and that is a big step into the direction of complete healing!'*
*R.L.*

Half a year after the attended workshops R.L. came for another consultation. A leaking intestine and panic attacks still troubled her when she had to go to the doctor's. We found that her body was constantly giving her signals that she had to realise her dream, her mission. From her childhood, R.L. had wanted to go dancing. We cleared her dream from the stress and the refusal, and gave R.L. the freedom to express her in dancing.

*'Here you find some feedback on the stress reduction and the extreme anxieties in the doctor's waiting room yesterday. After Thursday night's thorough PSYCH-K session I experienced improvement. I still have to do a lot of work on this anxiety and stress, but I am very pleased with the results. I did not have to go to the toilet four times and I did not have diarrhoea before I had to go to the doctor's!*
*Fortunately I was alone in the waiting room and I started dancing. I calmed down completely and in fact I went in quite relaxed. Isn't that super! This is unique.'*
*R.L.*

### Stopping a derailed stress reaction

In my practice I often meet people with fibromyalgia, high sensitivity, burnout or chronic fatigue syndrome, sometimes totally exhausted. Some exceptions aside – and I say this without any judgment – I experience them as 'unfree people', people who are captive to their own stress responses. Kind of victims of their own bodily stress responses. What once started with a belief like 'If you are tired, you have to rest', 'I cannot do this', 'They will laugh at me', … ends up connected to a traumatic situation and normal functioning has completely ceased. Taking their own position in society is valid for all other people, but no longer for them. They cannot do this anymore; their body does not function anymore. They are not capable of moving, undertaking action. They hardly or not at all take part in the dynamics of giving and receiving, which is typical of our human interaction and keeps it going. They feel that they only have to swallow. All impulses from the outside create stress. They continuously experience that stress and are no longer able to get disentangled from it. Their body is often completely out of balance: they feel pain; they have a badly functioning digestive system, allergies and lots of other diseases. From the morning till the evening they are exhausted and at night they cannot sleep. Because they are trapped in a circle of stress responses, their immune system is dysfunctional. Suggestions to stop this response encounter statements like 'this is impossible, because...' One disease cannot be cured because of so many others. The amygdala continuously discovers alarm signals. Both body and mind are exhausted. Often they just survive on food supplements.

These people have often exhausted all regular medical help and sometimes also quite a lot of alternative assistance. They have quite *consciously* tried out everything to get better and they have not succeeded. I am convinced that burnout, fibromyalgia, chronic fatigue syndrome and perhaps a lot more other diseases, which we generally call psychosomatic, arose from the *subconscious mind*. In my opinion these diseases have to be dealt with on the level of the subconscious mind. The problem is that often these people do not only generate stress, but also have so many habits of avoiding stress that the pattern is no longer to be breached with simple remedies.

Trying to help people with these complex complaints in individual PSYCH-K sessions is most of the time not sufficient. It is too little. Because they are living in a house that only consists of stress and limiting beliefs it is important to stay with them to continuously transform their stress. In order to break the habit of stress, they have to learn PSYCH-K themselves. Then the combination of consequent practicing themselves and being coached now and then, they will experience the best results[14].

If clients come to consult me about the problem of total exhaustion, I usually work with them in a few sessions and then they are ready to do the PSYCH-K Basic workshop. During the PSYCH-K workshops they learn to build up themselves afterwards.

## Experiments

Curious as I am about the limits of what can be achieved with PSYCH-K only, I agreed with R.L. to use just PSYCH-K. She herself asked me to try it out and she has committed herself to attending all workshops and to apply the process as much as needed. I am only present to support her in the background.

The turning point: because of circumstances she and I had to share the bedroom during a workshop. That is why we succeeded in breaching the *course* of stress at the moment when it was most needed, namely in the evening before going to bed. Without my presence this would not have been possible at that moment: she herself was panicking so much that the idea of doing a Balance was completely absent.

Private sessions and workshops together give the best results to tackle total exhaustion. In between the sessions the person can do Balances and during the sessions more general themes can be dealt with. So continuous feedback is possible in the moments when they would get stuck. While writing this book I came across people having to deal with total exhaustion. They were all part of twins in the uterus. These people often have anxiety attacks. For me it was a signalling to them that they were taking up too much space. Their system reacted to the 'vanishing twin' by making them look for the vanished twin. This way they expanded their search field far beyond themselves. They expanded their own space to the people around them. Their circle expanded hugely. As their territory expanded after the traumatic experience these people focus on all possible rejections from other people. They became hyper sensitive. This is extremely tiring. It is a reaction driven by fear and this is why they are exhausted.

My work hypothesis is that people who experienced trauma at an early age or who had to give up part of their childhood because of early responsibility for others (parentification)[15] can show damaged territorial behaviour. Their energy spreads far out of their own territory[16]. We are still animals in our cell memory and thus we experience fear when we tread on other people's territory. We can feel how the other person is going to push us back or reject us. We then protect ourselves with fear.

Then we take revenge for the rejection by others – whose love we desperately longed for – by depriving them of our love. I never saw this before, but to take away our love from another is the ultimate revenge. We punish the other for what he or she, real or alleged, did to us.

With PSYCH-K we have a tool that enables us to restore this energy field very easily.

The results of the experiments are promising. We discovered that total exhaustion – which goes hand in hand with continuous fear response, is probably related to the constant scrutinizing of the territory. People who are relaxed will be true to themselves and respect the territory of others, their space and their decisions. People who are anxious scan the surroundings continuously and are afraid of difficult reactions coming from other people. Balancing can transform this threatening reality to a reality that is open and loving.

So far we have explored the impact of beliefs and explained how PSYCH-K works. Now that we know how a former trauma can undermine our daily lives and ascertain how stress and total exhaustion function, we can go one step further and see how this stress works out in groups: drama. This is explained in the next chapter.

# 5. From Drama to a Learning Opportunity

*'We are already in heaven or hell, depending on our perceptions of reality.'* – Robert Williams

At the end of June I organized Basic workshops for two weeks in a row in Flanders. In the first week there was a woman who attended with her partner. She was so enthusiastic that she wanted to share this with her family. Upon phoning her sister-in-law, she heard that the family was in crisis. Because of his disturbing behaviour they wanted to send their twelve-year-old son to a boarding school. The sister-in-law contacted me and immediately decided to attend the Basic workshop together with her little son (L.). Mother, son and I myself stayed at the same house, so it was possible to give them some personal support during two evenings. The workshop brought peace and quiet in the family. Thanks to the responsibility that mother and son took for dealing with their own stress reactions, the drama the family had been entangled in, was changed into a learning opportunity. This situation is the motto of this chapter 'from drama to a learning opportunity'.

**Deepen the level of transformation from drama to opportunity**

As a theoretical framework we use a diagram from Alan Seale[1].
Seale draws four levels on which transformation can be achieved. Different questions are asked according to the level. Every situation is an opportunity to transform ourselves and we determine how thoroughly we want to deal with it. Do we remain a victim or do we become co-creator of our world?

| Level of Change | Questions | Effect | Awareness |
|---|---|---|---|
| Drama | Whose fault is it?<br>Who can I blame?<br>Why does this happen to me? | Power lies outside ourself | Victim |
| Solution | How can we solve this?<br>How can the situation get back to normal asap?<br>How can I get rid of this? | Control of damage, often without learning from the situation | |
| Choice | Whom do I choose to be under these circumstances?<br>What relation to this situation do I prefer?<br>What is my role in causing this situation?<br>Which steps will take to process?<br>What is an inspiring perspective here? | Taking Responsibility | |
| Possibility | How can this be an opportunity for me to grow?<br>What is happening here?<br>Where does this lead me?<br>What is there for me to learn here? | Broadening of the Counscious Mind<br>Personal Leadership | Co-Creator |

*From Alan Seale, Create A World That Works. Tools for personal & global evolution, Red Wheel, San Francisco, USA, 2011.*

### What is drama and how does it work?

Drama consists of stress reactions that link up. Do you remember the explanation on trauma? As soon as three sensory alarm signals are activated, we perceive the other person as an enemy against whom we have to set up a defence. Our defence is perceived by the other person as an attack, so that he/she too will go into defence mode. So drama is emotional and will threaten to escalate.

From our perception of enmity we think the other person started the hostilities but the drama originates in us. We start it to be able to channel the stress in our system. Sometimes this permanent stress reaction leads to physical exhaustion (flee and freeze reaction). Sometimes this stress will be directed at other people and drama is created.

All participants in the drama stand to lose. They are victim and perpetrator at the same time, but they feel they are victims only. This is how and why they can endlessly continue with the accumulation of pain, undergoing pain and causing pain. Until someone gets out of this drama cycle by ending the relationships, by ending his or her life or by starting a similar drama cycle somewhere else. This is the never-ending story of violence and destruction...

The only way out of drama is taking responsibility for one's own situation and break through the spiral of violence from there. PSYCH-K gives us the necessary tools for doing so. But let us first map out drama somewhat better.

In a drama everyone plays his appointed role in a jumble of interactions. In the interactional analysis these roles have already been described. There are the formal and informal leaders, the scapegoats, the lightning rods, the silent spectators, the troublemakers, the people in hiding, the anarchists, ...

Everyone plays their role, depending on their own personality structure and the games and tricks we learned at home.
Each role corresponds with certain beliefs.

- The formal leader: 'I settle things', 'You should listen to me', 'My will is law', 'I am the boss'.
- The informal leader: 'I know better', 'You should listen to me', 'I know what is the best for all of us'.
- The scapegoat: 'I am the victim', 'I am the scapegoat', 'I am guilty', 'I am responsible'.
- The lighting rod: 'I have to save things', 'I have to keep the peace', 'I set things right', 'This cannot go unpunished', 'Everyone should know this'.
- The silent spectators: 'There's nothing I can do about this ', 'I'd better keep my mouth shut', 'They don't ask me anything anyway'.
- The troublemakers: 'I get to profit from this situation', 'Everybody likes me', 'I set everyone against one another'.

- The people in hiding: 'As long as they don't take it out on me, I will be fine', 'They don't notice me and a good thing too! I'd better stay and watch from a distance'.
- The anarchists: 'I am happy things are not too tight here', 'All leaders are corrupt', 'I refuse to contribute actively', 'Better to have chaos than repression'.

*In a drama everybody plays their 'own role'*

René Girard, professor of sociology, wrote *The Scapegoat* in 1982[2]. In this book he explains the origin of the exclusion mechanism that is at work in stressed groups. He observed it first in a group of monkeys where there was no leader. It boils down to this. In a group without a leader, we all want to be the same, we all want to have and receive the same. In the meantime everyone wants to distinguish him/herself and emphasize how different we are. By wanting to be similar but different, stress increasingly grows in the group. The dynamics arise where 'everyone is against each other'. These dynamics are called 'symmetric escalation' which will last until someone has the courage to expel or kill the one that differs most of all. The scapegoat puts up with all the stress and is expelled from the group. By 'killing' the scapegoat, quiet returns in the group. The one who expelled the scapegoat becomes the leader. All the power games start all over again until a new scapegoat is expelled unless a good leader appears. This means a leader who can manage his or her own stress is needed. This leader sees no enemies, but only co-operators. As long as the leader pursues the good of all group members, the group will live peacefully. As soon as the leader loses his authority or is after his own profit, the scapegoat scenario will be repeated.

Obviously there are endless variations to this scenario: alliances will be made, fights between the formal leader and the informal leader will occur, and lightning rods will become scapegoats, ...

A good leader can cut through the drama, but he or she is not the only one. Everyone can bring about peace from his or her own position.

The family, to whom the boy L. is a member, is a loving one. All members of the family show a lot of commitment towards one another. This commitment cannot prevent the situation from escalating. In the family L. is the scapegoat, the father is the formal leader and the mother is the informal leader. There is a continuous squabble about leadership. The core of the fight is the education of the children. The children reflect the tensions between the parents. Between L. and his elder sister there is a continuous squabble, they can hardly stay in each other's presence. Between L. and his younger brother everything is OK, they like playing together.

**Working out a solution**

How can a drama be solved? The only way out of the drama is taking responsibility for mutual relationships and for our own stress reactions.

This means that we lead our relationships towards peace and refuse, constantly and consequently, to react out of stress. We take the decisive conclusion to keep whatever stress we feel to ourselves and to transform it. Each one of us does his own homework and takes the initiative to make it happen. In other words, we do not wait for the other person to begin the process.

The twelve-year-old son was the scapegoat of the family. In the evening at the end of the first workshop day we isolated ourselves to work together, just the two of us. When we did a muscle test in order to find out what we had to work on first: himself or the family system, we got a 'yes' for the system and a 'no' for himself. It did not matter to him, because we had agreed on doing whatever was necessary (and possible) in order to transform the situation. By muscle testing whether it was primarily a systemic or a personal problem, we respected the wisdom that was present in the boy.

In order to deal with the crooked relationships in the family system, I used a Balance for the family set up from the Health and Wellness workshop. Aside from the normal ingredients of a Balance, the idea is to create a family arrangement with little nametags. I decided to make a display of the nuclear family with the corresponding grandparents. The young boy put the tags on the ground, according to how he experienced the present family situation. In the meantime he told me that his mother had been very sad since the death of her mother, two years ago. This was quite hard on them. I asked him if since then the situation had become more difficult for him. He nodded.
By cautiously changing the positions, we moved to the situation in which he experienced peace. This situation we secured in his subconscious mind. The result is that from his subconscious mind an impulse comes into being in order to create this reality in the outer world.
After 20 minutes peace was created in him and with the family he belongs to.
The family system is one part of the puzzle, but it does not represent the whole picture. In order to evolve to a fundamental solution, the available family members and the relationships between them have to

be dealt with as well. The twelve-year-old son came first. What makes him the scapegoat, how much is his being different a handicap for the family? It appeared that since his birth he had reacted in an extremely allergic way, not only to several food products, but also to pollen, smoke and several herbs.

Within PSYCH-K we have our own view on allergies. An allergy is a stress reaction; more about this is to be found in Chapter 9 about health. If a child has allergies since birth, a trauma most likely lies at the root. From my practice I have learned that some people initially had a twin in the womb[3]. The fact that only one of the embryos developed can be quite traumatic for the remaining child. At first it experiences symbiotic unity with the other one and this other one 'disappears'[4]. Because our subconscious mind has access to all information from the conception until now, we can get to all necessary data through muscle testing. This can be important to transform the 'being different' of L. in such a way that neither he, nor other people suffer from it.

I asked L. if it was OK to test if he was originally part of twins. He agreed and one minute later it appeared that in the womb he must have had a twin brother. That created a trauma back then and in order to transform the trauma into peace, we did a relationship balance between L. and his not physically present twin brother. In Chapter 8 we talk about relationships and there we will go into what a Balance consists of. At the end of the relationship with 'the little twin brother' we celebrated. Then we tested again to see if L.'s relationship with himself was transformed. This was absolutely fine. Another 20 minutes and a lot more stress had been transformed from L.'s system. Now came the time to work with his mother. I asked him if I could share with her what we had discovered during this Balance with the family situation and the relationship Balance with his twin brother. He gladly consented.

The mother told me that her husband had to deal with a lot of stress at work. It has burdened him with heart disease, but he cannot force himself to change jobs. This stress had a big impact on the family. I showed her how L. had pictured the family relationships and how he feels when there is peace at home. She was shaken and saw what had to be done. We tested what was a Balance priority for her. That seemed to be the relationship with her husband. There was a lot of stress there. We don' t need to know consciously where it comes from or what it has to do with the situation in order to transform it. It is an emotional balance in which both partners again find peace with each other. When we left the room in order to find L., the mother said: "It will be different at home from now on." Although these words were spoken loosely, she made a choice here that gave perspective to the whole family.

## Choice

As soon as a first platform has been created where we can stand with some self-esteem, the players in the drama can choose to take up their own share. This self-esteem happens because we set in motion a situation that once seemed hopeless. We can find out what our own role is in the creation of the scenario. Instead of following the script, we can choose to go first in order to discover new possibilities because we know that perceiving a fellow man as an enemy springs from our own stress material. As soon as we transform the stress, the so-called enemy becomes the person we love again.

At the beginning of the second day of the workshop the mother and the son came into the room deeply affected. L. said that he had to do a stress Balance first, which he had learned to do the day before. His mother took a seat outside of the group in order to transform the stress acquired. Both chose to take up their own share in the squabble and transform it.

As soon as everybody was there, I asked him and her what had changed since the day before: "L. has slept through the night for the first time in months or even years[5]." The mother was touched when she told us this. She had been watching his quiet sleep: "How beautiful!"

My hypothesis is that L. had grasped the perspective on change. During the first day of the workshop he learned a process in order to transform his stress and during our personal session he got the confirmation that the family had a problem as well. He was part of it, but he was not the entire problem. This offered him peace – he could sleep now – and it gave him perspective.

During this second day of the workshop we learned how to create a 'vision of the future', the formerly described VAK (Visual, Auditory and Kinaesthetic), in which we shape the desired future. Because the group was unevenly numbered, I worked with L. His general objective was 'I am a good member of our family'. He could see it right in front of him: how he was going to play with his sister and his brother, how they were sitting at the table together and how quiet he was while eating and how they would play sports games together. He heard himself getting several compliments and felt really cool. The feeling that he is a good member of the family made him shine. His cells are jubilant because of the vision he has of what he later will be able to realize.

During the lunch break he came to me and said: "We could do some work tonight, but I would like to be alone with my mum. This does not happen very often and I really want to take this opportunity and enjoy her presence." I was so glad that he could express his wish all by himself and that he chose to enjoy the presence of his mother. In so doing he had taken a first step of action: he grabbed the opportunities that were offered to him.


## Opportunity

We know that there is always an interaction between the person and the group. If we do not have our whole brain ready thus causing stress[6], we are inclined to take up this interaction the hostile way. We attribute the enmity to the outside world and in this way make a difference between 'those over there' and 'I here'. If we are open, and thus in a whole-brain mode, we can choose to experience everything we go through as an opportunity to remove old stress material from our database. In this sense every incident becomes an opportunity for growth. This is not obvious, it asks for a steadfast choice to take on the sometimes-painful opportunities that reality offers us.

M.T. attended a PSYCH-K workshop abroad and was locked out by accident. What could she learn from this? Here is her story.

'The workshop was great for me. This was another level of doing PSYCH-K, but the organization and logistics were like "living the life of Riley". Because of this attitude the gate to the centre was locked at the weekend and the participants had forgotten to pass on the code. I had arrived last and everybody was already in so no one thought about informing me. This gave me a lot of information about myself: "I do not belong here, they do not want me, I feel excluded, ..." these are good reasons for doing Balances.

Through PSYCH-K I have been able to transform my cell memory of never processed losses. There were no words for the feeling I had been dealing with for years. The image of a painting that was hanging on the wall gave me a "butchered feeling"[7]. Just as there are no words for a mother who loses her child, I could not find a word that matched my past. Now at last I could give it a name. Although I had been working for years from the "Biology of Belief" by Dr Bruce Lipton, I have experienced that my subconscious beliefs had not yet been transformed. Since the application of PSYCH-K, the action plan included, the stress about this is gone. And this happened after a period of 38-years' physical and emotional pain.'
M.T.


Let us return to the workshop and the experiences with L. Because of a huge traffic jam everywhere in the country several participants could not reach the workshop location in time. We chose to spend some time demonstrating a relationship Balance, which is part of the programme of the Advanced workshop.

The evening before I had done a relationship Balance with L. and his physically absent father and we still wanted to do a relationship Balance with his sister. L. asked someone from the group to surrogate for her. Both tested weakly in each other's presence, which means that quite a lot of stress was present on both sides. This stress was transformed and another 20 minutes later L. and 'his so called sister' celebrated with a *high five*.

J.V., the participant who did the surrogation[8] for L.'s sister, sent me the next testimony.

*'During a PSYCH-K training a 12-year-old boy asked me to stand in for his sister, with whom he wanted a better relationship and who was not present. I gladly agreed. It went extremely fast, knowing that I was surrogating for his sister, the procedure also indicated clearly if it was safe and appropriate. This immediately gives you a lot of confidence in order to let the feelings happen.*
*I immediately felt that I stood above him and that I myself felt superior to him. The mother, who was present in the session together with her son, also told me afterwards that she had completely recognized her daughter in me from the behaviour I then showed. This also indicated that things happened quite spontaneously.*
*At the end of the relationship Balance I felt a lot of warmth and pleasure towards him. This was an emotional moment for me, to be able to feel the difference as compared to the beginning of the Balance.'*
*J.V.*

During some free practice time L. and I also transformed some allergies. Although this Balance is not taught during a Basic workshop, L. and I did use it in order to offer L. the highest possible opportunity to leave his position as a scapegoat forever.

In the course of the next week, the mother sent me an email.

*'We are genuinely enjoying the changes you have brought about! L. is really glorious towards his sister and brother. My husband doesn't really understand what has happened. He will notice with time!'*
*P.V.*

I do not agree with the way in which P.V. expresses this: L. has brought about these changes, not me. I knew that with PYSCH-K he could realize what he wanted most: creating peace in the family he belongs to. But it is he who did so, not me: he took the opportunity to tackle all the problem situations.

The end of this workshop was of course not the end of this story. In L's family a lot of work is still to be done. But as long as they do not completely butt up against each other, living together will be fine. If new difficulties arise, L. and his mother themselves can transform their stress, change awkward beliefs and create a new vision of the future. If they want to go on being coached for specific subjects, they will find a good PSYCH-K coach or do what they want to balance the relationships, themselves. In which case they will find space and time for a following workshop.

We spend a lot of time in life in drama and feeling victimized by the situation. Drama often goes hand in hand with immobility. We do not believe in the fact that things could be different. And this is the most blocking belief: 'I don't believe in the fact that this could be different'. As soon as we choose a solution, our life changes for the best. Maybe there is a blockage on 'being allowed to crave for something' or 'it is safe for me to be happy?' Who knows? But the person who chooses to find solutions will find them.

We are allowed to choose who we are and what we want to experience in a situation. With PSYCH-K every circumstance is a chance to grow and do good.
We can ask ourselves: what is the message behind PSYCH-K? How does it view people and the world? The answer brings us to the chapter 'Principles and Philosophy'.

# 6. PSYCH-K® Principles and Philosophy

*'Matter is just spirit slowed down enough to be visible.'* – Walter Lanyon

What I can appreciate about PSYCH-K is the extremely ethical attitude. Earlier I already stressed that only what the person him/herself wishes, or what is in his best interest, can be embedded in the subconscious mind[1]. From my PhD research I have learned that giving insight into the way in which you are looking at the world, is also an important factor in showing ethically correct behaviour. This happens in the Basic workshop. There we explicitly focus on the presuppositions underlying PSYCH-K. In this chapter you will get an insight into 'what lies behind it'.

The philosophy underlying PSYCH-K should be regarded as a whole. It is a philosophy with a lot of room; room in order to give meaning to what we usually call 'coincidence', space for other forms of life before and after this life.

## Being visible

While I am writing this chapter I feel my legs and arms itching continuously. I have the feeling that little spiders are crawling all over my body. But there is nothing there. Could this be a message from my superconscious mind? After all, my superconscious mind gives me messages through my subconscious mind that controls all my bodily functions. Let me test this. Indeed, I am not in a Whole-Brain State. This chapter is bothering me. I want it and feel that I have to write it. At the same time I feel some resistance inside of me I do not dare to acknowledge what I have come to believe

After my doctoral research as a Catholic theologian my life burst open. My research results progressed. What I know now about sound communication with the superconscious mind and the transformation of the nuisances in our subconscious database is still unbelievable or shocking to most people. Whilst writing this chapter, I tend to become visible. I am afraid of being laughed at and written off, shunned as someone who thinks and acts strangely. The fact that wonders are commonplace and accessible to everyone is at odds with how people are sweating away in order to earn a living and lead a meaningful life. Attached as we are to our difficulties, we do not believe (anymore) that we could make it much easier by using a little process. If I express what I am thinking, you will probably find me naive.

I stop writing and do a Balance with points of understanding and energy focusing. During this Balance 'energy of unconditional love and healing' are being added to the impeding points. The point that gets stuck is 'letting go'. I test weakly for 'I joyfully release the past and expect the best now and in the future'. So in this context I obviously do not believe this. I test strongly for 'I hold on for dear life to all that I do no longer need'. So, I cling to prevailing beliefs for fear of being rejected and spat out; I am afraid of being the scapegoat. I follow the procedure and three minutes later I test again. The point of understanding is strong as I test OK for 'I joyfully release the past and expect the best now and in the future'. My clinging to things tests weakly. During the Balance I saw the road wide open. Whoever does not believe and so rejects PSYCH-K, denies himself a valuable tool. That is fine, because it is a free choice.

Knowing that at first I did not endorse the philosophy of PSYCH-K even when I already was a Basic Instructor, I can let go of my 'need to persuade'. Initially I also had trouble with certain aspects of the philosophy. This has not stopped me from learning and passing on PYSCH-K. Perhaps as a reader you will also make this choice. Perhaps, just like me, you will first need experiences that will confirm that these principles are acceptable, before they can convince you.
Remember what it is I said in the first chapter? *Our beliefs are the short summaries of our experiences*. We can only be convinced of something, if we have experienced it. Whoever avoids the experience or does not want to enter it deeply enough, will not arrive at well-founded beliefs. Therefore I wish you a lot of transforming experiences. The beliefs will follow as a matter of course.

After expressing this, and after this transformation, I become brave and visible. I dare to comment on the philosophy underlying PSYCH-K. It is my experience that, the more my beliefs are in accordance with this philosophy, the faster I can bring about changes, both in myself and in others.

The opposite is also true. Whoever, on the basis of experiences, chooses not to make use of PSYCH-K, has every right to do so. It could be a fine choice, everybody chooses his or her own way – or the way chooses us.

B.P. has attended the PSYCH-K Basic workshop only, no private sessions.

*'A different way from PSYCH-K, a testimony*
*Perhaps you remember that I was on sick leave (and I still am) and suffered with heavy fatigue. I was also in a mourning process after the breaking up of my relationship with my friend (an 11-year long relationship), the third ruptured relationship in my life.*

*As you advised me then, I have systematically started applying PSYCH-K for about two months. All Balances for subconscious beliefs, all stress Balances, they all worked! Except for two things: the fatigue that did not end as fast as I had wished, the relationship with my daughter, which I wanted to be good... but it takes two to tango. Still, the attitude I took has had a positive effect in my relationship with her: I dared to express my pain and we had a good talk. I think this is the first step towards a more satisfactory relationship, at last.*

*I also had financial troubles back then. I had been worrying about it for weeks, but everything turned out right. PSYCH-K gave me confidence. And indeed, the solutions came, just by letting go of the worries and by living in surrender, the confidence that things would solve themselves or rather, that life would solve them.*

*Perhaps you still remember how religious I am. Well, since my sick leave, I have been praying every day. It is my first ritual in the morning. I light a little candle and write a prayer in my booklet. All these months*

*I have been writing page after page. And I came to the conclusion that prayer has the same effect as PSYCH-K. I remember well how you told me, when entering (time during a break): "B., what we are praying for, we can achieve ourselves." I rather found this a scary statement and I still think it is. Because I have discovered that I have exactly the same result when I am praying. I see the same positive effects. It is the dedication that makes a difference for me; the surrender and the confidence in Life itself. It is life in surrender, the receptive life that makes us receive a hundredfold. With both Jesus' life as an example and my deep faith I have come a long way and I would like to testify more, later. In fact it boils down to this: if you would just let go of the control you have over your life, you will receive godsends from heaven. Through your confidence in Life, Life itself comes to you.*

*My chronic fatigue syndrome is not cured yet, but I have received the faith that things will turn out well. That is very certain.*

*A man came on my path, with whom I have recently started a relationship. This happened at a moment I thought was not right for me and neither for him. However this is a godsend. By accepting this gift, quite a lot of movement has been brought in both our lives and has also given me new energy as well as a future.*

*In spite of the vision behind it and the faith in human beings PSYCH-K fades away for me a little as being something more technical.'*
*B.P.*


## We are all spiritual beings having a human experience

The fact that we are spiritual beings, which is why we have an intrinsic value, conveys that we are inspired. There is something inside us that drives us towards peace. That is our deepest longing: peace in and with ourselves, peace with others and with what transcends us.

B.P. describes the situation that I have gone through. Four years ago I would have called myself religious. I had, just like her, a relationship of prayer with the One I called God. I had a job as a pastor and conducted services in church. Now I would not call myself religious anymore, I just know. I know the divinity and can work with it. I can mobilize it in myself and in others. With Jesus as an example, I can through PSYCH-K activate the *self-healing* powers in people. I do not have to pray anymore, understood as 'begging' in order to realize something in my life. I know the procedure and I apply it.

Faith and belief are the same in that sense. When I previously said 'I believe', now 'I am convinced' that 'I am a good social worker' I can now check by means of PSYCH-K whether this is entirely present in my system. The fact that I can check whether a belief is also supported subconsciously for me is an advantage.

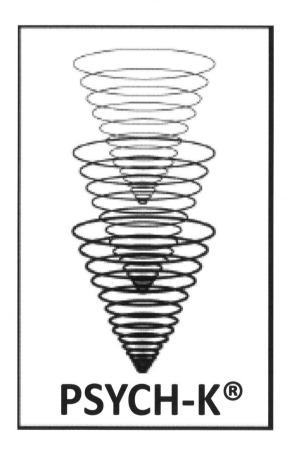

# PSYCH-K®

My 'system' is who I am: body, mind, and spirit. The spirals are expressed with the bottom spiral having the thickest lines, representing the body's density, the second spiral is less dense, representing the mind, and the third spiral is the least dense, representing the spirit. This is what the symbol of PSYCH-K expresses with the three interwoven spirals. Each component is a part of the whole person. That we are spiritual beings means that we are primarily spirit, a part of the whole. We are a bodily compact energy form belonging to the highest. The 'empty space' full of information is both in our atoms and in the whole universe.

The more we are at peace; the more we radiate spiritual life. With PSYCH-K we can convert spiritual language into facts. For me PSYCH-K is the translation of the spiritual in rationally, scientifically verifiable facts.

## We live in a universe with a meaning. Events happen for a reason

Because we can check whether an event has a reason or not, we discover more connections. I used to believe that we are living in a complying environment. We have food, drinks, love and power galore. Now I am discovering the synchronicity between events. From these experiences I trust the coherence that shows itself spontaneously.

Just as in the meantime I know from experience that my subconscious mind gives me signals – like for instance itches – so that I would consciously pay attention to something, I recognize the coherence between events. Yesterday B.P. sent me her testimony, so that I could use it today in the writing of this chapter.

Everything that crosses my path is an invitation to grow as a human being. I can do something with what I have been given. By paying attention, I also experience, just like M.T. in the previous testimony, awkward events as little presents along the way.

This is a PSYCH-K principle with which I have had extreme trouble; it was difficult to accept it. Why do we see so much misery, catastrophe, and death in this world? I do not have an answer.

If I work with clients who have an illness, and the person wants to know whether there is a hidden message behind whatever is happening, we can easily trace it. However I need to stress two things. First. Does the person want to know what a possible reason for this misery is? Second. I will be careful not to add meanings of my own. I cannot look into someone's soul or into the universe. I do not know what learning opportunities he or she will discover in a painful situation.

During two sessions I worked with a woman with terminal cancer. She wanted to know what stopped her from healing. She told me she lived in a split family. Once one of her brothers had hit their mother so brutally in a blind rage that she remained crippled on one side and could not talk anymore for the rest of her life. The family had been divided into two camps: brothers and sisters who still kept contact with the brother and the others who could not bear to see him. We discovered that her cancer had united the family again. By going to visit her, everybody got into contact with each other again. This discovery offered her the possibility of dying in peace.

No outsider can explain the reason for this cancer. At the end of her life she was grateful for it. She had realized what she dreamed of as a child: that the family would be united again. Was this the reason for the development of the cancer, I do not know, it is not up to me to make a possible connection here. Only this woman could make the choice.

I do not have an answer to the question of suffering in this world, unless I am trying to see it as a cry for peace. To this we can all contribute by transforming our stress reactions that produce enmity.

## The message conveyed by the challenges of life

Physical symptoms often are a messenger. The messages can relate to a belief that needs to change or behaviour that does not help others or me.

I have explained before that the subconscious mind controls our bodily functions. Our body function is at its best when we have access to all our capacity, when we are in 'Whole-Brain'. Self-Limiting beliefs and subconscious stress are unpleasant for the body. So it protests, it gives the signal that it cannot function optimally.

Pain is the most urgent messenger. In English the word *pain* can be seen as an acronym for *Pay Attention Inward Now*. Pay attention to the information that can be found inside now. If we tackle the problem without hearing the message, our body will have to send an even stronger signal, which may result in disease[2].

At the beginning of this year I had four teeth implants The dentist, who had attended a Basic workshop before, told me at the beginning of the procedure: 'You will not be troubled at all, because you have PSYCH-K'. This playful remark gave me quite an advantage. I thought 'Let me try it out'. During the operation I was lying as relaxed as in bed. As soon as I felt pain, I balanced it and the trouble passed. Afterwards I slept the anaesthetic off at home. I woke up with a terrible pain in my mouth. From sheer habit, our subconscious mind always sends us a habitual reaction first. I thought 'I must go to the chemist to get some painkillers now'. But then again I heard the words of the dentist: PSYCH-K was going to help me. While concentrating on the pain, I first did a stress Balance. I felt relieved and could think normally again. Then I asked 'What is it that disturbs me most?' 'The fact that something penetrated my body'. Then I asked myself the magical question 'What is it that I really want?' The answer came straight away 'I am untouchable'. This tested weakly; there was no harmony in my mind. While I was still lying in bed cosily and warmly, I did a New Direction Balance, a Balance from the Basic workshop. This requires a Whole-Brain posture while the belief is being repeated. For a few minutes a storm was raging through my brain. Experiences in which I let myself down (I had hurt my own inviolability) or in which others had doubted or attacked my integrity, everything passed under separate review. I kept on repeating calmly. As soon as peace had returned, which must have been after some ten minutes, I finished off the procedure. A celebration was required for all the pain had gone. The stitches inside my mouth caused a little discomfort, but that was all. I got the message.

It is very nice not to feel attacked anymore. It could not stop me from being afraid of showing myself, as became apparent at the beginning of this chapter. But it gave me firm ground under my feet when people effectively doubted me. That did not make me panic anymore.

The fact that challenges in our life may contain a message gives us a different view on symptomatic treatments. In doing so we are trying to silence the pain or the inconvenience before we have received the message. It is much more effective and healthy for our body to listen first to what our mind has to tell us through our body.

Sometimes we do a Balance for a symptom, like fatigue or for problems in a relationship. If we do these Balances in order to get rid of the symptom as soon as possible, these Balances may give a certain relief, but will not have the long term desired result.

I have been working with a woman who had been suffering from chronic fatigue syndrome. By attending 'Other Life' and the PSYCH-K workshop she had recovered considerably. She was shining. There was just one problem left: every morning she woke up in order to have regular bowel activities. So she had to get out of bed and that bothered her. Quite often she could not fall asleep again and she felt she might have too little sleep. As we were looking for messages, we found quite an astonishing one. The message was that she had to go to work. This woman received sick pay and this financial advantage stopped her from going to work. If we look at this message on the level of symbolic language, it is quite obvious. 'The time of sleeping is over, get back to work', says the superconscious mind by way of her body. As long as this message is not answered, the symptoms will continue. If she ignores this inconvenience, her physical symptoms will probably continue to increase, becoming even clearer and more insistent.

Symptoms are like messengers: they want the message to be heard.

## Partnership guides the healing process

Partnership means that both partners have an equal contribution. When I am working with clients, they are my partners for the whole process. They determine the content and I know the process. I am relying on them as far as the content is concerned, and they know they are in good hands during the process.

The language that is used in PSYCH-K Balances stresses this dialogic process. Together we are doing muscle tests and we do them together. The partner is the one who says whether he or she tests strongly or weakly for a belief we are checking, and then I agree with it or not. As soon as one of us is in doubt, we repeat the test. PSYCH-K is done together with someone, not to or for him.

The most important resources necessary for change are embedded in the person who is changing, not in the facilitator. The real power for change is in the person, not in PSYCH-K. PSYCH-K is just a key used to disclose and activate that power. By means of PSYCH-K the deepest wisdom of the mind and the corresponding self-healing capacity of the body are being activated.

## Knowing what you do not want is not the same as knowing what you do want

I have already told the joke of the waiter and the chef in the restaurant. If the waiter does not know what it is the client wants to consume, he cannot serve it. It is therefore not enough to just remove a problem without replacing it with the things we really want. Hence that desired beliefs in a PSYCH-K balance are always formulated as an affirmation, as something we want to do.

I for one can entirely support this principle. Far too often we spend our energy complaining and moaning and we forget to form a vision for the future. If we do not have a clear objective of what we want to achieve, we are very unlikely arrive there. The destination is too vague.

It is like asking a taxi driver to take you somewhere. If he receives a vague address from you, you will arrive in places you did not ask to go.

When I gave a PSYCH-K demonstration in a group that had not asked for it, I felt that it would be better to find a belief to implement in myself rather than to ask a group member as a volunteer. Without much thinking I chose 'I have too much time'. In the weeks after, some clients cancelled their appointment. I arrived much too early at meetings... I had to learn to deal with a new phenomenon in my life: having too much time. The destination I had given was vague. I should have chosen 'I have sufficient time for assignments I have to carry out' or 'I have the feeling of having too much time'. I am curious to know what these beliefs would have had as a consequence.

Leaving pain and sorrow is still heavily burdened with the energy of these emotions. Moving into the direction of joy is much different. There is a longing that attracts us, something that is good for others and ourselves. This already gives us joy beforehand and even more when we arrive at the destination.

## 'Everything should be made as simple as possible, but not simpler'

Albert Einstein has never known how much impact his statement 'every-thing has to be made as simple as possible, but not simpler' would have. I have heard him quoted countless times.

The PSYCH-K Balances are very simple. The youngest participant in a Basic and an Advanced workshop was 10 years old and did fine, often even better than most grown-ups. This is because Balances are easily learned and applied. The procedures are simple enough. They are printed out on one or two pages and most facilitators plasticize them for convenience and continuous use.

Change can be that simple. You follow the procedure and there you are. It is important not to add something to the procedures, nor to leave anything out. Every sentence is important. Adding something is extra ballast; leaving something out disturbs the process, and can make it less effective. Because in the whole world the same procedures are being followed, their energetic field of consciousness is increased. That is what we, the Certified PSYCH-K Instructors and Facilitators, experience. It gets steadily easier for participants in workshops to learn the process and the transformations happen more quickly all the time.

## The subconscious mind needs different tools

There are eleven PSYCH-K Balances with only a couple of recognized varieties. In the Basic workshop we learn the New Direction Balance and the Resolution Balance. In the Advanced workshop the spectrum widens with the Verbal and Non-Verbal Rapport Balance, the Balance with Belief Points and Energy Focusing, the Core Belief Balance, the Relationship Balance, the Life Bonding Balance, Ear rolls, Figures 8 and Cross-crawls.
In the three other workshops we teach variations on these Balances. A Balance for the Transformation of Allergies, a Spiritual Core Belief Balance, an Optimal Health Balance and an Alternate Life Balance.

It is the subconscious mind that determines which Balance is needed to transform stress, a belief or a situation. Through muscle testing we know which tool the subconscious mind needs to cause lasting changes. The whole spectrum of Balances is completed with a *sacred* or *secret* Balance. This is a very fast process of transformation that can be applied in all conditions. Participants are taught this procedure at the end of the Advanced workshop. By the time we have experienced all of the different Balances, the subconscious mind has become accustomed to quickly and easily implementing changes in the subconscious mind.

## The belief of being separated from the divine is the core of all difficulties and challenges in life

We are one; one in body, mind and spirit. We were one matter once. Our personal Higher-Self is connected with all other people and the cosmos. We share the mind, the breath, and the enthusiasm with everything alive on earth.

PSYCH-K is permeated by this idea of unity. Moreover, it is much more than a belief or a thought. It is the tool with which we are working. From this unity we can in full respect stand in someone else's place energetically, so that we can balance the relationships. From this unity we can contribute to the life of animals, to organizations, to the earth, and to the universe. We can even work from within this unity. If a person makes a mistake, I wonder 'What is it that makes me create this problem?' The answer to this question is often quite enlightening. It opens possibilities of new solidarity, without judgment. It is neither you nor I, who creates this reality; we are shaping it together. We are taking part in each other's reality: I by writing this book, you by reading it.

As soon as we relapse into the illusion of dividedness, we lose a great part of our potency. It is a reaction of stress, a reaction in which we see the other as an enemy and treat him as such. What springs from separation, often creates chaos.
Let us not confuse dividedness with uniqueness. Every one of us is both unique and related. This is an expression of our *Divinity*. As soon as we defy one of these poles, our uniqueness or our relation, we will harm our humanity and the largest opportunities that have been granted to us. Reality is one and complete. By applying PSYCH-K, we are taking part in this unity and wholeness, in body, mind and spirit.

The ethical quality of our contact with each other will increase, if we address our prejudices. We reveal to each other what our position is in the world. After this has been done we can move one step further in the expanding of our thinking and the opportunities that our human existence offers us. Get this!!! From the connection with each other the world opens up to a new life (together)!

# 7. Surrogation

'PSYCH-K is *a quantum physical process, that moves energy with intention.* It is a non-local, as well as a local process.' – Robert Williams

## Testimony

I do not know M.L. personally. She has attended PSYCH-K workshops with a colleague in the Netherlands. As we share one list with PSYCH-K facilitators, she has also received the request for testimonies for this book. M.L. considers herself as being highly sensitive: she can feel how her children are doing when they are not with her, but with her ex-partner. Before she attended a PSYCH-K workshop, this high sensitivity was a burden for her, now she can work with it.

*'Once a psychologist told me: "You feel people's sorrow, don't you? But can you leave it there?" Then I could not. Now I can, but only after I contributed to help them. My tool is the ever clear, ever available, ever sound, ever simple and always attractive PSYCH-K method.*

*Two examples: for six years I have been living separated from my ex-husband and children. I feel when my 8-year-old daughter misses me and I bring balance in her energy with my muscles as substitutes for hers.*
*I can also feel when she senses that her father at a certain point is "weak" (in stress) and then I Balance my ex's energy – again with my muscles as substitutes for his.*
*When my daughter is with me again, I tell her when I felt that she missed me before going to bed or the fact that she felt her father's lack of confidence. I teach her to distinguish with her own muscles – what comes from her and what for example belongs to a little girlfriend of hers or to her father. Some things may be damaged in different areas with them and could have nothing to do with my daughter.*

I presented to my daughter what I had written down. She found it correct as to the feelings of her own sorrow and being better at identifying the stress of other people.

Perhaps you can use this story; perhaps you might think it is directed too much at highly sensitive people. My thoughts about this are nevertheless that it is high time for highly sensitive families to receive tools, simple enough to apply them in education, and rich and sound enough to be able to bring help to the people around the highly sensitive persons.'

M.L.


## Surrogation, a gift to others

'After the Basic course I sent you an email, because I suddenly had very limiting thoughts that would not leave me at all, until you went into surrogation and things went much better two days later. Once in a while this will happen again, but only sporadically. Just because of these awkward thoughts immediately after the course I have done nothing at all and I wanted to give it a rest. I think a little bit because of fear. I do not like the idea that you have to practice daily after the course, but I understand that without these exercises you cannot master the method well. I haven't yet practiced, but I am considering attending the practice days and perhaps repeating a course. By nature I like to notice tangible evidence. During the course I have been working on my claustrophobia. I thought it might have disappeared but this is not the case. This is very discouraging to me, because formerly I had read that PSYCH-K works quickly and powerfully and that we sometimes need only one session to make phobias and allergies disappear. This makes me doubt the effectiveness of the method and its possibilities, although I think PSYCH-K is so beautiful!'

V.V.D.


Because I went into surrogation for V.V.D. in order to transform her limiting thoughts, things went much better for her. By nature we want to contribute to the lives of others. We wish our fellow men all the best. Especially the people we are concerned about most, can count on our personal commitment and attention. If for some reason they are not present or accessible, we feel powerless to relieve the sorrow they are going through. By going into surrogation, we can – in utmost respect and recognizing the personal responsibility of the other, help transform the sorrow that he or she is going through. V.V.D. is responsible for looking at the messages and advantages of her claustrophobic behaviour and for practicing herself. When she was in trouble, I helped her transform her limiting thoughts by substituting for her.

We went to see a baby who had been born far too soon. At last the baby girl was at home and she flourished. Sometimes however she started moaning, without any reason at all. When we arrived, the little girl was asleep. She had just eaten. While we were talking, I saw her little face distorting with pain as she moaned in her sleep.

I asked the mother if she would be willing to do a surrogation for her little daughter. The young mother had never before heard about PSYCH-K, but she wanted to try it out. Because the baby cried with pain just after being fed, I suggested testing the belief 'It is safe for the stomach to empty'. She tested weakly for this, so it was a 'no'. By means of a New Direction Balance, this belief was replaced after five minutes. The child was relaxing visibly. We had to laugh about it. As soon as the mother opened her eyes, she said: 'while she was in the incubator, she was too weak to throw up. She would have choked. That is why she had a catheter in her stomach. Through this catheter she was given food. In order to prevent her from throwing up, the remainder of the milk was drained out of her stomach after half an hour'. Now I understood the pain of the little girl when her stomach was being emptied. Her subconscious mind had connected the emptying of the stomach with being unsafe, being hurt (the catheter perhaps sometimes stuck to the stomach lining). By doing the balance we undid this connection.
We tried to look for other messages connected with this pain. And there were some: the little child felt guilty about not growing quickly enough. We transformed this into 'I am growing at my own pace and that is fine'. By doing these Balances we prevented the little girl from developing any more stomach troubles in her future life.

Let me add another baby story. In an Advanced workshop in which surrogation is being taught, there was one participant short in order to do Core Belief Balance. I took the place of the missing participant.

By doing this Balance we embed the foundations of our life. We only have to do it once. It is like stabilizing a house. As soon as the foundation is there, the building can safely be erected. In the close circle of my friends I could not think of anyone for whom I had not yet done the Core Belief Balance. Suddenly I realized that someone in my family was pregnant. I could do a surrogation for her little baby, still to be born. What an experiment! Especially because It is my belief that little babies have an undamaged, 'pure and free' beginning. As soon as the ritual of surrogation was done, the Balance was carried out. Most core beliefs were OK in the system, except for 'I can' versus 'I cannot'. As a little baby I felt some insecurity about as to whether I could stay or not. As soon as I felt this feeling grow, I remembered that the father of the baby had been born after a pregnancy of six months only. His survival had been critical. The experience about the insecurity of survival was part of the cell material of the father and had been passed on as such at the conception. This stress had probably been part 'of the genes'. At the end of the Balance there was peace and celebration! The fear had been broken. It was my contribution to a pregnancy that ended happily.

Here are two more stories about an older man after which I am going to sketch the philosophical background of surrogation.

An older friend of mine was troubled by fits of anger after several CVA's (cerebral vascular accidents). Just like all of us, he had met with several traumas in life and he was trapped in bad memories. This was very difficult both for himself and for the people around him. He was angry all the time.
When I was on my way to pay him a visit, I wondered how I could help him. I went into surrogation and tested 'I only remember the beautiful memories'. Before bringing this in balance for him, I ended the surrogation and tested this belief for myself. I tested weakly as well. The rule is that we never try to Balance for someone else if it

tests weakly in ourselves. So I first balanced this belief for myself, went into surrogation again and embedded the belief in my friend.

Afterwards I went to drink something with him in an outdoor café. He asked me: 'Tell me something more about that PSYCH-K method you are working with'. I told him about limiting beliefs that can burden our functioning, like for instance being troubled by painful memories. He told me there and then that he had no care in the world: 'I only have good memories'. He admitted consciously his subconscious was programmed differently. We spent a fine afternoon together.

*When we receive energy from the other person it is like a cloak draped around us, so as to be able to serve him or her*

When a friend of mine was dying I also went into surrogation. I could not be present physically, but I could help him. When the nurse told me on the phone that he went into death agony, I went into surrogation. I tackled all the beliefs that entered into my mind concerning dedication, letting go, being forgiven and forgiveness, finding peace and passing into the light. I asked the superconscious mind what he needed and did a Balance for this. I felt things becoming peaceful; everything had been 'accomplished'. 30 minutes later I received a phone call with the message that he passed away. He had crossed the threshold.

Surrogation is a delicate matter. It raises a lot of questions. In order to carefully reveal the basis of surrogation, I read some philosophy. In surrogation it is about the highest good of the other one that matters, not of myself. The French philosopher Emmanuel Levinas has developed this in detail[1].

## Levinas: philosophical background of surrogation

Levinas, one of the founders of relational ethics, devoted a booklet to surrogation[2]. For him substitution what we could translate as surrogation is the necessary answer of the person to the fellow man who is being persecuted and oppressed. The suffering of the other person concerns us. We let ourselves be touched, we take his/her place and allow it to fundamentally take precedence over our own desires. The need of the other one appeals to us, teaches us and commands us. It is not we who determine what we want to do about this person: only what he or she needs, determines what we have to do. In that sense surrogation is the foundation of our own humanity. By answering it, the best part in us will prevail.

For Levinas the call of the other person brings us in the position of debt. Because his or her suffering touches me as a facilitator he or she takes precedence over my own desires. According to professor Roger Burggraeve, a Flemish ethicist, the term 'responsibility' contains both the debt and the personal responsibility[3]. According to Levinas the fact that we owe the other person the relief of his suffering, comes first and is the foundation of who we are. The question that arises is; are we concerned about ourselves or do we radically give priority to the other person? The answer to this question qualifies us as a high-minded human being or not.

For Levinas the call of the other one's face even arouses the humanity of the I[4]. I am not just saying 'Here I am'. By accepting the other person, I become unique. By turning, away from myself, towards the other I am the one changing[5]. I myself become different from whom I was before. From a self-centred person I will become someone who is truly human. And so the best in us comes up. If, however, I withdraw from this call, I am withdrawing from my own true humanity, from my own destiny of being human to the other person. Responding to the other one's call is an inner obligation; it owes the other one the answer 'Here I am'. I put myself aside, I put everything I think I know about the other person aside, and I let him speak for him/herself. I'm listening and will do what is needed[6].

The other person can only refer to him/herself, can only belong to him/herself. This transformation for me contains both his or her body, (in)-ability and vulnerability, his or her 'being' and all that is irreducible to him/her, including his or her own responsibility towards others, which he/she has to carry in his/her turn[7].
The other person has the authority to show him or her the necessary respect and does not actively claim it[8]. The relationship that shapes the human being, therefore, is not the relationship with him/herself, but the relationship with the other person[9]... The other person comes first: even though I reach out, I cannot keep a hold on him or her.
This is the attitude that is necessary in surrogation: we follow the other person in his or her inalienable self. We follow and use the dynamics present in the other person without taking control over it.

For Levinas the responsibility surpasses the relationship, because this is ingrained in the human being. This means that I owe an answer, irrespective of the nature of the relationship. Levinas radicalizes the responsibility that I have not asked for but which I am placed in, because the other showed him to me, until being responsible for the other person[10]. This means that I make room in myself for the other one, so that he/she could receive all space possible to come out well. I passively withdraw so as to be able to fully respond[11]. I am not taking responsibility *for* the other person, but I am emptying myself in order *to carry him*, and in carrying him I am becoming my true self.

The surrogation, as it is made possible through PSYCH-K, is the ability to follow and carry. By taking the other person's place, we accept him or her, both in good and evil. We are following the other one's direction, as it is presenting itself. The objective is to enable a state of complete peace within, with others and all around.


## A 'sacred' ritual

Q.R.S. attended all PSYCH-K workshops.

*'I notice that, just as when there really is a person in front of you, I remain a facilitator when I go into surrogation.*
*In my head I keep tuning in to the other one (who I am myself in surrogation), I am listening openly to what comes up and at the same time I am ready for the other person, without judgment.*
*I invite the other person in me, reassure him, ask questions or offer quiet space just being there.*
*I notice that, when my thoughts go astray or become judgmental, the other one in me reacts to this, sometimes rejecting or indignant. Even if there is a surrogation for a "thing" like for example a house, these reactions will keep coming as well! This is quite extraordinary.*
*It is nice for me to feel the other one's emotions and feedback in my thoughts, words or behaviour right away.*
*I love "playing" this game of good fine-tuning.*
*Sometimes I go in surrogation for someone from my parallel lives. It is possible that an issue within myself has been healed at a certain level but that another piece of the puzzle is to be found in another life. I know this because a certain belief tests strongly for myself and weakly for the person in the other life. I assume that by healing this other me*

*(who is a part of myself) deeper layers in myself are being healed. I find the use of PSYCH-K fascinating!'*
Q.R.S.


It should be clear that the ritual you go through to go into surrogation for someone is 'sacred'. 'Sacred' in the sense of inviolable. We receive the other person's energy as a robe that wraps itself around us in order to be of service (see drawing).

If we violate the inviolability of another person by controlling him/her, surrogation will automatically be interrupted. The awareness of the essential inviolability of the other person is part of the initiation of the ritual.


The ritual in itself is quite simple. As usual we will make contact with the subconscious mind. Next we will ask the permission from our own superconscious mind and then from the superconscious mind belonging to the person we are going into surrogation for. The permission of the superconscious mind is the guard. If it is not OK for me to take the place of this person, I will get no permission. If it is not OK for the other person, we will also get a 'no'. This double-check is necessary as a security.


Next we will test whether surrogation has been happening. As soon as we are installed, the balances are performed as if the person were present himself.


To do a Balance for someone else is an act of love. We spend time from our own life on the growth of our fellow being.

While I am writing this, I can see my childhood friend before my eyes. She took her own life two years ago. I am going into surrogation for her and feel what she needs. 'I am going to the light' is what I feel I have to test. It tests 'weak'. I bring it into balance. As soon as it is in balance, 'I am in the light' tests strongly. 'Is there something else to be done', tests 'weak'. I end the surrogation.

The minutes that I have spent in surrogation for her have helped her. I do not know exactly how though but I added energy to her system. She is welcome to it; she has suffered enough.

G.B. has attended several private sessions, including the Basic, Advanced and Divine and the PER-K workshops.

*'I always had a bad relationship with my sister for as long as I can remember. Since 1995 I deliberately had no more contact with her. I have never trusted her; there has always been something about her that subconsciously and consciously repelled me (repel factor).*
*We did a Relationship Balance together and you went into surrogation for her. I wanted to have a better understanding of our relationship...*
*It appeared that my little sister has always been jealous of me — because I had been brought up by my mother's grandparents with love and care and often stayed at my aunt and uncle's place*
*Unfortunately my sister has not received any love from her own parents and that is why she has become hard and pinches things that do not belong to her in order to compensate for her lack of love. This is neither ethically justified nor fair, but for her this behaviour is quite normal. She is extremely materialistic and has taken funds from my mother's heritage that were not meant for her and has passed them on to her daughter.'*
*G.B.*

Some people think that every human being has to go his/her own way in life, has to learn his/her own lessons. In a sense I agree with this. Surrogation is an interference with someone else's path of life. I see this quite differently though. We are all connected with each other. What we contribute to each other strengthens the whole. We are not separated and no one has to go his/her own way in order to learn his/her lessons alone. A helping hand is welcome. Imagine that we had to live without each other's help! The criterion is that the suffering of the other one sets our hand in motion, not our own needs. This is the crux in Levinas' philosophy. In G.B. there was a longing for understanding and peace with her sister. That is what we went for. If we feel uncertain about our own intentions, we have to bring them in balance beforehand. We can for instance use the belief 'My intentions are pure' or 'I only give what the other is asking for'.

In our world I notice that we would rather look the other way than take up the suffering of another. We are turning away from the suffering around us. That is what Levinas calls indifference or 'killing one another'. So we are wronging our own humanity and the other's. We owe each other our love as it determines whether we are completely human or not. I see many more dangers in indifference towards each other's suffering than in contributing too much to each other's life.

## 'Love thy enemy'

Let us go one step further. Imagine we have an enemy, someone we really don't get along with. As I have discussed before, we can lose ourselves in the *drama* and continue to impersonate a victim: 'Poor me, X does not grant me life'. We can transform this in for instance 'X is happy with me'. All alarm signals that have led us to perceive X as the enemy, are being transformed by it. We can also keep looking for *solutions* and set our subconscious mind on another perception of the situation. A stress Balance for the situations that have got out of hand before, can take away all sensory alarm signals related to these situations.
We can also *choose* the relationship we want to have with this person. 'I have a fine contact with X' would then be a fruitful belief, or if we do prefer not to see him or her anymore 'I accept that X and I have split up'. Imagine that we decide, in accordance with the Christian wisdom, 'to love our enemy'. We will then see this enmity as an *opportunity* to bring 'I love X' into our system. Or more extensively, 'I am a loving human being'.

We can still go one step further. We can see people as blindly influenced by their sensory alarm signals and serve them by adding love to the system. Then we go into surrogation and we do the Balances that serve them most, like a Balance with the Core Beliefs, a relationship Balance of that person with themselves and a relationship Balance with ourselves. This way we will find a basis for removing enmity on the opposite side.

If we do not want to interfere with their system at all, we can even let their superconscious mind choose what they need. Without knowing what it is, we can do a Balance for this. So they will perfectly get what is needed. The time we spend in surrogation adding energy or love to the life of someone we wrongly thought of as being an enemy, will transform both our lives.

Surrogation is almost a fixed ingredient of relationship Balances. Often one of the partners is ready to get over the drama and look for solutions, choices and opportunities. The absent partner is then represented by someone, for instance the facilitator, who will go into surrogation for him or her. By using relationship Balances, PSYCH-K can contribute dramatically to the creation of peace in a relationship. That is the subject for the next chapter about relationships.

# 8. Peace in Relationships

*'When you remember your divine origins, through the love you share with others in a relationship, peace becomes the foundation of that relationship.'* – Robert Williams

Participants to the workshops have sent a lot of testimonies concerning this subject and the next two chapters. This is quite logical as relationships that have been ailing for years can be healed in a remarkably short period of time, often in less than an hour. This remains spectacular[1]. That is why a Relationship Balance is the designated instrument to realize peace. Key elements of the relationship are dealt with during the Balance. The stress is being transformed and the relationship is changed for the better. There is a choice for the future.

I.P. attended both the Basic and the Advanced workshop. She is part of a practice group. She did this relationship balance in the Advanced workshop.

*'One of my most beautiful experiences with PSYCH-K was the Relationship Balance with my father. During this Balance so many emotions were released and I was deeply moved. It really was a revelation and liberation. So much stored pain and sorrow was released.*
*After the Balance I felt a burden was lifted from my shoulders straight away. I could feel the liberation. My life has become so much lighter ever since.*
*Moreover, the relationship with my father is much more sincere. We are able to see each other and meet each other in love and respect.*
*I am very grateful for this.'*
*I.P.*

F.V.H. attended the Basic workshop once and the Advanced workshop twice.

*'PSYCH-K has strengthened the connection with my daughter: a lot of limiting beliefs have been balanced, so that there is room for positive and clarifying communication, in which feelings are being given the necessary attention and a kind of acceptance is growing between us.*

*The connection with my father gained more space by doing a Relationship Balance. For me the conscious mind has been strengthened in order to stay within my own power in relationship with him. Now I have more peace, where first there was merely a struggle for the right to exist.*

*By applying PSYCH-K I myself have reached the essence of the resistance within myself in relation to people and other things, in which now the next insight is beckoning and a door is opening. That makes the control and fight within myself in relation to everything that exists (of sorrow, loss and deep pain) confidently lead to acceptance and healing.'*
*F.V.H.*

W.V.H. has attended the Basic, Advanced and the Pro workshops. She has a practice of her own.

*'Another example of a very beautiful session is found in a Relationship Balance between a grandmother and her granddaughter. The granddaughter of 16 is with me for a session, because she misses her grandmother very much.*

*I go into surrogation for the grandmother. As soon as I am in surrogation, I feel incredibly nervous. I notice that I have a very special connection with my granddaughter. During the Balance I also have to come up with a belief as a grandmother. During this part of the Balance I feel myself flourishing like a flower and I experience complete liberation. I can break away and follow my own path. All nervousness is dropped and I open my eyes as a changed person. Further in the Balance I feel my granddaughter breaking away from me and standing in her own power. We are both liberated in this session. What makes this session so immensely special to me is that this grandmother had already passed away. I experienced that after her death she was still*

*trapped in her life here on earth. In this session she was completely freed. It showed me that the workings of PSYCH-K are infinite. It does not only affect the here and now, but also the present, the past and other realms.'*
*W.V.H.*

L.J. has attended the Basic and Advanced workshops.

*'Our son and his girlfriend asked me to do a Relationship Balance. They have been together for nearly two years now and they are getting along quite well with very few quarrels that are quickly patched up. However, they had also read and heard that after about two years the hormones involved in being in love diminish and that they would then get a different perspective on the relationship. Their viewpoint was that it would be better to do a Relationship Balance and to get an insight in the subconscious mind instead of just adopting the attitude of wait and see. They were both convinced that little or nothing would show, because they were getting along so well.*
*They were both surprised by the result, especially our son who received a number of "opportunities for growth" (some matters in the relationship caused some stress he was not aware of). Both could recognize themselves in the explanation of the result. It was quite beautiful that they did not condemn one another, but took this as an opportunity for growth, for clearing stress and still for improving their relationship. Since then they have grown enormously, they seem to be even closer and still they give each other more freedom. This is so nice to see!! I wish I would have known this earlier, it would have saved me a lot of trouble.'*
*L.J.*

As a doctor in relational ethics, I am greatly concerned about relationships[2]. I can enormously enjoy people who are getting along well, whereas my heart sinks when people treat each other like mere objects. By analyzing consultations for the quality of their relations for five years, I have become extremely aware of the power of words. Words can create or destroy. We, human beings, are the guardians of these words, we can mobilize them as we see fit. If we are open, supportive words are more likely to flow from our mouths. If our system goes into defence mode, we automatically open up our box of tricks containing the fighting, fleeing or freezing possibilities. If we want to create peace, it is important to fine-tune our subconscious automatisms. The Relationship Balance is a great help in doing so.

**The power of words**

A.M. attended the Basic, Advanced and Divine workshops

*'At the age of twenty I decided to have my first name changed. It felt as if the name, chosen by my mother, did not really fit my personality. I decided to choose my own name and to continue to live by it. In a PSYCH-K session it suddenly dawned on me that in this way I had excluded a substantial part of myself. For years I had had to fight doubts, I could hardly make choices; I had continuously been looking for myself. By means of a Relationship Balance the equilibrium was restored and I was able to make peace with the part of myself that I had been avoiding for years. It felt like a "sacred moment", so essential, so close to myself, ... a magical reunion.'*
*A.M.*

Words create reality, perhaps because they have a direct impact on the water that runs through our body[3]. In that sense they directly influence our whole existence, without detours. That is why declarations of love have such a deep impact. The whole body is vibrating with them. The opposite is also true, of course. Spiteful remarks make us shrink. Dr Bruce Lipton discovered that words open up or close down the cell membrane[4]. They are the keys that can open or close our doors. Words are bearers of energy; they represent materialized meanings. That is why it is necessary to completely respect the words of other people. The beliefs that they choose to Balance or the words that are being spoken in a Relationship Balance belong to them. It is quite important not to add nor leave out anything for they know best what is most valuable[5], what exactly needs to be said or heard now in order to flourish.

Some words go straight to the soul; they touch different energetic layers. This applies to the words that are being spoken in a Relationship Balance. The partners in the relationship are asked to decide what they wish to say or what they want to hear. The words that are chosen can be likened to those of a vow, an oath that is taken.

Here is one example. There are 15 minutes left for practicing after an Advanced workshop; one small group has finished too soon. One participant would like to do a quiet Relationship Balance. As I am preparing to write this book, I ask her to go into surrogation for this Balance. There is no stress between the book and myself; it really feels fine. In order to improve the relationship between us, we both choose a sentence that we want to hear from each other. From the book I want to hear 'I am a success'. The book wants to hear from me 'You are travelling all around the world'. Whoops, this sentence expressed by the book stirs up some fear inside of me. I had thought about writing for a small audience, with only Dutch-speaking people, and I had never thought of having this book translated. Now the book repeatedly asks me, with meaning and loving intention, to promise 'You will be travelling around the world'. At first things go roughly, full of fear, but then things get smoother. At the end there is a celebration: the book is a success and travels all around the world. What has started as a quiet Relationship Balance, without a lot of emotions, has had a deep impact on me.


## Checking for stress between us

E.K. attended the Basic and Advanced workshops. She has a private practice.

*'Let me talk about the experience I had with a Relationship Balance with my daughter E. (with someone in surrogation) concerning the theme "stress and food".*
*I noticed that I still wanted to decide what E. put on her sandwiches and how many sandwiches she ate. I always subconsciously kept score. I kept watching her. That aroused tension. She is sixteen and therefore*

*this is no longer a good idea, neither for myself and definitely nor for her.*

*In a Relationship Balance I have been able to transform the stress and fear of the beliefs concerning eating badly and putting on weight. I have replaced them with trust for her own judgment capacity and that it is quite OK to learn for herself, especially by trial and error.*

*My present was to experience the trust that I had given her and the trust in life and myself. The fear and the control issues disappeared. I am glad about this and I notice what good it does her and us. To be together at the kitchen sink preparing our lunch for the day for example is a real joy nowadays.'*

*E.K.*

The objective of a Relationship Balance is to deepen the understanding between two people by identifying and transforming the issues that challenge them. This comes about by weakening the non-verbal sensory alarm signals that have crept into the relationship[6]. The brain of the partners will be fully activated again, so that both can mobilize their full rational and emotional potential in the relationship. The objective is to trigger a Whole-Brain State whenever the one partner sees, hears or feels the presence of the other one.

Apart from the fixed ingredients, as discussed in Chapter 2, the Balance consists of five specific steps. First we have to find out whether the partners are already in a Whole-Brain State in relation to one another. Being in a Whole-Brain State means that there is no significant stress between both of them. We can check this by letting them look deeply into each other's eyes for 30 seconds, while listening to the facilitator's words. If a partner tests strongly at the end of this half-minute, then he or she does not feel stress towards the other. If a partner tests weakly, this muscle test indicates that there is conflict between the two hemispheres of the brain. In the contact with the other one there are (verbal) limiting beliefs or there is (non-verbal) stress in the system.

My husband and I apply the Relationship Balance in order to keep our relationship fresh and loving. As soon as I notice that things are not running smoothly between us, we do this Balance in order to weaken the static. If things go roughly, I take for granted that he is the culprit. As soon as we receive permission from our superconscious mind and our subconscious mind to trace and transform the stress, we deeply look into each other's eyes for half a minute. I usually assume that my husband is going to test weakly. Of course I should know better. Don't I know the theory? It is my alarm bells that turn him into the enemy. He tests strongly and I test weakly; it has always been the same. This sobers me up and is at the same time quite liberating. We continue to Balance for another few minutes and everything is lovey-dovey again.

## Discovering and transforming the problem

If one of the partners tests weakly, there is stress in the relationship on that side. Either both partners test weakly, or one of them or neither of them. For the relationship it is not important who tests weakly. The important thing is that the stress be transformed and that both can openly invest in the relationship again.

A Relationship Balance is by no means a way of fixing a relationship. Relationships come into being and are maintained by decisions that the partners make. Decisions are made by the conscious mind, not by the superconscious mind. All in all a lot of our decisions are directed by subconscious impulses. We want to be responsible beings. Deciding which relationships we want with someone is as such a conscious act. With PSYCH-K we can decide lucidly and sensitively. By being 'in balance' with one another, we can soberly and sensitively discuss in a Whole-Brain State how we want to get on with each other. If we are not in a Whole-Brain State, our subconscious stress impulses command us. As I have explained before, during subconsciously directed defensive reactions we do not show the best part of ourselves. We had better be in a Whole-Brain State and get on with each other candidly. It is less hurtful, and does justice to the other person.

While the partners are just looking at each other, we try to determine what the current problem is. Is it a matter of lack of self-respect, reproaches, lack of love, unfulfilled needs, not being able to let go, being difficult, blocking learning opportunities, avoiding responsibility, refusing to change, distrusting choices, being worried or not trusting life?

If we know what the theme of the stress is, we will transform it in each partner separately. It matches the vision of PSYCH-K that we ourselves have to take responsibility for who we are in our reactions. Every one of us has to do 'his/her own homework' and weaken the sensory alarms that are in our system.
Peace begins by not passing on the problems that concern us, but begins by tackling and solving them ourselves.

Formulating this description lasts longer than transforming the themes. Usually the transformation only takes a few minutes.

As soon as the stress concerning the other person has been removed from our system, the contact is quite different. We are looking at each other with a fresh look; we feel the view the other person has of us is different now. This remains a fine experience for me over and over again. Knowing that transforming one's own stress can create a totally different kind of energy in the relationship is also a stimulating conclusion.

One more testimony. R.V.D. has had counselling four times; she has not attended any PSYCH-K workshops. First we did a Core Belief Balance, and then mainly Stress and Relationship Balances: with herself, with her daughter-in-law and afterwards with a girlfriend of hers. Here is her story.

*'I would like to write down some impressions, because I have received much benefit and even a little magic from PSYCH-K.*
*I have already told you about the fairly awkward relationship with a girlfriend and with my daughter-in-law. By looking at them in another, more positive way, I have experienced some positive initiatives they took regarding me, without myself expecting these in the least.*

*I am not looking forward to my birthday party (70) on Sunday. We are expecting some 55 people. I know quite well that I am going to shine for all the joy of my life and I am going to give a short speech. I feel I am a privileged woman... because of three great sons, three beautiful and wise daughters-in-law, seven dear grandchildren and a husband who has been loving me dearly for more than 50 years... (speech abridged).*

*Doing PSYCH-K with you has really helped!'*
R.V.D.

When each partner has shed his/her own stress, we will test again whether there is a new full flow of energy through the previously mentioned problem areas. Then we will even take it a little further. While in this step we have been working with each partner separately, in the next step the relationship will be settled.

## The individual bonding process

If both partners have sorted out things with themselves concerning the other one, the connecting process will follow. The relationship, the connection between the two of them, is a separate entity. A love relationship is different than a cooperative relationship. The connecting process aims at restoring the specific character of the relationship.
I myself, think this is very special. A Relationship Balance with a child provokes completely different feelings than a Relationship Balance with my husband. Other aspects are addressed in me.

Before peace is possible, we need words: connecting words. Who tested weakly can choose what he or she wants to hear. If only one of the partners tested weakly, he or she can also choose what he has to say to the partner. The sentences spoken have to be short and meaningful.

At the moment when the person is in a Whole-Brain State, he or she perfectly chooses what the soul needs to hear in order to be healed completely. Asking for and receiving forgiveness are often the first sentences that come up. Most of the time these are not what the partner really needs to hear. It is rather an intermediate stage; these words have to be spoken first. The most meaningful words are those that offer perspective. They are sentences that build a new kind of energy in the relationship.

During the individual connecting process one partner just accepts what the other partner brings in. The words are spoken with meaning and loving intention while both partners look at each other and make movements in the shape of figure 8's. By bringing in this sign of infinity, all sensory data are being brought in balance with the chosen affirmation. Both the verbal and the non-verbal aspects of the relationship are being healed. Both on the side of the giver and of the receiver blocked emotions can be released. That is why the process may be emotional. After that relaxation begins.

In turn the partners take the role of the giver and of the receiver. So even at the deepest level the dynamics of giving and receiving, as known from contextual assistance, is activated again[7]. Because the partner can choose what he wants to say, the other person hears what pleases him most, what is most essential. The partner isn't left guessing. As the partner himself is in a Whole-Brain State, nothing should stand in the way of giving the other one what is beneficial to him/her.

### The collective bonding process

When each partner has separately given and received, the time has come to confirm the dynamics of giving and receiving for both parties

The partners hold each other's hands and in turn speak the sentence that the other one wants to hear. In the meantime they are looking into each other's eyes and are respectively focusing on the face, the sound of the words and the spot of the body where they feel the other person most. The sentences sound like a song that is being sung back and forth. Meanwhile lemniscate signs (horizontal figure of 8 signs) are being drawn in the space between them. So all sensory data –

visual, auditive and kinaesthetic – are being brought in accordance with the statements.

The liberating effect of this collective process is hard to express in words. All aspects of our humanity are being addressed: the eyes as a window of the soul, the holding of hands as an expression of the body, the words that touch the cells, the lemniscate signs that transform the visual, auditory and kinaesthetic data. The whole system – therefore the whole human being – as body, soul and mind is involved in the bonding process.

As soon as this connecting process is completed, the partners deeply look into each other's eyes for 30 seconds, just like at the beginning. Major sources of conflict and stress have been transformed in the relationship. Not only have the individuals transformed their mutual stress; the relationship itself is often transformed. At last there is (again) breathing space and room for peace between them.

In the testimony of R.V.D. she says that the initiative came from the other people: '… I even received some positive initiatives from them directed at me, which I didn't expect at all'. R.V.D. had consulted me; her daughter-in-law and her girlfriend were both not physically present. In order to heal the relationship, I went into surrogation for them. And still, afterwards, initiative came from the daughter-in-law and the girlfriend. R.V.D. describes this minimally: of course it is her perception. Perhaps these women also took the initiative before and she had not been aware of it. This is quite possible. Nevertheless, because the energy of the relationship has changed, wonderful things can happen. Without knowing about the Relationship Balance that has been done, the absent partner often takes an initiative that was previously unthinkable. This is one of the wonders that a Relationship Balance may provoke.


## Relationships are being touched for peace

Relationships tend to strive for joy and peace. Not in the passive sense; they are aware of active giving and receiving peace dynamics from both sides. In joy and peace the relationship can develop its highest potential. A lot can then be realized.

Because we are in relation with everybody around us, we can do Relationship Balances with living, dead or children not-yet-born.

With A.V.G. we did two Relationship Balances, one with herself and one with her daughter.
*'I am going to play it by ear and announce a couple of remarkable changes. I can look someone in the eyes without being intimidated and second, after the Relationship Balance I did with myself, I am no longer afraid of myself. The result is that I can function in a small group and dare to express myself.'*
*A.V.G.*

With clients I am inclined to do a Relationship Balance between the person and him/herself first. As long as we do not have a balanced relationship with ourselves, all the other relationships are burdened as well. Such a Balance can be immensely liberating. Where before there was fighting and disagreement with oneself, the Balance can create personal peace.

With N.V. there have been several coaching contacts. She has also attended several workshops.
*'In our relationship there is peace at last …*
*During the individual sessions I have worked, on the relationship with my mother together with M.R. No matter how hard my mother and I tried, almost every contact we had ended in a painful and/or offensive remark. Step by step M.R. and I have removed the stress from this relationship. The final liberating breakthrough came on a practice day, when my former and other lives and those of my grandmothers were dealt with. Even if I do not fully understand all this, the relationship with my mother has never been better.'*
*N.V.*

The relationship with our parents can profoundly influence and help to shape us into what we are now. That is why this connection with them is dealt with most in counselling sessions. Our parents have of course also been shaped by their own parents. Our grandparents have passed on their cell material to our parents. This is going on and on. Our family history with all the connected beliefs, expressed in the cells of our body, carries material that has been passed on from generation to generation[8]. Though we do not have access to the experiences that are underlying these beliefs, the beliefs can still exert their beneficial or baleful influence. We are aware of some beliefs, for instance that in some families daughters can be treated as inferior beings. If this was also transmitted in our family from generation to generation, the relationship between mother and daughter will be burdened with this.

Relationships with lovers are also a recurring theme in counselling. During the session there is room for surrogation if necessary, so that the relationships with former, current and future lovers can be brought in Balance.

From the chapter 'From drama to learning opportunity' we have learned that a drama that has not been transformed can be transferred to following situations. We tend to repeatedly create the same problems. By creating peace with our 'ex', the current or new lover is given every space. The old problematic energy is no longer between our loved ones and us.


## Relationships with children

During a second counselling X. told me that she has already known me for a long time. She had once before seen me in an interview for a group counselling of women after abortion at the Centre for Relation Building and Pregnancy Problems. She tells me how the abortion has remained an obstacle in the relationship with her husband, whom she has now divorced. It is comforting for her that the abortion has been talked about at the end of the relationship, but it is still gnawing at her. We touch on the subject at the end of the session and I suggest that she reads the book I wrote about this[9]. When she feels that she is ready for it, we can do a Relationship Balance with 'the child that was never born'[10]. During the Relationship Balance there is an enormous flow of love between the mother and 'the child that was never born'. The connecting process is both forgiving and also promising. X. has been promised a new life.

X. visited me one more time. She has a new partner with whom she can share her life in a different way.

Whether our children are still alive or not, the connection with them is very strong. I have done several Relationship Balances with our children myself, both while they were present but also in their absence. Someone will have to go into surrogation.

The most lasting impressions are the Relationship Balances with 'children that were never born'. From my work in post-abortion counselling I know that the greatest suffering from this relationship springs from the love that cannot flow. There is an enormous love both from the mother and from 'the child that was never born'. Reproaches stand in the way of this love. The objective is to bring peace and quiet to this relationship. We have to continue to promote the love that springs from this here and now.

I am so grateful that with a PSYCH-K Balance we can heal wounds that are not accessible with other methods. In the introduction I have stated that I wanted to start post-abortion counselling in a different way. I would do Relationship Balances, with the person and their own self, with 'the child that was never born', with the father and Stress Balances for the situation in which the abortion was carried out. The results of this counselling would now be far greater than what we could achieve a couple of years ago. Relationship Balances are equally beneficial in situations with i.e. miscarriages, handicapped children, stillborn children and in situations in which a woman could bear no children at all. So peace is being created with all those children, those who came and those who were expected without coming.

## Relationship with an 'invisible' twin brother or sister

G.V.L. came for a first counselling session and we balanced his relationship with the twin partner that he had known in the womb. Afterwards G. attended the Basic workshop.

*'What I especially remember from our meeting, is the fine valuable feeling to find out that you knew the phenomenon called twin syndrome, whereas most therapists have not even heard about it.*

*For many "VTS cases" (Vanishing Twin Syndrome) it is always difficult to make a distinction between which part, which characteristic belongs to myself and which part belongs to the twin. Because you were able to take the position of the twin, many things that really belonged to me became clear. The exercise then has produced an increase of my self-respect. PSYCH-K has then, through you, made it much clearer to me where my self-respect was lacking.*

*It has brought me more inside myself, closer to myself, so that it becomes clearer now who I really am. Because twins happen to lose themselves sometimes.*

*This was the conclusion of the session: for myself "enjoy and be happy" and for the twin "see you later". This has given me such a feeling of enlightenment that I first went for a drink in a nearby pub before I could drive home again.'*

*G.V.L.*


It goes without saying that any family relationship can be balanced, with brothers and sisters, with grandparents, uncles, aunts, and all people that have played an important family role for the person. The Balance can be done, as I have described before, either with currently living people or with deceased family members by way of surrogation.


### The relationship with 'abuse'

I regularly receive women who have been sexually abused for counselling. Besides several other Balances that can bring them at peace with themselves, I will at one point suggest doing a Relationship Balance about abuse. Such a Balance does not only picture how much the abuse has permeated this woman, at the end it will bring her peace. That is the objective.

I go into surrogation with 'abuse' myself. At the beginning I feel very invasive, big or even overwhelming. At the end I feel that I have no hold on this woman. The abuse energy has really been disconnected from this person. The energy has also become insignificant, it is no longer asking for attention.

In 'abuse' I also experience a switch in my role. Whereas at first I receive far too much room to play, at the end of the Balance I experience myself as someone who challenges the woman into powerfully expressing herself.

The statements that were chosen in three different situations are: 'Enough now, go' versus 'X., I am letting you go'; 'I need my own space' versus 'You are untouchable'; 'I totally release you' versus 'Only my own energy surrounds me'.

PSYCH-K, and more specifically the relationship Balance, works quite powerfully at the non-verbal level. This changes the person's energy.

## More relationships in balance

Relationship Balances can be done with everything we can give a name to. Because we do not only relate to people, but also to feelings, to sleep, to organisations, to financial institutions, to nature, to humanity as a whole, ... and to the divine. I will discuss the latter in Chapter 12 'PSYCH-K unleashes Love'. But here are two other testimonies.

G.S. attended the Basic, Advanced, Pro and the Health and Wellness workshops.

*'I did a Relationship Balance on the situation between Palestinians and Israeli people; we usually do Balances for ourselves but there is more to be done. One of my daughters is married to an Israelite. When they are fighting in Gaza, I feel concerned. There is little I can do so I did a Relationship Balance for Peace for the peoples of Israel and Palestine. We worked on "letting go of the past". I do not know if they felt something when the negotiations took place but I was relieved to have done it.*
*I did a Balance with L.D. in a family setting. The Balance was incredible; I put everyone in a circle. During the mourning period surrounding my mother's death (May-August 2014) everybody shook off the remnants*

*of tensions and so we were totally present for my mother and father. Any light resistance that I felt was defused immediately and transformed in positive action. The other people felt the same. These are baby steps, but each tiny step from every one of us make a huge difference.'*
G.S.

M.V.D. attended the Basic, Advanced and Divine workshops several times.

*'About trauma: I often use PSYCH-K as an addition when working with people with traumatic experiences. Here too I noticed that the process is speeded up by the use of PSYCH-K. It quickly removes the emotional burden from an experience (Stress Balance). After that there is space for further research and processing as well as a new perspective.*
*I notice that forgiving and setting free continues to work (deeply) even in me, it removes issues more and more, so that freedom is created in order to live as the real you and to experience control over your own life.*
*In the case of abuse and other traumas the experience of impotence is very intense and PSYCH-K gives you something tangible with which you can begin to believe in your own influence and power.*
*With everything happening it is always of the utmost importance to me to take into account the transcending factor as well, so that an experience does not only solve something, but also brings something; what is the message? I want to discover what my share is, what I am responsible for, how I can grow from this. This helps me take responsibility and transcend the "level of drama".*

*Finding messages in any experience has also been facilitated by PSYCH-K; the system points them out! People, whom I am working with, give me feedback about it being so fine that a question or a theme when working on it, is dealt with quite thoroughly; all messages and advantages are being transformed and it means a big clean-up; of course we must work on it, but without digging too deeply! For instance in the case of physical symptoms, a specific fear, repetition of something that is not wanted. What I find so beautiful is that gratitude* can be created for all that exists; this means acceptance at a deep level.

Again and again working with surrogation, will give me special experiences; I have already been a horse, Buddha, the Origin, a dog, fathers, mothers, deceased persons, children, money, work, organs and other body parts, blockages, eating disorder, the person himself, an apparatus, etcetera. It is quite beautiful to see that the person with you immediately notices the subtle shift in energy, attitude, facial expression, radiation and linguistic usage. People say for instance; "Well, that is how my father always acts". Mostly it will bring deep, experienced insights, awakening and transformation.

In our practice my partner and I myself are working together with couples, using incidental questions or sometimes more intensive processes. When we do a Relationship Balance, in combination with counselling, this gives us marvellous results! Quite recently a client has called this an "APK for the relationship"[11] (this term we will put on our website); it quickly traces growth opportunities and deepens and confirms the connection.

Also with regard to relationships of parents and children, family relationships, friendships and collegial relationships I gladly and often do a Relationship Balance, because of its effectiveness.

About astonishing experiences: a seven year old little boy who after one session with the mother and one session without her was freed from his fears and can now be a wonderful child again. Someone else experienced the presence of an angel during a Balance. People who discover their own value, who take care of themselves, who follow their hearts and find their own way. Young people who become powerful. People who break free from addictions, fears, phobias, panic, trauma, ... People who in a constructive way take big decisions about relationships, children, destination and philosophy of life. Relationships that become deeper and more loving; families that function much better. People who after a session suddenly are free from eczema or earaches. Physical complaints that lessen, like a woman with a serious leg injury who was able to walk much better after one session; my migraine that disappeared by trusting the wisdom of my body. Really *touching is the 80 year old woman, who had the courage to overlook her past and "clean it up", so that she is no longer haunted by ghosts from the past.*

*Divine: this retreat has deepened my connection with the higher, the All, my divine spark. I can work more and more and be in the now, from a growing confidence that everything is perfect the way it is, so that more than often I am "fine", even if I am not fine. In the course I attended I learned to trust the course of the process of the other person and to actually leave the responsibility where it belongs; I was very much aware of the fact that this kept demanding my alertness; PSYCH-K clarified this for me. By bringing together more light and peace in the world, heaven and earth get closer. In my opinion PSYCH-K can largely contribute to this and it perfectly fits this new age; it is time to start living from the heart and we should do this together; together we are one, each with an authentic value.*

*I have so many experiences that I find it difficult to choose; I have been applying PSYCH-K for over one year and a half and I do this once or more times a day, for myself, my environment and my clients, so this really adds up!'*
*M.V.D.*

PSYCH-K has more to offer than just solving difficulties. It brings us home within ourselves and with others; we learn lessons of life, so that we can grow spiritually. In other words, PSYCH-K transforms at the level of opportunities, as every situation is a challenge to grow as a human being[12].

In the last chapter I will rather stress the transcending connection. Let me first focus on the matter from which we are built, namely our body. The next chapter will therefore deal with health.

# 9. A Healthy Mind in a Healthy Body

*"Disease is often a spiritual wake up call for an individual. Pay attention to symptoms as messengers from your Higher-Self, before you kill the messengers and miss the spiritual gift they bring." – Robert Williams*

M.T. travelled to Marseille in order to attend the Health and Wellness workshop there. This was her fourth of five PSYCH-K workshops[1].

'While travelling with the TGV (fast train) from Marseille to Brussels, we had only just left, and a woman came into our carriage to ask if there was a doctor among us, because help was needed for someone who had fainted. There was no doctor, so I presented myself, as I am a nurse. We had just received our first-aid training in PSYCH-K and I was able to start practicing right away. In the meantime the man had recovered consciousness, he had felt some pressure on his chest and felt sick while heavily perspiring. He had a fast pulse, I guess from experience about 100 per minute, but it could be felt clearly. He knew kinesiology, but muscle testing was impossible for him under the circumstances. I quickly put him in a whole-brain position. In the meantime I kept controlling his pulse, which immediately calmed down. When he opened his eyes, his queasiness was gone. He felt better, but still quite weak. I reassured him that this was normal. In the meantime I had called for a doctor to be at the next station. So, without medication, or any other means, it is possible to, but only with the person himself, clearly remove the important stress factor. It was a beautiful experience, because when working with PSYCH-K, I normally don't use my nursing skills. So I didn't know the results of a Stress Balance are measurable by taking somebody's pulse.'
M.T.

## The effect of a previous trauma on our current health

A.X. attended two private sessions and the Basic workshop. She wrote the extensive testimony at the beginning of the chapter about trauma. Afterwards she added this.

*'I used to have trouble with my sinuses; I often had to use steam baths. Now it does not trouble me anymore. How do I think this is possible? After the Balance with the Core Beliefs here at home I suddenly went through a memory of abuse. I again experienced an ejaculation and of course I had to throw up and the vomit also came through my nostrils. Since then I have had no more trouble with my sinuses, only when I have the flu, but never without a reason anymore. The pain that started each time, felt as if a tractor had driven over my face. And there was never the least bit of mucus, the sinuses just started swelling and being irritated.*
*My husband has also noticed that I do not experience this trouble in winter anymore. There can only be one explanation, which is the new experience after this session with you.'*
*A.X.*

From my research, which I have described earlier in the second chapter about trauma, it appears that the previous loss of control can bring our body to a traumatic feeling again at any moment. These traumatic reactions come into being because at least three sensory alarm signals will start. The active alarm signals cause the same reaction in the body as during the trauma. If it means feeling panic, panic will come up again; if it means dizziness you will feel dizzy again. If the reaction included running away or a beating, the body will follow that same scenario[2].

B.H. has learned to stop her stress response with 'Other Life'. After that she attended a PSYCH-K Basic workshop. She went into private counselling to address her lung problems.

*'In January 2014 my breathing felt constricted. After the result of the lung test there was 10 percent of COPD (Chronic Obstructive*

Pulmonary Disease), this was quite a blow. No matter what the general practitioner prescribed – inhaler a, inhaler b, then inhaler c followed by inhaler d – nothing seemed to help. Then he went for antibiotics, but nothing happened. I only became more and more ill (a lot of stress). One day I saw the doctor working during weekends, who said: "You do not have a lung problem, but you have the birch syndrome." This is a problem of the bronchial tubes due to an allergy and also to food allergies. According to the doctors it cannot be cured. Then I got Prednisone directly in the nose, but nothing happened. In the meantime I could hardly breathe, doors and windows seemed shut tight.

Then I went to see E., a very skilful PSYCH-K facilitator in Doetinchem. The cause of my problems was a car accident in which I had lost my brother when I was aged 17. My mother blamed me for the accident. That caused six years of stress at home, until I left.

E. did a 2-hour Trauma Balance and addressed some other items that happened after the accident in the next hour. And you will not believe it. E. lives beautifully in the midst of pastures, and as I walked outside, for the first time in six months she was able to breathe freely again. I still cannot believe it!

But still my brain was trying to pull me back over and over again when I felt stress and so I had to use the Alexander concept some 25 times a day, because the anxiety is closely related to stress. These days I only have to use the Alexander concept 4 times a day and soon I am going to see E. again for the home run. Up till now I have seen her 3 times.

I do work a lot with PSYCH-K, because it doesn't stop at half measures. For me, PSYCH-K, combined with "Other Life", is a gift from heaven.'
B.H.

In physically painful conditions, like what happens after an accident, with a disease or with violence quite some loss of control may be experienced. Then the current bodily reactions are accompanied by bodily reactions as felt during the trauma.

When I only just had my own a practice and even before I was working with PSYCH-K, I. came to me for counselling. 25 years ago she had experienced a serious accident. The fact that she had come out of the wreck of her car alive, after she landed under a lorry and had survived several operations was a miracle.

Although she had continued to live a normal life, the woman now, in her menopause, showed extreme problems. Due to a burnout she was no longer able to work. The worst were the hot flushes as she experienced acute mortal fear while undergoing them

With the knowledge I had then, we had to bring the sensory alarm signals into the conscious mind, so that a memory could be created and the body would no longer go into alarm. Little by little we tried to reconstruct the accident[3]. By keeping on clustering the different sensory signals into a memory, we tried to form a picture with all puzzle pieces and find the most traumatic experience. That was when she got stuck under the lorry, jammed under her steering wheel, with a smashed foot, knee and hip. With the will to survive she wrestled herself free from this trap and pushed the door open. The last thing she felt before fainting was the breeze of the warm summer wind.

Every time I. had a flush, she experienced the same warm breeze and her system went into agony. By this technique of regression she was freed from the agonies. The corresponding beliefs, however, had not been transformed. With PSYCH-K we can do both.

N.V. did the Basic, Advanced and Pro workshops.

*'I used to regularly have a sore throat. The doctor could detect neither a bacterial nor a viral infection. When I told M., she suggested we should do a Relationship Balance with my throat. In the future I know that, whenever I have a sore throat, I will have to take the time to listen to it. Often my throat has to tell me something. Once the message is received, the pain automatically disappears, unless I really have to see the doctor, which my sore throat also will tell me.*

For months my left ear had been irritating me sometimes mildly sometimes seriously. Medically speaking nothing seemed to be the matter. In a PSYCH-K workshop I learned to work with messages, secondary gain and actions. Because I really had been fed up with this awkward experience of "spitting movements" inside my ear, I went to look for a possible message. And indeed, there was one: "Let go of the past." My ear could not have been clearer.'
N.V.

I.W. only attended the Basic workshop.

'Whenever I slept less than 7 hours a night for a few days in a row, I became ill. I got a sore throat, was short of breath and I got several physical complaints. With PSYCH-K I have been working on the belief: "Even if I sleep less than 7 hours a day, I will always remain healthy and function optimally." Since then I have never had these complaints again, even if I sleep less than 7 hours.'
I.W.

J.S. only attended the Basic workshop. This was presented in two parts: first a two-day weekend, and next a practice day on the next Saturday. On that last day the participants learned how to discover hidden messages underlying their complaints and how to make use of these advantages.

'On the first day of the course I asked you what was the best: doing a Balance for my whole health or a separate one for my high blood pressure? You advised me to work as directly as possible. It immediately worked and my blood pressure went down.
But after a week things did not work anymore. The next weekend we learned to do a VAK to the Future. Then it became clear to me that my high blood pressure was a reaction coming from myself. It was like a cry for help. I could not handle things any longer; I had had enough. I also understood then that it was a way to hide, like a victim. In fact I was blackmailing my husband, so that he would not become angry again, because the cardiologist had also frightened him by telling that my heart condition was very serious.

*In this course I understood that I was the one and only who could get out of this situation and I was the one who needed to change. I understood that I kept attracting these things, perhaps through my experiences as a child. But this is no longer necessary.*

*I am so pleased that I am no longer dependent on what someone else is saying, but that I can change myself and that I am fully responsible. That I think I am worthy full of joy and can also radiate this.*

*My husband is reacting quite differently now; our relationship has improved a lot. And fortunately, my blood pressure and heart are much better now.*
*This PSYCH-K course liberated me also in other items. I am very grateful for being able to learn and grow. I want to advise everyone to attend this PSYCH-K course. For me it was unnerving, but also a joyful experience.'*
*J.S.*

Our body is the only tool that can make clear what the subconscious mind tries to signal when something is not well[4]. Far too often our body irritates us, it does not function the way we think it should. Most of the time this has to do with a wrong interpretation. Our body makes something clear to us. Sometimes that is a limiting belief that opposes the beneficial functioning of a part of the body. Bruce Lipton claims that 'the biggest impediments to realizing the successes we are dreaming of, are the limitations that are programmed in the subconscious mind'.

From our education quite a number of limiting beliefs may have been programmed in our subconscious mind. For instance 'only the doctor knows what makes my body ill'. Or 'If I get something, it is always serious' or 'They will not find it'. More fundamental beliefs may have been embedded into ourselves for generations, like 'A man is made to suffer' or 'In our family they all die young'[5].

G.B. attended the Basic workshop, the Advanced and the Divine workshops twice.

*'I cannot talk about my sleeping problem as I still fall asleep in the morning, nor can I talk about speaking in public, because I have not yet had the opportunity to stand in public. After a terrible car accident and a lot of surgery PSYCH-K has helped me to accept my face as it is.'*
G.B.

P.B. came in for several private sessions and attended the Basic, Advanced, Professional and Divine workshops.

*'I have had trouble with my blood sugar levels for years. First I had to take medication so I was able to keep it under control for a while. But then my blood sugar levels remained so high that I was told to inject insulin. That is why I started working on this with PSYCH-K. By working on this for quite a long time, we arrived at the heart of the matter. We started by removing the first layers until we reached the core. Since then my blood sugar levels have gone down so much that I had to reduce the medication. But as my blood sugar levels kept decreasing, I do not have to take any medication at all anymore. And no I am no longer a diabetic patient!!!'*
P.B.

Sometimes we have to dig a little before we find what is really the matter. In PSYCH-K we call this puzzling 'looking for messages'. Together we have developed a strategy in order to trace these messages easily.

K.V.O. attended the Basic and Advanced workshops.

*'I am attending the Advanced workshop. M.R. tells me about the influence of PSYCH-K on my health and she says: "Just do a Balance for what you expect from your body". "Yes, yes, why not..." thinks my critical I. "If only it could be that simple..."*
*But I want to try it out. Because I have had constipation for years, I do a Balance for "I have regular bowel activity every day". The Balance is happening quite fast. Believe it or not: during the Balance the word*

linseed occurs to me. Apparently my body needs this in order to have regular bowels. Isn't this funny! Ever since I add linseed to my food daily and I can go to the toilet regularly now!'
K.V.O.

D.B. did the Basic workshop twice and the Advanced workshop once.

'The constipation problems started 1 and a half years ago after doing a detox. I got supplements and used suppositories costing 22$ apiece. I drink up to 2 litres of water per day. There was but one solution left; having an enema administered regularly and this gave me haemorrhoids.
I went to my GP for advice and started being scared. He prescribed another kind of pill but this didn't help either.
So I went to the hospital in Leuven to have a colostomy. I had a small polyp removed, nothing major. I was referred to a different specialist for an appointment on the 17th of October. In the meantime I did a Balance for: "Everyday I go to the loo easily and use linseed". I also looked for messages but couldn't find any. Nothing helped.
About a week prior to the 17th of October I did a Balance on: "I am easily defecating, eating linseed soaked in water overnight". THE NEXT DAY I DID AND I STILL DO.
I had to tell the specialist that I was able to go easily every day now because I drank soaked linseed regularly, for I didn't dare to tell him about PSYCH-K.
I once got a serious scolding from a physician when I told him I took alternative supplements at the time of my breast cancer bout.
This professor congratulated me by saying: "Congratulations Madam, you cured yourself".'
D.B.

## We don't have to experience the trauma again in order to transform it

In contrast to other methods, in PSYCH-K we are not looking for what may have happened before but we are looking for the beliefs that are present now because these beliefs are often manifested in the body. Bruce Lipton claims that the beliefs we hold influence the body more strongly than the normal functioning of our cells. Talking to our subconscious mind does not help: it is like talking into a tape recorder to change the recording, without hitting the recording button. According to Lipton the cells are forced to stick to the subconscious programme[6]. It is our undermining beliefs therefore that can make us ill.

F.D. attended the Basic, the Advanced and the Divine workshops.

*'People around me might say that by becoming an adult my life has changed. Prior to PSYCH-K partying and working a lot under the influence of cannabis, alcohol and cigarettes had determined my life. After the acquaintance with PSYCH-K I found the power and the will to give my life a positive turn. Now, after one year, I am welcoming my first child in a sound and pure family. No more addictions! I am a healthy father.'*
F.D.

Fortunately, with PSYCH-K we do not have to experience the whole trauma again in order to neutralize it. We are just giving the subconscious mind the task to find and transform the sensory alarm signals. That was what M.T. did in the train from Marseille. Despite the fact that she could not test the fainted person with kinesiology at that moment, they brought back the man from his body's re-experience of the trauma. She was able to assess this from the speed of his pulse. M.T. never knew what kind of trauma this was.

L.J. attended the Basic and Advanced Workshops.

*'My husband was operated on twice within a year on his back from a double discus hernia. Before both operations we had followed quite a number of therapies that all had helped a little, but we could not ease the pain. To his astonishment, he experienced even more pain in his back after the second operation and the removal of both hernias.*

*I attended the Basic PSYCH-K course and applied the Stress Balance and the New Direction Balance with my husband and immediately he felt a decrease in pain.*

*Two weeks later I attended the Advanced course and I did a Relationship Balance with my husband's boss. Our son went into surrogation for the boss and it turned out to be quite an emotional Balance. Immediately after the Balance my husband felt much better and he had almost no pain anymore. Since that day, whenever he feels pain in his back again, we do a Balance and the pain vanishes. We have noticed that whenever he experiences stress, it shows up in his back.*

*The procedures are clear and the Balances are very purposeful and effective. Both my husband and myself have already attended a lot of courses about personal development and we are really impressed by the way PSYCH-K works. It is an extremely fast way in which we do not have to go digging in our negative emotions but in which we are focused on what we want to achieve. It works so well that in the meantime my husband has also registered for the courses.*

*Our son came home and showed us his right shoulder, which was hanging much lower than the left one and of course as a result his back hurt. We went looking for the underlying message of this lower shoulder and we found that some burdens are emotionally too strong for him to carry. We did a Resolution Balance and a New Direction Balance. After the session his shoulder was at the correct height again. This happened two weeks ago and everything is still fine!'*
*L.J.*

In order to diminish the influence of the sensory alarm signals with PSYCH-K we do not need to know what happened[7]. Surprisingly even with insight, combined with actions and commitment, seldom produces lasting results.

N.V. attended the Basic, Advanced and Pro workshops.

*'Fear of hands*
*During one of my physiotherapy treatments it showed that I might have*
*a fear of hands. This also seemed to be the case in my subconscious*
*mind. One balance later this fear had completely been transformed.*
*Since then every form of bodily tenderness is much more enjoyable.'*
*N.V.*

A.V. attended the Basic workshop.

*'I had been having health problems for almost half a year: Pfeiffer*
*and a (chronic) ear infection. I tried everything: regular health care,*
*acupuncture, chiropractic treatment and osteopathy.*
*I had registered for the basic training of PSYCH-K and I did not look*
*forward to the weekend at all. How would I be able to make it through*
*these two full days?! I was so tired, really exhausted.*
*But still I went and it is undreamed-of how my energy has grown and*
*how my complaints have vanished! Whilst on the way towards the*
*meeting I only had 30 percent of energy, when I came back it was at*
*least 85 percent and it kept on going up even more.'*
*A.V.*

When on holiday in Bulgaria we walked into a local shop. While we were
looking around, I became dizzy and felt sick. I told my husband and we
went back to the car. I did a stress balance there. This is a fast process
in which I focused on the dizziness. I asked my superconscious mind
for permission and engaged my subconscious mind in transforming
the alarm material. I was in a whole-brain position and concentrated
on the dizzy feeling. After three minutes I was myself again. I felt that
my body was shifting a little and then I was completely back. Literally
and figuratively I had been cleared. It is with joy that I could consult
the map as we were driving further.

## Developing fear and behaving accordingly

Our conscious mind likes telling explanatory stories, because they give
us something to hold on to. I do not know what happened to me in that

little shop,. I became dizzy and it has been cured. Without PSYCH-K I would have felt dizzy and sick a lot longer. I would then perhaps have told a story about the circumstances. For example that 'I find these little shops musty, not fresh'. Our conscious mind likes giving an explanation of why something is as it is. That gives us something to hold on to in uncertain times; times in which our alarm is switched on. Of course my beliefs about these small shops are not respectful to the people there, but most of the time we do not notice this.

As soon as we start believing our own story – we are convinced that things went the way we tell it – our subconscious mind will scan the surrounding world for correspondences. Know that composed stories are told with more dogmatic assertion than stories without underlying alarm signals. That is because the conscious mind, in contrast to the subconscious data, has to keep up the story[8].

From the first chapter we remember that a belief is a conclusion or short summary of an experience. If, as a conclusion of my dizziness, I had accepted the belief that these little shops in Bulgaria are musty and not fresh, I would not have visited little shops in Bulgaria anymore. The belief 'In Bulgaria little shops are musty and not fresh' is still looking for a further confirmation and I will find it. The behaviour of avoidance that we develop in this way can considerably impede our life. Our already little world then becomes even smaller and smaller. We are developing behaviour of avoidance: fear for fear[9].

By connecting the belief 'In Bulgaria little shops are musty and not fresh' with the experience of dizziness – and we know now that our subconscious mind is the champion for making such connections – going into a little Bulgarian shop is connected with this bodily reaction. The sensory alarm signals are attached to the belief and together they are responsible for quite a fuss in little shops. When having a similar reaction in Belgium afterwards – e.g. this little shop reminds me of the one in Bulgaria – we will create more and more situations that trigger these sensory alarms. We can break this impeding circle by doing Balances.

During the transformation of stress we now and then highlight limiting beliefs. These beliefs have been stored during the original stressful situation and most of the time they have to be transformed separately after the stress balance. If not, the beliefs continue to control the future behaviour[10]. The stress will then have been removed from the situation, but as long as the beliefs remain active, the self-destructive behaviour will be repeated. Sensory alarm signals are connected with more and more situations. It is like an expanding inks stain.

This mechanism leads us to the transformation of allergies.

**Transforming allergies**

N.V. attended the Basic, Advanced and the Pro workshops.

*'Enjoying scampi again...*
*Some three years ago I could not eat scampi any longer without feeling sick and tired for the rest of the day. Crustaceans have never been my "cup of tea", except for scampi, jumbo shrimps and langoustines, which I liked a lot. Being a sceptical person, I accepted the challenge during the Professional workshop though. It seems incredible but it is true, during the workshop I ate prawns without feeling sick at all. It took some more time to adjust, but now I fully enjoy a scampi salad again.'*
*N.V.*

Allergies come into being because a traumatic experience (loss of control) is being connected with the food that the person is eating at that moment or the substances present in the air. As soon as the subconscious mind connects the stress of the person or the situation with the food or the substance, an allergy is created. Formerly in Chapter 8 we have met N.V. in connection to transforming stress in a relationship. The relationship with her mother was a heavily burdened one. During a day out they ate scampi's for lunch. A simple argument later in the day resulted in an intolerance for scampi's. But this we don't need to know consciously in order to get rid of the stress.

A Balance for transforming allergies is unique, because first of all we have to look at the person or at the situation the allergy is connected with. Then we try to establish peace with this person or this situation. Next we will check whether the apparent allergy is resolved. We talk about an apparent allergy because in fact it is stress or trauma that is connected with food or with the substances that created the allergy. It is all about stress connected by the subconscious mind to the food, the pollen or something else. If we disconnect the links by establishing peace with the person or the situation(s), the allergy will come to an end.

E.G. has attended the Basic, Pro and Advanced workshops. The Balance for the transformation of allergies is taught in the three-day Pro workshop.

*'From the moment I attended the Basic workshop I started applying PSYCH-K daily. Every day I experience a stressful moment usually even more than one. I am actively looking for non-supportive beliefs, and I find quite a lot of them. The fact that I am allowed to celebrate after every Balance makes things much more enjoyable.*

*One of the most striking changes in my life is, that since the Pro workshop, the allergy is gone... I have done a Balance for hay fever and another one for a house dust mite allergy. The result was remarkable, at least for a couple of days.*

*When I started sneezing again in the course of the next week, I was a little disappointed at first. But then I realized I was sitting next to a bunch of flowers. Could this be the cause? Was I allergic to this? Yes, so I did another Balance, then. The following day I started sneezing when I was sitting next to an old cupboard. I tested strongly for "Apparently allergic to this old cupboard". I transformed this allergy too. Since then I have realized, that whenever I start sneezing, I get a signal that something has to be transformed. I have transformed several "allergies", from what seems an allergy to a towel to an apparent allergy to the place where I am working, to newspapers and even the desk of a colleague. For about two months I have been dealing with "allergies" daily. Now I just happen to sneeze now and then, but each*

I have also transformed all my allergies. Before I knew PSYCH-K I used an antihistamine and a spray to keep my bronchial tubes open, because I was so allergic to several trees, but now I am free of medication.

I have to mention a special detail: we generally like a lot of things that are burdened with only one or two sensory alarm signals. This is because these sensory signals 'affect us'. They carry an attraction just like painful stories in our lives attract us. I think it is because they call up our attention because of the alarm they are charged with and we should neutralize it. As our body directs us to be relaxed, our system ensures that we grasp the things that cause us (light) stress. The chance increases that at a certain moment a third alarm signal will be activated and then the body will ask for complete removal of all the signals.
You could wonder and ask yourself: people, who are allergic to certain food products, generally find these extremely delicious.

I used to be very fond of nut-paste. Every morning I had a sandwich with it. Nut-paste has been part of my fixed morning ritual for years. The Organic shop knew the amount of pots I bought there and when a new kind of nut-paste came out, they gave it to me to try it out. At home I ate a sandwich with it straightaway. It was the best nut-paste that I had ever tasted, the pure taste of hazelnut. As soon as the paste entered my mouth, my mucous membranes started swelling. I felt them growing larger and larger. I took a second bite of this delicacy and did a Stress Balance in the meantime. I would not spoil anything as delicious as this. As soon as the Stress Balance was finished, I felt more relaxed, but the allergic reaction was still there. I tested whether it had to do with a person or with a situation and I trans-formed the situation. I saw myself standing at a row of hazelnut trees as a young child. What happened there – I don't know what – I didn't need to relive it in order to change it. Two days later I tried to eat my usual brand of nut-paste. It did not taste half as delicious as before. It had lost something of its attraction. I also finished the new nut-paste but it didn't taste as miraculous good as the first taste.

Allergies, as E.G. describes, may have to do with almost anything, even with nice things. When I was in training to become a PSYCH-K Pro Instructor, someone from the group had to choose and pick an allergy for a demonstration. She had never been allergic and at first could not think of anything. Then it occurred to her 'I am allergic to love'. She tested strongly for this. She was so surprised about this that she wanted to share this with us. I also tested strongly for an 'allergy to love'. How did we manage to develop this? Perhaps we had been punished or humiliated unexpectedly – so we must have suffered loss of control. Even though we were acting quite lovingly towards animals or children? Or perhaps love might have been burdened with stress during our life? Who can tell? We quickly transformed this 'allergy to love'.

I would like to conduct a double-blind research with doctors into the effect of PSYCH-K on allergies in comparison with the traditional way of treatment. The only problem here may be to find an ethical commission at a hospital ready to support this project. Imagine that all allergies could be transformed without medication... What a splendid prospect!

### 'No need of medication to make it through the day'

M.M. attended the Basic and Advanced Workshops.

*'Before the Advanced workshop I really needed 2 to 4 Tylenol tablets in order to get through my working day. At home I seldom needed them though I often had headaches. After the workshop I can now get on with my life without taking Tylenol at work. What a relief. So many things have changed in my life. The nice thing is that I once was a people-pleaser but this is over now. I can become very cranky though; I notice that a lot of things are changing and when things get out of*

*hand I do a Balance. Things are back to normal for me again. So many nice things happen!'*
*M.M.*

We often use medication in order to silence the symptoms. When we do a Stress Balance during a headache, we do actually solve something: the sensory alarms are being eliminated. After that, treatment of the symptoms is redundant. The signal is gone[11].

### 'Smoking is dirty and it stinks'

Y.B. had attended the Basic, Advanced and Divine workshops. She works as an acupuncturist.

*'On my way to the Divine workshop (January 2014) I defiantly bought a packet of cigarettes. I smoked very little, in fact only with colleagues or friends, but... what do you do, when you crave for them and do not have them?*
*The first day I readjusted the belief from "Smoking is relaxing and fine" to "Smoking is dirty and it stinks". The rest of the weekend I did not feel any need for smoking. On a Tuesday I arrived at school where I am a lecturer and I walked past the smoking room, a covered area outside. Usually someone who has just given up smoking likes the smell of smoke, but... unconsciously I thought: "Hell... it stinks" and immediately after "Hurray... it worked!!!"*

*As an addition to my treatments with acupuncture I am also applying PSYCH-K. When someone is convinced that he or she will not be (completely) healed, this will always work to his or her disadvantage. So I usually plan a PSYCH-K treatment, when this limiting belief is present.'*
*Y.B.*

This story needs no further comment. Y.B. only transformed one belief in connection with smoking. It is a belief, though, that makes it easier for her to stay away from smoking.

**Through PSYCH-K the competence of health workers is expanding**

S.V. is a physiotherapist. He has attended the Basic, Advanced, Pro and Health and Wellness workshops.

*'In the first year that I was working with PSYCH-K, after I had attended the Advanced workshop, I was injured while I was doing fitness exercises. There was a loud crack and suddenly I felt a piercing pain in my right knee.*
*As a physiotherapist I immediately had the reflex of examining what had happened. Which tissue had been damaged and in which way? How could that have happened during that movement? But I could not find a clear answer. It was not my kneecap, not my meniscus, nor a ligament.*

*After a short period of physical rest I started a revalidation program. But the pain would not disappear. So I decided to tackle the pain with PYSCH-K. I concluded that my superconscious mind wanted to signal that I had to receive a message. After I understood this message and had balanced for the necessary issues the pain soon disappeared.*

*But a few days later the pain increased again. First I tried to do some physical rehabilitation, but finally I ended up with a message again. There was a lesson I had to learn. This pattern was repeated several times. The pain almost disappeared completely, but then returned and forced me to go into confrontation.*

*At a certain moment the pain returned quite acutely during a long bike ride, which I had been looking forward to for some time. The pain was so fierce that it seemed impossible for me to finish the ride. At that moment I understood that my superconscious mind used the pain in my knee to make me aware of certain things and that it would go on repeating in the same way until I did something about it.*

*Through Balances I then made the deal that I wanted to be informed in another way about confrontations, which are necessary to be addressed.*

*I decided to listen more intuitively to whatever is happening to me, so that there would be no need to convey these messages through pain or physical restraint any more. Even if physical pain is now the last option, I prefer these messages to be brought through intuition, through people from my neighbourhood or through recurring themes in the media. Since then I never had any impeding injury anymore.'*
*S.V.*

Does the entire health care system have to make use of PSYCH-K? I do not think so. As it appears from Y.B.'s story, health workers can expand their specific competence by applying PSYCH-K. Everyone can use his or her competence and the results of the treatments can be improved by supporting beliefs. If the client chooses to commit himself completely in order to help a treatment to succeed and to change the limiting subconscious beliefs, the path is clear[12].

Sometimes a disease is a symptom of a broader dysfunctional system. Then it can make sense to discover and transform the beliefs underlying the present dysfunction.
When the Balance with the Core Beliefs was only used experimentally – Rob Williams, who was at that time working as a psychotherapist, had only used it with a friend and with himself. A woman with Crohn's disease came to him for a consultation. She was completely devastated. Rob suggested trying out the method with her. She agreed to do the Balance with the Core Beliefs. About two months later, she returned to the medical clinic where she had been diagnosed with the disease, for a check-up. There they could not find any trace of Crohn's disease. Instead of admitting that apparently a "cure" had taken place, they claimed that she must have been misdiagnosed, or that her x-rays had been somehow mixed up with someone else. They confirmed that the woman did not have this incurable disease and that this diagnosis had been wrong. And so they could do justice to the situation and their own belief that 'Crohn's disease is an incurable chronic disease' remained intact. The idea that there had been something like 'a cure' was kept out of sight.

## The belief may determine whether we live or die

If we are convinced that we, just like our parents, grandparents or extended family will die of a heart attack, our body will prepare itself for this because our beliefs will determine how our cells will behave[13]. Even if this contradicts our usual bodily functions, 'cells are forced to follow the instructions of the big boss which is the nervous system'.[14]

I noticed the opposite. I experimented with beliefs like 'I am young in spirit and have a healthy body', 'I am energetic' and 'I enjoy the power of my body'. The result is that I feel young, energetic and powerful. I can move mountains. Of course I also did an Optimal Health Balance, where the beliefs for a long and healthy life have been embedded into my subconscious automatisms. I am looking forward to the results...


## Mentally healthy

G.C. did all five PSYCH-K workshops.

*'The biggest result I have already obtained with PSYCH-K is recovering my self-respect and self-confidence. Hiding myself and feeling inferior belong to the past, which is clearly noticeable in my new open and radiant attitude. Often changes do not show immediately and you consciously have to look back in order to find out how subtly and unnoticed these new characteristics or beliefs have automatically crept into your life.'*
*G.C.*

G.C. has suffered from chronic fatigue syndrome for 30 years. With 'Other Life' he stopped the stress response and then he consequently worked to give himself another life with the help of PSYCH-K. I met him prior to his 'Other Life' training and I have followed his progress in all the PSYCH-K workshops. Formerly he seemed to me someone without energy or backbone. In two years' time he has become a very handsome man.

## A healthy body as well

For years I have suffered from spastic colon, a disorder in which the little muscles of the large intestine get cramps, just as this can happen with muscles in the calves. I suffered so hard that I had to faint before the cramp would stop. For years on end I had to take two pills a day. Since I have been practicing PSYCH-K, I have only had spastic colon twice. By doing a Balance during the attack of pain, I was able go to sleep afterwards as usual. By doing a Balance during the pain, all sensory signals have been transformed. I am curious to find out if it might return.

Does PSYCH-K only help with stress related illnesses or also with 'purely' physical ailments? In fact, we must reverse this question: are there 'only purely physical ailments', diseases that are only related to the body? The question itself disputes the unity between body, soul and spirit. As described in the chapter on the PSYCH-K principles and philosophy, we assume that we are one: everything we experience in our body also comes into being through our spirit.

My husband's back was stiff while he was loading the car. He was supposed to help our children to build their house. First I gave him the necessary bodily help. He got to lay on his belly on the ground with a cushion under his stomach, so that the back muscles could relax. In the meantime I first did a Stress Balance. Then we kept looking for messages and advantages from this back blockage. We could not find any. In order to have his back completely relaxed, his subconscious mind chose another Balance for a New Direction, in which we integrated enneagram messages into his subconscious mind[15]. After one hour and a half of attentive love my husband was fit again. His back had been cured. Without any problem he could do his building work for the whole weekend.

## PSYCH-K effectively activates the self-healing capacity of the body

The self-healing capacity of our body is immense, especially if it is supported by the right subconscious beliefs. Prior to (and also during) disease it is sound to embed the right beliefs into our system. With 'right' I mean all beliefs that support 'I am healthy'. Moreover it is important to realize that our subconscious mind can only use bodily signals to indicate an imbalance. This imbalance can both involve the body or the mind.

In March, I got a sore throat. In order to take care of this, I did a Relationship Balance with my throat. That was quite an experience. There was no stress in my throat, but there was some in myself. I had a problem concerning self-respect, I blamed my throat for being sore, I did not like my sick body, I thought my needs were not being met; I clung to the past and wanted to keep everything as it was. My sore throat expressed the underlying message of a lack of self-respect. This was transformed. During the process of connection I told my throat 'I will take good care of you', and from my throat the message came 'I will only swallow what is good for me'. In the time afterwards I noticed that I became more selective in accepting things about myself. I only swallow what is good for me. And I have taken good care of my throat: hot tea and honey did the trick.

The best belief that can help you cure a disease with medication, an operation or another treatment is 'This means will help me get rid of the problem'. If you are not convinced that this might help, the cost will bring you little return.

## Placebos and nocebos: the power of enhancing and the force of limiting beliefs

In his text 'Placebos: the effect of a belief', Dr Bruce Lipton describes the research of Dr Bruce Moseley, an orthopaedic[16]. The latter divided the patients participating in a research that he conducted into three groups: a group in which the knee joint was being scraped, a group in which the liquid of infection was washed away and a third group in which only an incision was done to make a scar. This last group in fact underwent a fake operation. All three groups received the same care afterwards with an exercise program.

The result was that the placebo group showed as much improvement as the other two groups. The completely positive effect of the operation was clearly due to the placebo effect. A similar research has also been carried out with other diseases. Bruce Lipton does not call this placebo any longer, but an effect of belief. That in fact is the point: believing that something works makes it work. We still have to embed this belief into our subconscious mind otherwise everything remains in the category *wishful thinking*. Only thinking or repeating beliefs consciously does not have the same result[17]. The beliefs in our mind – in our subconscious mind that is responsible for the automatic impulses – directly influences our biological functioning[18].

If our body is dominated by limiting beliefs, it will produce a *nocebo* effect. If you and the people in your environment– especially the doctor and your close family members – believe that you will die of a disease this will probably happen. Lipton says: 'your beliefs work as the filters on a camera and change the way you are looking at the world. And your biological functioning adjusts itself to your beliefs'.[19]

The particular aspect of PSYCH-K is that we ourselves can choose from which impulses we want to direct our body: will it be self-healing or self-destructive stimuli, will it be love or fear. As soon as our life is impulsively adjusted to love, our body will react with health. If we are determined by fear, we will develop several diseases. Therefore Lipton concludes: 'It is not our genes, but our beliefs that direct our life'.[20]


**Be sure to have healthy beliefs in a healthy body**

In the process prior to a Candida treatment, I promised myself not to eat sugar for a long time. I had embedded the not so handy belief 'Sugar is poison for me' into my subconscious mind.
A week later my husband and I were eating out in a restaurant. After some hesitation I ordered an ice cream to round off the meal. As soon as the waiter came with the desert, I had to run for the toilet. When seeing 'the poison' that I was going to eat I, immediately got diarrhoea. My body had already started the evacuation.

Of course I have changed the belief into 'My life is perfect while eating only natural sugars'. So I am not inclined to use products with sugar either and at least they are no longer making me sick.

You must have noticed that I like exploring the limits of the possibilities of PSYCH-K. I have the feeling that I am only just at the beginning. I know that some of these stories may look exaggerated or bizarre. For me they are just assessments, with every time the realization – just like Y.B. when she was walking past the smoking area – 'great it worked!' I keep being surprised every time.

For personal growth and development we use the name 'PSYCH-K', for the same method in a business environment we use 'PER-K'. This is what the next chapter is about.

# 10. PER-K, PSYCH-K® at the Workspace

*"Our goal is to help business people change their perspectives about business. When business people wake up to this potential, we can create a sustainable economy and ecology. PER-K® can play a key role in making this change possible."* – Robert Williams

J.D.V. has a coaching practice of her own. She has attended all PSYCH-K weekends.

*'I have assisted my husband while he had to cope with the fact that after 20 years of service he had been fired in an extremely awkward way. I used the Balance with family constellations and I have made a Balance for his relationships in work myself. Furthermore I have been working with him for a positive mindset and on a special way to apply for a job. He has found a great new job and he says he has never felt freer especially after all our work. He says he has gone from hell (his old job) to heaven with this job. The management of his new job sees the employees as their biggest asset. He has been received with open arms.*

*On his advice I have written a protocol about what we did and I am going to see how I can help other job seekers.*
*It is essential that those who have been fired first try to cope with all feelings and patterns of their dismissal and transform them into positive patterns. During the Balance with a family constellation my husband saw – like a flash – that the way in which he had reacted to the conditions of his old job was caused by a pattern that had sprung from his early youth and that he had unconsciously repeated for years. He said: "It was such a revelation that I saw the desk moving up and down and I needed some time to cope with this." This understanding has set a lot of things in motion. By Balancing the work relationships we have created a new possibility for a job in which he would be appreciated. And that has come true completely.'*
*J.D.V.*

## PSYCH-K for working conditions

PSYCH-K can also be applied for working conditions. Quite a number of participants in PSYCH-K workshops have an independent practice and are applying PSYCH-K in order to help their clients.

M.V.D. attended the Basic and Advanced workshops.

*'PSYCH-K has given my community and myself so much that I do not know where to start! Even my work as a PSYCH-K facilitator has been enriched. I am applying it in combination with, among other things in depth counselling (transpersonal counselling), with which it fits in perfectly, because it is also directed at the diverse layers of consciousness and at connecting with and trusting in the own wisdom and sense; the transcending; the observer; the understanding that everything is perfect as it is.*
*Often there is a shift and an expansion of the conscious mind, and through PSYCH-K this is strengthened and the process is speeded up!*
*Focusing on where you want to go and letting it grow healthily using your own power, also perfectly fits the therapy aimed at solutions.*
*Sometimes I wonder: does PSYCH-K fit the counselling in depth or is it the other way around? Where are the limits of PSYCH-K? It is a field of infinite possibilities.'*
*M.V.D.*

S.S. has attended the Basic, Advanced and Divine workshops.

*'I have been taking anti-depressants for 29 years because of depressions, perhaps because of a family-based predisposition in combination with circumstances. One year before I started PSYCH-K, I stopped taking anti-depressants. It has been a difficult year, but since I have started the PSYCH-K process, the quality of my life has gradually improved. Now I am feeling better than ever and I am literally in motion – a gigantic progress if you know what being depressive means: not being able to move. The depressions are history and the road is clear again. I have made more progress than ever before.*

*When I just started working with PSYCH-K, I did a lot of Balances that had to do with my wish of being able to have my own practice and training office. But I did not dare to give up my steady job. Now, after two years, I have lost my job in health care due to government savings. Is this bad? My partner and I have started a counselling practice and a training office. We are now receiving unemployment benefits giving us the opportunity to start our own company and realize our dream. Meanwhile we have fourteen clients and we have just finished a number of training assignments. So be careful what you wish for as you just might get it.*

*In our counselling practice I often work in a solution-oriented way. Through counselling we usually quickly arrive at the core of the matter with the client; we find new insights and new horizons are opening up. We always apply PSYCH-K in order to "fix" new directions and to end the sessions. What surprises me though is that by working in the sphere of PSYCH-K the ego and the corresponding impediments are put "out of action": the thinking mind is off and the process is running a lot more smoothly. Even the space in which we are working becomes lighter all the time! That is why we have made this the slogan of our practice: "Become lighter". And this is what our clients experience as well.'*
S.S.

F.H. has attended the Basic, Advanced and Divine Workshops several times. She also attended the Pro workshop. F.H. has an independent practice.

*'I have applied PSYCH-K in order to quickly find a steady job. I started by doing a VAK to the Future, in which I have formulated and defined my objective. My objective was to find a steady part-time job so that I could combine the coaching practice with my husband and three children. I had given myself a month for doing this. In that month I have been looking intensively for vacancies on the Internet, using my network, by phoning, writing, in short I did everything that was necessary. I treated all limiting beliefs and setbacks I experienced with PSYCH-K Balances, so that I could take action again with new inspiration. I also prepared*

for interviews this way. After exactly one month I was offered a steady job at a school. So I have received more than I had thought possible: the job was only 5 minutes away on bike from my house. The activities were scheduled in the mornings, so that I had all afternoons free for my coaching practice and all school holidays free for my children.'
F.H.

G.S. has attended the Basic, Advanced and the Health and Wellness workshops.

'I had been troubled by the daily schedule at work for some time and by the job itself, I had difficulty in finding the right balance between physical work, brainwork and computer work. I was usually too tired from doing one or more tasks incompletely. I was so tired physically or psychically that I completely collapsed too soon every day. My longing, my dream is, like a Buddhist "monk", to do various things every day so that this variety would allow me to keep going for a whole day. At the beginning of my holidays I did a Balance with an intention and this worked immediately: funny, now I stop doing one thing and automatically I am able to finish a totally different thing. I also make time for a long walk in between activities.'
G.S.

K.G. has attended the Basic, the Advanced and the Divine workshops.

'While I was doing a "VAK to the Future" I had given myself three months in order to find a new job. After two months a job crossed my path, which I accepted gratefully. Unfortunately the job was far too heavy for me and I did not like the director's approach.
A month later I unexpectedly received an email from the first company where I had applied for a job. It was the job I really wanted to do, I had the qualifications for it as it was a job in education! I did not hesitate for one moment and I took the position right away!
I have been working there for eight months now and I really feel pleased and happy; I feel myself radiating so that I in turn can make other people happy!'
K.G.

196

## PER-K, how it is taught

PER-K, to be pronounced as 'purk', the business version of PSYCH-K, uses a different approach in the workshops, but as for process it is the same. Only the language and the goals are different. PSYCH-K is directed at personal growth. PER-K focuses on production, exceptional leadership, excellent management, top sales results, effective communication, team spirit, health and well-being in the company, and of course also on transforming stress into success[1].

PER-K is taught in separate workshops for people who are working in companies or who have a company of their own. Ideally PER-K is being taught *in-company*, to a team within a company.

In companies and organizations it is possible to realize the full potential of the company or the organization through PER-K. In this chapter I will focus on both possibilities.

## The impact of beliefs and stress on the quality of work

J.G. came for private counselling twice and attended the Basic workshop.

*'For 5 years I have had a partnership (ltd) with a man of 25, who in the meantime became my best friend. I myself am 35 years old. I am a rather emotional person and he, 10 years younger, is quite the rational type. This led to a conflict model in which we started working alongside each other and not together any more He took the attitude of "You cannot hurt me", so that I started generating stress.*

*A construction site involving cooperation, produced stress, stress that grabbed me by the throat. All the things we had together: the company, the contracts with customers, bookkeeping, ... produced stress in me, while he seemingly quietly kept going. This went so far that I wanted to quit as a self-employed person and went to my bookkeeper for advice.*

*He told me that I was doing a good job and that me and my partner were really building up something solid. He advised me to look for help.*

*At that moment I had contact with a girlfriend who immediately told me about PSYCH-K. She had already talked to me about years ago, but at that moment of my life it did not seem relevant. Now I could see no other way and I accepted her offer, knowing that she was the only one giving me a tool that I would accept, even undergo. I attended the PSYCH-K Basic workshop in February 2014. The cooperation with my partner seemed to come to an end and we had taken a break for a couple of months.*

*In the workshop and also in the two private sessions that I attended with M.R. afterwards, we had been working on relationships. What I wanted was to not have any stress when I was with my colleague. We agreed on the formulation "I feel good in the presence of my colleague".*

*Two weeks later we started the activities of our little company we had been fighting over for four years again. After one day of work he told me that I had become much calmer. In the following weeks I noticed that we were growing towards one another, that we had exciting talks about life, that we no longer work for ourselves but for each other and that we were developing a deep friendship. His rational side seemed to be moderated, or at least I feel it as less threatening.*

*We have become friends; dear friends and we also express it. Every week he tells me "You are now calmer and less serious", and I tell him then "You have become more open and more emotional". Oh yes, after four years the stress of bookkeeping, telephoning, contacting, in short, the tasks that running a company brings, is gone. I start living again, I am a revived independent person in a partnership, and I am enjoying it thoroughly.*
*PSYCH-K transformed my fear of people into the power to inspire people.'*
*J.G.*

The quality of our work is optimal when we fully concentrate on it and are emotionally involved in what we are doing. Expressed in 'brain language': when our left and right hemispheres are being activated, we perform maximally. For we need both our reason to analyze and evaluate and our emotions to keep working in a motivated and involved way.

Limiting beliefs and stress reduce the quality of work. Although when stressed we are doing our extreme best, the quality of our performances is reduced. For research has shown that when we suffer from limiting beliefs or stress we over activate one hemisphere and almost completely switch off the other one.

In case of *emotional stress* the emotions take almost all space. As a result the concentration at work decreases. The brain needs extra energy in order to deal with simple affairs. This is quite tiring.

In case of *rational stress* the emotions disappear. The person is totally involved in the contents of the work and loses normal commitment. This has negative effects, both on the work relationships and on the private ones. The person is not happy in his environment.

*Limiting beliefs* work in the same way. Because they oppose who we really are, sober-creative beings, our limitations also create resistance. One example: if someone has the belief 'I do not dare to share my ideas in a group', the wish not to have a problem with this is also present. Everything that opposes our nature – which is complete potential– calls up resistance.

Another example: whoever has to write reports or texts regularly, is familiar with *writer's block*. Suddenly nothing works, no single letter will appear on the screen. We try to use several tricks in order to write, but the quality remains limited. This goes against our capacities. If I integrate into my system a supporting belief like 'I know perfectly what I want to write under this title', the text will flow from my fingers.

Do you want the get rid of limiting beliefs and stress in only a few minutes? It is possible! Learn the PER-K process, apply it and within minutes you will work optimally. Whenever you produce quality, both rationally and amicably, working is a joy.

## PER-K: from willpower to automatic behaviour

Up till now we thought that only forced willpower would lead to good results. Still, research has shown that our behaviour is determined by at least 95 percent from our subconscious impulses and only 1 to 5 percent by what we consciously want.

95 percent is doing the job automatically, 5 percent is willpower. So it is in our extreme interest to set up our automatisms for working effectively. If the 95 percent is in the way, our hands will produce nothing; our mind is occupied. We keep going, but we are not really working. We do know the procedures, but we get stuck at the first step.

As soon as we have typed the right destination into our automatic pilot system (our subconscious mind – our GPS) it will lead us to wherever we want to go. Still, we have to do the driving ourselves: paying attention to changing conditions, noticing blockages and detours, taking time to get there and enjoying the changing outlook. The result of correctly adjusting our subconscious mind is: a productive and successful job and a quieter life.

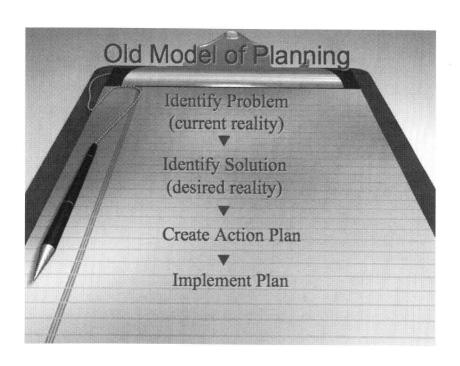

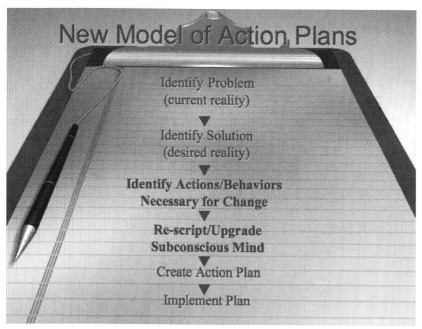

*Old and New Model of Action Plans*

Do you recognize this? You set yourself a goal and whenever you want to start, your heart is sinking. You look for distraction: There is something more urgent to do first... The results are corresponding. You want to do this and you know that it is the best you could do now, but you hardly do it if ever at all. You are underperforming both at task level and in the team. The solution we usually try to apply is to try even harder. This will inevitably lead to exhaustion.

'Trying harder' tires you even more. It is much more interesting to give the right instructions to our subconscious mind right away. For instance, we can replace the belief 'I first have to clear everything before I can start something new' with 'I enjoy beginning something new'. Perhaps there is another belief that is bothering us? We look for an alternative that makes us enthusiastic and embed this into our automatic pilot. Carrying out this process usually only lasts a couple of minutes. The time we will gain is many times larger than the time we spend doing a Balance...

The most efficient thing to do is to master the PER-K process yourself, so you can bring yourself in a Whole-Brain State again and therefore be in optimal condition in any situation that asks for it.

### Results after a PSYCH-K or PER-K Balance

In *"Neuroscience Reveals the Whole-Brain State and Its Applications for International Business and Sustainable Success"*[2] Dr. Jeff Fannin and Rob Williams describe research with 125 people. Their brain activity has been measured and fixed by means of an electroencephalogram (EEG), prior to and after a Balance[3].

The left light grey activity shows that only half the brain functions; the left and right light and darker activities show the result of the brain after a Balance of a couple of minutes. – The difference in grey hue is not so visible in the next figure. You can download the whole article in colour at

http://www.freefullliving.com – page Science.

Under the figure you will read the story about the person whose brain prints these are.

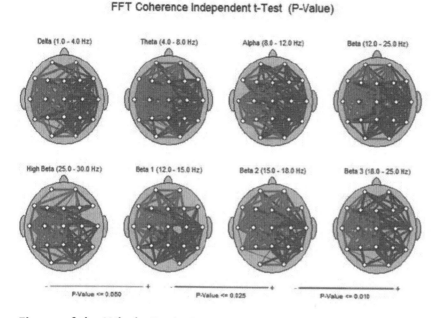

FFT Coherence Independent t-Test (P-Value)

*Figure of the Whole-Brain State, resulting from a PSYCH-K/PER-K Balance*

'This woman had been an office manager for over ten years. Her dominant pattern before the PER-K° Balance was facilitated, (seen in light grey), is left hemispheric. Very logic oriented, her management style was "my way or the highway". Her approach was demanding and she expected others to do exactly as she commanded. Most of the people that worked for her did as she asked out of fear of reprisal from her or at times, experienced her uncontrollable anger. After the PER-K° Balance, the dominant pattern, (seen in dark grey), represents access to the emotional/right side of her brain, augmenting the qualities and attributes of her left hemisphere. The result was that her consideration of others was noticeably better, and her interpersonal relationships at home and at the office improved substantially. Her leadership abilities began to flourish and she became well liked. In addition, the office ran smoother, with greater efficiency and productivity. Her shift toward a *Whole-Brain State* created a new attitude toward others, fostering a more congenial work environment. The overall shift in the attitude of her employees toward her was supportive, resulting in a more positive feeling about the work place.'[4]

**PER-K, areas of application *Exceptional leadership***

*'The goal of most leaders is to cause people to feel reverence for the leader – the goal of the exceptional leader is to cause people to feel reverence for themselves.'* – Christopher J. & P. Nelson, *Seven Secrets of Exceptional Leadership.*

'Exceptional Leadership' ratifies a participant in order to reach the highest level of his leadership. The latent, subconsciously hidden talents get required room to develop. By harmonising subconscious beliefs with conscious objectives, everything that stands in the way of effective leadership can be eliminated. Participants will receive examples of beliefs that they can integrate. They will develop the skill of formulating and implementing their made-to-measure beliefs themselves. 'Exceptional Leadership' is developed both for newcomers and experienced leaders. In a workshop you will learn how to develop your leadership to its full potential.

Some examples of beliefs:

| *Self-limiting beliefs* | *Beliefs for success* |
|---|---|
| 'I make the decisions, it all depends on me.' | » 'I delegate responsibility to others when it is opportune.' |
| 'When I share power with others, I fail to reach my objectives.' | » 'By sharing power, I will enlarge the possibility of reaching my objectives.' |
| 'When I show weakness or vulnerability, I lose the respect of my employees.' | » 'As a leader I confidently deal with my strength and vulnerability.' |

| | |
|---|---|
| 'When I avoid making decisions, I avoid making mistakes.' | » 'I trust the decisions I make and I take responsibility for the results.' |
| 'Changes worsen the situation.' | » 'Changes optimise the situation.' |

### Excellent management

*"We doubt that a well-intentioned, just-try-harder approach will fundamentally improve the quality of executives' decision making... training must be broadened to include what is now known about how our minds work and must expose managers directly to the unconscious mechanisms that underlie decision making."* – Banaji, Bazerman, & Chugh, Harvard Business Review, December 2003.

'Management for Excellence' introduces the power of the subconscious mind to the participants to enable them to react to exceptional situations, rather than showing just habitual reactions. Because our behaviour is determined by our beliefs, successful people have habits that fulfil their lives; they do not have to fight a daily battle. When subconscious beliefs go against conscious objectives, self-undermining thoughts rise up and self-sabotaging behaviour is the result.

Some examples of beliefs

| *Self-limiting beliefs* | *Beliefs for success* |
|---|---|
| 'When I ask for help, I lose face.' | » 'Asking for help is OK with me.' |
| 'I cannot trust others, they will turn against me.' | » 'I see and expect the best in myself and in others.' |
| 'When at the top I know everything best.' | » 'I accept that there are different ways to do things.' |
| 'I know how someone else should do the job and let this be known.' | » 'I put the right person in the right place. He knows his job.' |

'When I spend too much time coaching another person,

they might steal my job later.'

» 'I admit the advantages of training colleagues to be good managers.'

### Top sales results

'PER-K for Top Sales Results' is developed to broaden and support the effectiveness of existing training skills in sales. Participants will learn to harmonize their subconscious mind with their intended objectives. Successful people have more beliefs like 'I can' than 'I cannot'. This psychological advantage can make the difference between a good and an excellent salesman. By replacing undermining subconscious beliefs with consciously desired goals, self-sabotaging behaviour will be changed into success-promoting action. That's how success will become a 'self-fulfilling prophecy' instead of a daily struggle!

Some examples of beliefs

| *Self-limiting beliefs* | *Beliefs for success* |
|---|---|
| 'No matter how hard I try, it is never good enough.' | » 'I do my best and it is getting better and better.' |
| 'My fear of rejection keeps me from having success.' | » 'I am calm, full of confidence and energy when I am making telephone sales.' |
| 'It doesn't make sense trying to reach my quota, I cannot make it anyway.' | » 'I trust my possibilities and I can do whatever I have in mind.' |
| 'When wanting to finalise a sale, the buyer will probably cancel anyway.' | » 'When I make an offer to a client, I will create a win-win situation.' |
| 'Because I work better with stress, I will always procrastinate.' | » 'I am working quietly and steadily and everything is ready in time.' |

### Effective communication

*'Effective, two-way communication demands that we capture both content and intent and learn to speak the languages of logic and emotion.'* – S. Covey, *Principle Centered Leadership.*

'Effective Communication' helps participants to expand the possibilities of communication with individuals and groups. It develops more cooperation between the left (logical) and right (emotional) brain hemispheres. By strengthening the connection between both brain hemispheres, well-balanced patterns of communication are established. People, who communicate successfully, will use, when having contact with others, both their logic and their emotions, which increases their effectiveness. By means of 'Effective Communication' you learn to replace your disturbing beliefs with beliefs that will improve your communication skills. For those who want to conquer their fear of public speaking this workshop is a necessity.

Some examples of beliefs

| *Self-limiting beliefs* | | *Beliefs for success* |
|---|---|---|
| 'I do not give my opinion about others, for they will think I am mad.' | » | 'I give my opinion openly and honestly, clearly and in confidence.' |
| 'If I compliment people, they will think that I want something from them.' | » | 'I feel comfortable when I congratulate someone.' |
| 'It doesn't matter what I say, people do not listen.' | » | 'What I have to say is important and I expect to be heard.' |
| 'I do mind giving criticism, it is hurtful and makes things worse.' | » | 'I communicate my criticism in a delicate and empathic way.' |
| 'When others don't agree with me, I think I am wrong and they are right.' | » | 'What is right for me, is fine with me, even if others do not agree.' |

**Team building**

*'Even when I walk in the company of three people only, I can learn from them. I can imitate their good qualities and unlearn the bad ones in myself.'* – Confucius

PER-K helps participants to tune their personal attitudes, values and beliefs to effective group interactions. Mostly people in-group behave in the same way as they do (or did) at home in their family. Quite often such behaviour is inadequate in a professional sphere. Participants will learn to become aware of their behaviour and to conduct themselves in such a manner that they can connect in their own way. Effective teams work on the basis of faith, mutual respect and commitment with regard to commonly accepted goals. In order to increase this essential quality in a group and to support people in developing themselves in this matter, participants will learn to align their subconscious script with consciously desired values and behaviour.

Some examples of beliefs

| *Self-limiting beliefs* | | *Beliefs for success* |
|---|---|---|
| 'Other people always have better ideas, so I will keep silent.' | » | 'My ideas and actions are important for the team's success.' |
| 'When I contribute more than others, they will think I want to put them in a bad light.' | » | 'If I am capable of it, it is fine for me to contribute more than others in the team.' |
| 'I cannot trust others, they only work for themselves.' | » | 'I trust other people and I give them the benefit of the doubt.' |
| 'I keep what I think to myself in order to blend in.' | » | 'I am honest about my own vision, even when others see things differently.' |

| 'I have to protect my ideas, otherwise others will take advantage of them.' | » 'I share my ideas and experience so that other team members and myself can benefit from them.' |
|---|---|

### Health and well-being

*'The simple truth is that happy people do not get sick. The attitude that someone has with regard to himself, is the most important factor in health and well-being.'* – B. Siegel, *Love, Medicine & Miracles.*

'Health and Well-being' equips the participants to develop more respect and self-consciousness concerning the coherence between body and mind. Stress and toxic beliefs can have a dramatic effect on our mental and physical health. Participants will get access to beliefs that adjust their immune system. The objective is to develop an 'immune competence'. More well-being means more productivity, less leave of absence thus less need for health care. Less absence results in more productivity and less costs. So it is important to explore the connection between body and mind and enjoy an improved health, happiness and energy – as well for yourself as for your employees.

Some examples of beliefs

| Self-limiting beliefs | Beliefs for success |
|---|---|
| 'What I think has nothing to do with being ill or healthy.' | » 'I recognise the power of my thoughts and their influence on my body.' |
| 'I see what is going wrong even before I see what is going right.' | » 'My spontaneous attention is directed towards the positive and sound aspects in my life.' |
| 'My life is full of stress, things always head the wrong way.' | » 'I am focused and full of energy, my life is one big success.' |

| 'I keep my feelings to myself, there is no room for them in my job.' | » | 'I can express my feelings openly and easily.' |
| --- | --- | --- |
| 'I have no time for eating well and doing sports, but my body can cope.' | » | 'I choose healthy food and activities that stimulate my well-being.' |

### Transforming stress into success

*"If you are distressed by anything external, the pain is not due to the thing itself, but rather to your own estimate of it; and thus you have the power to revoke at any moment."* – Marcus Aurelius

'Transforming stress into success' gives participants the possibility of identifying the most important stress factors in their lives, both personal and professional. By using the PER-K 'Whole-Brain' process, participants will learn to use the energy that is lost by stress in order to find constructive solutions to their problems. The key to success is seeing difficulties as opportunities, as challenges that stimulate creativity. Participants indicate that – through 'Transforming stress into success' – they feel calm and comfortable in situations in which they would normally panic.

Some examples of beliefs

| *Self-limiting beliefs* | | *Beliefs for success* |
| --- | --- | --- |
| 'No matter how hard I try, it is never good enough.' | » | 'I do my best and my best is good enough for me.' |
| 'I am mostly tense and anxious when something changes too quickly.' | » | 'I am calm, confident and full of energy when I am challenged in life.' |
| 'I feel bad when others treat me wrongly.' | » | 'I have the power to decide with regard to others how to act or react.' |

'By worrying I show that I care about others.'

» 'I am relaxed, I do my best and focus on solutions rather than on problems.'

'Life is a battle. For me it always turns out wrong.'

» 'I am creating my life by my thoughts and actions. I do have the power to change.'

## One more testimony

Luc Limère is a PER-K catalyst[5]. This means that he has attended the three-day 'PER-K is essential to success' workshop. Besides this workshop he has also attended the PSYCH-K Basic, Advanced and the Divine Workshops.

*'There are so many trainings so many tools and tricks for companies, that people can't see the wood for the trees anymore. Often they choose a quick win, which later appears to be a waste of time. I seldom happen to hear about a method of which I think: this could be different; this method seems to be more sustainable and applicable in our corporate world.*
*Still notwithstanding some question marks, I will investigate it. After having attended PSYCH-K training myself, I was a little more enthusiastic. Especially because I could apply the method to myself quite easily and could immediately experience the measurable differences in my community.*

*However the great breakthrough came when I started applying PER-K with the managers in my coaching practice. Those were strong personalities, operational whiz kids and members of management direction who had already done and seen everything. At least that is what they said. However they kept bumping into limiting beliefs, which made their life and work very difficult.*

*Like a sales manager who just recovered from a burnout. He was very much aware of his own limiting motivation "perfectionism", but he did* not know how to deal with it. By balancing this belief into a quality and talent instead of a pitfall, his attitude has strongly changed. I have heard that now he is even trying to convince his colleagues to let go of their perfectionism. And he can do this, because he is imbued with this and his new belief is "hardwired" or reprogrammed in his brain.

I am so glad that I happened to meet M.R. as the stimulating power behind PER-K in our quite traditional Belgium. It is through professionals like her, that the business world will get access to this new neurological technology with which we can finally let go of our old patterns. This way we will make room for renovation within ourselves, so that we can also pragmatically apply it and shape our teams, customers and all stakeholders so they can benefit from it.'
Luc Limère

# 11. Infinite Possibilities

*'Everything is possible but not everything is probable. Let's stretch our reality and leave it to the Universe, then see what happens.'*– Robert Williams

In a phone call with Rob Williams, the founder of PSYCH-K, I talk to him about this book, the titles of the chapters and the contents. He stops at this chapter 'Infinite possibilities' and says: 'For 26 years I have been curious to know whether there is a limit to the possibilities with PSYCH-K. So far I have not yet discovered any. There is not an area in which we cannot apply PSYCH-K. This keeps me curious and open to all new things that are waiting to be discovered.'[1]

## With only 11 Balances we create infinite possibilities

With only 11 procedures or Balances we can create infinite possibilities. The client chooses what he or she desires the most, and that's what we focus on and realize.[2] Because our desires are so assorted and differ from moment to moment, there is quite a range of possibilities.

M.V.D. has an independent practice. She has attended the Basic workshop three times and the Advanced workshop twice. She also attended the Divine Integration Retreat.
She is a member of a practice group that gathers every six weeks to practice PSYCH-K.

*'My experiences with PSYCH-K are so diverse, both for myself and for the clients and others in my community that it is a challenge to choose from them. I will do my best (and my best is good enough)[3]. Let me give a small random selection.*

*PSYCH-K has astonished and left me in awe. I have the feeling of holding gold in my hands: infinite possibilities to powerfully and*

*effectively deal with challenges and blockages, for my community, my clients and myself. Although it is not a magic wand, it has brought larger and smaller miracles into my life. I knew that the subconscious mind controls us to a large extent, and I also knew how to make things move a little and how to work with all layers of the conscious mind. The power and speed with which this is happening in PSYCH-K, gave me an even more profound confidence about handling things. I can transform whatever does not serve me anymore and I can live more genuinely. I know who I really am, independently from the "stories" about my life and myself. How liberating!!*

*A week after the Basic workshop, I started my own practice after years of dreaming about it. Suddenly all I needed automatically came unto my path. PSYCH-K perfectly fits the way I look at the world, it connects a lot of profound insights from diverse trends by which it builds a bridge in my work with people and it happens to be thoroughly founded. Ever since I have been living with PSYCH-K I have more confidence, especially in my own intuition. It is easily passed on to other people; I have far more energy, notwithstanding a serious chronic disease that seems to determine my life less and less. I have pleasure, satisfaction, connection with myself and others, more self-respect, I am recovering more quickly, I can handle more, I make better choices and am taking more care of myself. I discover the message in experiences far more quickly and do something with it, I feel more and more like a co-creator of my life. People in my community are struck by the quiet, confident happiness I am radiating.*

*In my work as a counsellor/coach I notice that I experience far more confidence in the process of the other person, which gratifies us both. I see people experiencing quick to very quick changes in blockages that have been there forever. This even happens with people who have gone through a lot of therapies and are extremely sceptical. I often hear after one or a couple of sessions: "it cannot be that easy?" Sometimes people seem to be waiting for things to go "wrong".*

*Some examples of changes: a boy who after some sessions did not have panic attacks anymore, obtained excellent marks at school, could in a relaxed way give a presentation in front of the class and did several things he had no longer thought possible.*

*A woman, who continuously experienced very high stress and now can be calm and talk, can study again and do nice things.*

*A woman, who was depressed and is now enjoying life again. People who could easily stop smoking or give up other unhealthy habits, and who find them-selves worthy of being cared for.*

*Someone who after the PSYCH-K session had a constructive relationship for the first time and people who after a session could handle a challenging situation in a relaxed and confident way, like examinations, job interviews, talks in which bad news must be broken and presentations.*

*People who finally dared to follow their passion. I see people crawl out of their shell and doing what suits them. People who find the meaning of their life and spiritually deepen their path.*

*People especially have far more confidence in their own capacity to be influential; they discover their own power and potential.*

*What often strikes me is that this also benefits children. Sometimes children come to me, but often I can already do something only with the parents, so that changes will be effected in the children and lots of things will change for the better. The parent can process the reflection and has more confidence in the child and his or her course of life. This way the world is becoming a little more beautiful and light!'*
*M.V.D.*


It is striking that about 10 percent of the only 616 people who have attended the PSYCH-K workshops in Flanders and the Netherlands (July 2014), have an independent practice in which they professionally make use of PSYCH-K. Most of them had this practice before; others have started one after the workshops. This is a remarkable conclusion. PSYCH-K is quite new. Since 2008 Dutch-speaking workshops have been monthly organized in the Netherlands; in Flanders this has only happened from 2012 onwards. Now there is a growing offer of workshops.

From this I conclude that professionals feel attracted to the method and want to learn and use it. With PSYCH-K they feel better equipped professionally to help others. Not only do the speed and the simplicity appeal to them, the possibility to work with people who, as M.V.D. says, have had problems for years, as well...

K.G. did the Basic workshop twice and the Advanced workshop once. He puts it very simple, as it is.

*"With PSYCH-K problems can be resolved, which otherwise remain. I recommend PSYCH-K for people who are troubled."*
*K.G.*

**Working with children and teenagers**

W.V.H. has an independent practice. She attended the Basic, Advanced and the Pro workshops.

*'After a phone call from a desperate mother, the next day (at the beginning of March) there is a ring at my doorbell. There she is with her 15-year-old daughter. The girl is very depressed her face is a blank. She is in an examination year, but she is convinced she will fail because she has been playing truant too often and she has no courage left. Moreover she is behind schedule. She has been going to a psychologist for a year, without any effect. The medication has already been increased twice, without effect either. So let us try PSYCH-K (on the advice of a client of mine, who has also been seeing me with her daughter).*
*During the introduction I notice that it is hard to establish contact with her: she shrugs her shoulders continuously and is hardly answering my questions. I suggest that we start the session; in this case we will do a Core Belief Balance.*

*As we are trying to integrate the positive belief statements, I see a miracle happening right in front of me. The light in her eyes is coming back. She starts radiating from within and her whole attitude is changing. She is relaxing and starts laughing. And indeed, she starts talking! All this is happening within 15 minutes. One hour after the beginning of the session I tell her that things are finished for now, she is disappointed. "You seem to be lying quite comfortably", I tell her.*

216

*"Yes, indeed. In fact I would like to go to school tomorrow", she tells me then. The mother starts crying spontaneously.*

*A week later they come to me for the second session. The daughter is going to school again, she has stopped her medication and she is feeling good and strong. She still has little lights in her eyes and the talking is still there... After the second session there were no further sessions.*

*In June I received a card and a cake delivered at my home. The girl passed her final exams! She is doing fine and she is going to study to be a veterinary assistant.'*

W.V.H.

M.C. is a teacher at a primary school. She has attended the Basic and Advanced workshops.

*'In my class with children of 7 or 8 years old there was a boy last year, who was hindered in his homework, because he thought he was not allowed to make mistakes. A Balance for a New Direction gave him a relaxed feeling and ever since he has been able to do his homework with confidence.'*

M.C.

There is nothing that makes me happier than working with children. They feel strongly that PSYCH-K is really helping. Because their left hemisphere is far less trained to critically question – or even undermine – things, they surrender to the dreams they can achieve with PSYCH-K. Transformations happen even more quickly with them; they have to transform a smaller database than the adults.

Because PSYCH-K is a method of doing, they like it more than just 'talking about things'. That they do dislike. Often children like choosing Balances in which they can move. They can perfectly imagine what their life would be like if they did not have one problem or another, and while talking they can see it happening in their imagination.

**PSYCH-K workshops are open to young people from 10 years old onwards**

F.T. (10 year old) has attended the Basic and Advanced workshops.

*'The funniest thing in the Basic workshop was doing the Solution Balance. I very often repeat it. I also did a VAK to the Future for group work in class. I used not to like that, but now I really do. I even have a nine grade for this.*
*In the Advanced workshop I found the Balance with the Core Beliefs most special, because it is impossible to compare yourself with who you were prior to it. Everything was nice, even in the Basic workshop.'*
*F.T.*

L.T. (15 year old) has attended the Basic and the Advanced workshops.

*'The Basic workshop was an experience that opened my world. It was nice to learn to Balance but I also liked the difficult long scheme of messages and advantages a lot.*
*The Advanced workshop changed everything. You can do the Balances very quickly and there are even more Balances. The most special one was the Life Bonding Balance. I saw my soul descending into myself. Also the Core Belief Balance in surrogation for my grandfather was*

quite special. This gave me a strange feeling, like you are yourself but in someone else's body. I like working in the garden now, which in fact is my granddad's hobby.
Since using PSYCH-K my stress at school has decreased a lot.'
L.T.

S.T. (18 year old) has both attended the Basic and the Advanced workshops.

'The most important thing for me is that I know that I can always do a Balance, no matter what is happening.
This is the way I used to find my student digs in Leuven. I desperately wanted a room in the American College, but the number of available rooms was limited and I had to write a letter of motivation. I tested strongly for "I have a room there", but I received a negative answer. After that I remained strong for "I have a room in the American College". A couple of weeks later I received an email. Someone had cancelled and now the room was mine! This was quite special.'
S.T.

PSYCH-K is accessible to everyone. Young children from 10 years old onwards can attend the workshops. They learn the process quite quickly; they immediately feel that it suits their wishes and their longings.

G. (12 year old) attended the Basic workshop with his mother.

'My little son G. was bullied at school and he did not feel good. He did not like going to school. By working with PSYCH-K he started liking school again. The teasing and the bullying remained, but his reaction was better, so the bullying ended sooner and he was able to meet other friends, so that he felt he "belonged" too...
I have a very open relationship with him and he told me that the boys no longer really bully him at school. That same week I received a phone call from a mother, whose little sons were at the same school (in a lower class) and they told her that my son was bullied at school and that they did not like this at all. She wanted me to know about this,

*because she was concerned. I found this quite bizarre, because G. had just told me that he was not bullied any longer. I discussed this with him and he said that the behaviour that the two boys had described was correct, but that it no longer bothered him so he just ignored it or answered something back and turned to his friends. His perception has clearly changed.*

*He has to go to a new school (secondary) now and I clearly notice that he is not apprehensive about it. He is positively looking forward to meeting new friends. The fear of not belonging somewhere appears to be totally gone.*

*Whenever he feels that he has certain emotions, he immediately does a stress Balance and that helps him tremendously.'*

*I.W.*


*'PSYCH-K should have to be part of the teaching package in every school in the near future.'*

*R.L.*


When youngsters from 10 years old onwards take part in the workshops, I foresee a little corner for them, which I arranged with comics, so that they can dive into them when they finish early. PSYCH-K is not only extra cool for children; it also raises your playfulness, you're daring to try out things, experimenting and invent silly desires. It is a nice game with fantastic results.


## PSYCH-K as a playful way of preparing yourself for getting what you desire

C.Z. has attended the Basic workshop.

*'On a Saturday I arrived at the PSYCH-K practice day and I had to wish for something. What could I wish for? What would I apply PSYCH-K on? Something tangible? Next week I am going to a lecture of Bruce Lipton (the man!!) and I think that what I would like most for now is this man's signature and a picture of the both of us.*

*Before the big day I was very nervous but on the day itself I was waiting next to the queue (not in the queue), leaning on my crutches and I just kept waiting quietly. Bruce himself was covered in sweat and patiently addressing everyone. As the last one I bumped towards him. Someone came to me spontaneously and asked me if I wanted him to take a picture with my iPhone.*

*I was so happy. I have 5 photographs and one great signature. I was very calm (No nerves) and after that I talked away with the man next to me. That is unique, because I am always very reserved, like a closed book. Not anymore. Everything seems to come to me. Great!' C.Z.*

In the book *The Alchemist*, Paulo Coelho describes a man who goes out of his way to find a treasure. He leaves everything behind for this. Finally the treasure seems to be hidden behind the fireplace of his house. In order to find what he desires, he has covered this very long road. He has become much wiser: the treasure is hidden 'in his own house'. That is how I feel. Because I had a lot of trouble with myself, I have followed an intellectual, emotional and a spiritual education. I got started and I have found that everything I desire is 'in my own house'. PSYCH-K is the process with which I can dig up every treasure that is attractive to me.

In *The Alchemist*, one sentence is repeated that made a lasting impression: "And, when you want something, all the universe conspires in helping you to achieve it."[4] Expressed in terms of PSYCH-K: as soon as our subconscious mind is totally in line with what we want and deeply desire, we are 'tuned in' on the universal creative energy. With PSYCH-K we transform our subconscious mind and we influence the collective subconscious, as well. Then nearly everything is possible.


## PSYCH-K connects us to the Universal Energy

B.X. has had one private session and has attended the Basic workshop.

*'On the last day of the Basic workshop I did a Balance for my dwellings (I am now renting a place and this has produced stress for a long time). From the Balance came the first step of the action plan: doing an analysis of strength and weakness about buying or renting a house*

*or a condo. I did the Balance and this came out: buy, a house in good condition, with some space to sit outside.*
*You can guess the result. The day after I noticed a small house on a house market Internet site that completely met the result of my exercise (before that I was only looking for condos). I went looking at it on my bike and this is a funny detail: the phone number of the owner ends in the four digits of the PIN code of my bankcard. I had a good look at the house and the next day I went to visit it with a friend, the day after with a girlfriend, I made a bid, which was accepted. Done!! J'*
*B.X.*

P.V.D.W. has attended the Basic, Advanced, Professional and the Health and Wellness workshops.

*'In the Health and Wellness programme I had a beautiful experience with a surrogation. I wanted to do a Relationship Balance with my father. My partner received no permission to replace my father however she received permission to stand in for me and I received permission to stand in for my father. For me this was a wonderful healing experience. My partner, just like me, was in a Whole-Brain State; so was I, as my father. I could feel how much he loved me and that he was sorry to have been worrying about his own pain so that he did not have time left for me. This feeling was quite enriching. This experience made it clear again that the Higher Self has a "higher objective" and that asking permission is important.'*
*P.V.D.W.*

From the Christian tradition we know that 'whatever we ask will be given us', we are living in a benevolent universe.[5] The only thing that matters is asking for this to our higher conscious mind so as to be able to rephrase the question if this doesn't match the wider perspective of our superconscious. In Chapter 2 'PSYCH-K works quickly and powerfully', I have described that receiving permission from the superconscious mind is a required element for the procedure of a Balance. At the moment I only emphasize the need of this in order 'not to harm' and to make sure that the Balance comes first. But there is more.

The effect of connecting with the superconscious mind is being able to plug into this highest benevolent energy. It can direct the attention of others and ourselves to the fulfilment of our desires. Receiving permission from the superconscious mind is a fundamental part of a Balance, not only in order to avoid the minimum of harm, but also in order to make our desire energetically heard in the universe and check whether it is in accordance with the All-mighty (higher consciousness). This still means that we have to act though. It is my deepest wish for PSYCH-K to become accessible to all, but I have to take action first, for instance by writing this book.

In workshops I am meeting with people who will have nothing to do with this superconscious mind at all. They ask me if I want to arrange an introduction or workshop for friends, colleagues or family in which this is not mentioned. They are afraid that their community will reject this helpful method because of the mentioning of this aspect. If I were to accept their request, I would be fundamentally disloyal to who we are as human beings – a part of the whole – and I would react out of fear rather than out of love. I am not afraid (anymore) to talk about the superconscious mind at all for we all are part of it. If we fine-tune ourselves to it, we are connected with all people and with creation itself. Not only are all possibilities within reach, but also – as it appears from the many stories – it is automatically given to us.


**Making Music**

N.V. has attended the Basic, Advanced and Pro Workshops.

*'Playing the piano: reading the scores without stress...*
*In the Advanced workshop I appeared to experience stress when reading and expressing visual words and sentences. This was quite surprising. If there were an account of stress in communication, wouldn't it rather be in connection with the auditory? The stress was transformed. I no longer thought about it, until I was sitting at the piano at home. I realized how much more I could enjoy my playing this*

*instrument. The proof of the pudding was the next piano lesson. For the first time in my life I played a complete piece in a very relaxed way.'*
*N.V.*

In the Advanced workshop we learn to do a Balance in order to make our verbal and non-verbal communication free of stress. It is a Balance that makes our life very easy, even if we do not always see the connections with PSYCH-K afterwards. When I read this testimony for the first time, I could not discover where the link was between the Rapport Balance that was done and playing the piano. This was because I could not imagine what we have to do in order to be able to play the piano: as it happens we are reading the musical words of notes. If there is stress in the reading, this may have consequences for the fluency with which we will play the piano.

*'In the PSYCH-K Advanced workshop I learned how to do "co-surrogation". I thought I might try this out. At that moment I was studying Bach's Aria from the Goldberg variations and I was inspired here by the CD recording by Glenn Gould in 1981. No sooner said than done. I went into co-surrogation with Glenn Gould and have played the Aria. It was quite an experience. Even though my head and fingers had to do the job, I had the feeling of being on cloud nine all the time.'*
*N.V.*

PSYCH-K offers us the possibility not to have to play alone. We can call in the composer of the piece himself in order to add more quality to the piano music. That is what we are doing when we are going 'in co-surrogation'. We completely remain ourselves but we tune in on the composer or on the piece. I am curious to find out what someone experiences when going into surrogation with the musical work...

### Understanding a foreign language

B.W. has attended the Basic, Advanced and Health and Wellness workshops.

'When I was reading about PSYCH-K in Bruce Lipton's recent book, "The Biology of Belief" I wanted to learn the processes straight away. Through the Internet I found out that there was an English-speaking workshop in Madrid a couple of weeks from now. In the Basic workshop I immediately had some wonderful results for everything I undertook. There was a free day before the Advanced workshop started, so I decided to see an exhibition of quantum physics. All the information appeared to be only in Spanish, a language that I had never learned, so I did not understand what was written at all. But convinced by the miraculous power of the processes of the past days, I thought: "No problem, I have PSYCH-K." I walked out again, did a Balance for "I understand Spanish", went in again and I understood what was written. The meaning of the words was clear to me! What an extraordinary experience!'
B.W.

During A PSYCH-K Balance we are linking ourselves to the superconscious mind. In that sense we have all the knowledge of the universe at our disposal. Indeed, these are astonishing accomplishments!


## "Cleaning" a house before the sale

When my parents' house was sold, someone asked us to pass on an energetically 'clean' house. I went into the corner of a room and went into surrogation for the house. I felt quite solid. 'I only take the good memories of the people who built me and who have lived here' tested weakly. I did a Balance for this. As soon as the Balance was done, I jumped up and opened the windows. All painful memories were floating away into the open air.
Afterwards I drove past the house and if felt friendly. It is quite a special experience, when I tell you that I have never dealt with energetic cleaning or anything like it. I rather feel more like a scientist than an energy worker. But in fact I seem to be both.

**Working with horses**

Here are four testimonies about PSYCH-K and horses

R.M. has attended the Basic, Advanced, Pro and the Divine workshops.

*'A report about the experiences of my daughter M. and her horse Aquiona. Four years ago Aquiona came into the life of the then 26-year-old M. Aquiona was a five-year-old mare that had hardly been ridden and was known for her difficult, unpredictable character. M.'s former horse Owin, was an easy tempered gelding. Everyone advised M. against buying Aquiona, because she had not been riding on horseback a lot in the last few years, as she needed the time to study. And indeed, there were numerous problems: the mare was very difficult to ride; she was surly, rigid and often uncontrollable. A change of trainers and moving to another stable did not bring any improvement. Finally after two years of messing about M. wanted to sell Aquiona last year. I, as a father and PSYCH-K facilitator, had already pointed out to her the possibilities of doing a Balance, but at first she did not like the idea. Finally she agreed, it was a last resort. Together with another experienced PSYCH-K facilitator we then did a Relationship Balance, between M. on the one side and the colleague as a stand-in for Aquiona on the other.*

*In fact it was quite a surprise that we discovered that Aquiona wanted a good relationship with M. but that there had to be mutual respect. All experts were convinced of the fact that M. had to be much more authoritarian towards Aquiona though and that she dealt with her far too softly.*
*The changes were sensational. From the first day after the session Aquiona changed completely. She was cooperative, she let herself be ridden well, she learned quickly. For M. the sale was off right away. M. and Aquiona are having a great relationship now and together they are competing in several races, where they already won several prizes. Since then M. has also got a better understanding of Aquiona and more insight into her character.*

*Sometimes there are little things we bump into, like when she entered the trailer to go to the first race. We knew that something must have happened a long time ago, because Aquiona refused to step onto the trailer. After a balance, in which M. herself went into surrogation for Aquiona, she stepped onto the trailer without hesitation.*

*So, for some smaller problems with which she is confronted with her horse, M. herself regularly goes into surrogation and then all the little worries are straightened out.*

*I am convinced that PSYCH-K would also work for top horses, with which several problems occur during races and such events. I had a talk about this with the national coach of the Dutch dressage team. However it is very difficult to convince the conservative equestrian world of something great that works so easily.'*

R.M.


G.B. has attended the Basic, the Advanced twice, and the Divine workshops.


*'Armando, my two year old foal was much neglected during the first 18 months of his life and had a shortage of vitamins and minerals. I saved him from the slaughterhouse.*

*He had been hospitalized in De Morette from the beginning of December 2013. He kept having diarrhoea and losing weight. Moreover his red blood cells count kept diminishing. The veterinary surgeon suggested doing a lumbar puncture before Christmas, in order to find out if he suffered from leukaemia.*

*We went into surrogation and decided not to have this operation carried out. He was far too weak for this and I was concerned for his fragile health. The medical experts were never able to find the cause of his disease, in spite of several medical tests.*

*In surrogation we have asked him if he wanted to live or die, and Armando said: "I want to live!" That made us decide to fortify him and no longer to look for diseases. He then received several blood transfusions and he started producing red blood cells again. On 15 April 2014 he left De Morette. His recovery has taken four and a half months. He has gained some 55 kg and he is eating his fill.'*

G.B.

M.M. also has a story about horses. She has attended the Basic and Advanced workshops.

*'At a later age I started racing with my little horse. Before PSYCH-K came into my life, I was sitting on my tiny horse, me a trembling little piece of a man and I kept thinking: "What do I have to do this for in heaven's name? Is racing fun? No, not really. On the road with the horse in the trailer used to be a terrible journey!"*
*After the PSYCH-K Basic workshop I was still a little sceptical. I thought: this is not going to help me to race.*
*On the morning of a race I did a Balance for inner peace. I will never forget this particular day. After I had checked in, I came to the trailer and saw my little horse hanging with both forelegs over the pole, which had to keep her steady in case of an unexpected stop. Panic? No panic at all, no stress. I started thinking logically about how I was going to solve this. Well, some twenty minutes later she was behind the pole again. After she had been checked, I did the race. My little horse was fine and I quietly finished the race. Later on someone said to me: "You were so calm!"*
*Great! Now that I am writing this, I have to smile behind my computer!'*
*M.M.*

H.V. attended the Basic, Advanced and the Pro and Divine workshops.

*'I had a touching experience with a surrogation at a riding school with a beautiful mare and her rider, who did dressage. In the previous months contact had worsened between the two of them, and a lot of time and energy had already been spent in trying to improve it.*

*They called me and asked if PSYCH-K would work with horses. I had never worked with horses before and was not at all used to dealing with horses. At home we were told to keep our distance Up till now I always distanced myself from these animals for more than 1.5 meters. I felt that it could work if I prepared well. On the Internet there was a lot to read and I prepared myself with a couple of Balances. I felt quite at ease and sufficiently prepared right away in the first session.*

*In the stables we did a Relationship Balance between mare (with me in surrogation) and rider. During the Balance I felt how the horse changed inwardly from feeling stressed to complete calm! We remained in surrogation until the moment rider and mare rode off together. They had found a permanent new harmony together.'*
H.V.

Horses are known to be very sensitively accessible. It is no wonder that the four PSYCH-K facilitators had such a special effect. PSYCH-K has a lot to offer to horse trainers. Now horses are being used to draw attention to people about how they react to rejection or acceptance of horses. If horse trainers would use PSYCH-K they could go one step beyond. The information retrieved from horses can lead to transformation to a more open and stress free life.

## Working with different animals

N.V. has attended the Basic, Advanced and the PSYCH-K Pro workshops. *'One of my mother's dogs had the disagreeable habit of starting to bark each time we came across other dogs in the street. I really was fed up with this and went into surrogation. During the surrogation itself, something remarkable happened. This dog, which had never before tried to get closer, came leaning towards me and looked me tenderly straight in the eyes. I had good hope for the next walk. Unfortunately, the evening itself, the belief and the accompanying VAK did not produce the desired effect. I kept asking my mother later if anything had changed, but no success. Until now that is, about two months later. My mother had been travelling to some family members who also own a dog. This had always been a problem in the past. But this time there was none. Everything had gone smoothly. Both dogs could perfectly get on with each other, which had never been the case before. Recently I had to go to the vet for a check-up for my mother's dog: quite cooperatively it laid on its back to have her belly shaved and examined. My mother was thunderstruck. Could there be some peace in that little dog's body at last?'*
N.V.

We do not know at which moment a Balance is integrated. This can be immediate, and sometimes it takes time. We do not know what the result of a Balance produces in the animal's system, only that it is most likely to have a positive effect. As we have seen before, other messages or advantages may be connected to the barking. If these are not brought into balance or released, the behaviour will persist. Whether there are results or not, this does not tell anything about the activity of the brain. As shown in Chapter 10 'PER-K, PSYCH-K in professional situations', changes are visible on an EEG and the results are visible. But sometimes behaviour is connected with other factors, like beliefs or other situations.

**Asking for money in times of poverty**

D.S. has attended the Basic and the Advanced Workshops. His starting point was bleak: no income, a threatening bankruptcy, living isolated in a one-room flat, and a very limited perspective. During the workshops he was in a constant panic. It was a hard job to help him in order not to drown in his problems. To be able to survive he had to ask people for financial help which he did not dare to do at first. His prior objective was having enough money for food.

*'On Monday I did both a Stress and a Relationship Balance together with L. Whether there are any connections I am leaving that up to you to decide. Most things proceeded normally, but I found it strange that everything started the day afterwards for me.*
*- The National Health Service paid €67.*
*- An amount of about €60 has also been paid in my account, but I forgot its provenance.*
*- The water company sends me a letter that I would receive €122 (They wrote I would have to wait for two months to get it though).*
*- Yesterday I rang at six people's doorbells and asked for €1. Two people gave me €1 and €3. That touched me deeply. A third person wanted to help me, but she had no coins at home (and I believed her). On top of that I had two nice conversations. The other people were rather*

*aggressive or said that they received no help either. But the fact that all these people also had problems gave me quite a shock.*

*Yesterday I visited L. again and this time the contact was much warmer after the Relationship Balance. Phone contact with L.S. went much smoother.'*

A week later he wrote the following.

*'Meanwhile I have done two more rounds and some people gave me €10 and even €20. The average I can collect during a walk of half an hour is over €30. And all this started after the Relationship Balances.*

*The Social Security Service will pay me with retrospective effect and my sick leave has been advanced to 1 February. That is quite remarkable, because this was the only point I had not completed in the VAK to the Future. Apparently this visualization during the VAK was necessary in order to receive more sick pay. The medical advisor considered my situation serious and urgent.*

*Sometimes I even receive more money back than what I paid for, without my noticing it. Quite nice! Last night was the first night that I saw that things would be all right and that I was able to make plans. My first successful plan was to try to get a basic income. That is only the beginning of a whole number of items on my list, because a lot of money is involved and debts have to be paid. This was already straightened out this week.*

*I want to become better at counselling top firms in informatics and telephone protection and sustainability in infrastructure and architecture. The protection of smartphones and tablets will become an interesting work area.'*

D.S.

The fact that someone is living in continuous chaos and panic and succeeds in controlling his own life again by means of PSYCH-K has my deep admiration. I appreciate this man and I am glad that this process offers hope in hopeless times. We still have a long way to go, but the road is becoming clearer. This man is very talented.

Formerly, everything was dark and he was on his own. Now D.S. is reaching out, he is creating relationships and in doing so he also creates a new future.

**Bothered by heat?**

L.M. has attended the Basic, Advanced and Professional workshops.

*'From childhood on I could not stand heat, even when I was standing in the shadow. As a grown-up it became even worse. I was feeling short of breath in a temperature around 30 degrees (or more), and suffered bad moods because of this. Between noon and 5 p.m. I did not come outside and regularly I was in bed, completely wasted.*
*When the last heat wave was announced, I thought: let me handle this with PSYCH-K. After a session with messages and advantages and a Balance for solution all the elements tested strongly.*
*This was quite remarkable in itself, but I still thought: I'll believe it when I see it. The next day it was very hot. I noticed that I was walking through Vilvoorde alive and kicking at noon, and it was over 30 degrees. This was really a wow experience!*
*After two more weeks, with a lot of warm days, I can confirm with pleasure: it still works!'*
*L.M.*

We have repeatedly indicated that inconvenience, pain, trouble, … are symptoms of stress, coming from a brain that is underactive. There are experiences – or expressed in brain language 'sensory alarm signals' – that are wrongly linked to situations that are readily occurring. We do not have to know what these situations are, but we have to know whether these signals also contain a message from the subconscious mind or that we unconsciously keep up this trouble, pain or inconvenience because of the advantages. If we bring this into balance, the bodily signals often disappear.

*'Limiting beliefs of which most of us are not aware of, are dealt with in PSYCH-K. It is quite wonderful to bring yourself more in balance by a simple balance exercise, just through using your own brain.'*
*R.L.*

We can even go one step further. Sometimes we see someone for counselling who is presently troubled by something. I will order the subconscious mind to go to the origin of the problem. Most of the time there will be no conscious pictures of this. We do transform the stress that is sticking to the original situation and this way clear a great deal of the inconvenience. For problems that have been there for quite a long time, we will look for further messages and then we finish. 'Finish' means that we continue to live and are looking forward to experience how we will react if 'the nasty' situation should present itself again.


## No more sickness of heights

M.V.S. has attended the PSYCH-K and the Advanced workshops.

*'My husband always has sickness of heights when he is standing 4,500 meters high, then he becomes very ill. Usually he needs two days to get used to it.*
*We worked on this with PSYCH-K beforehand and he walked on the Mount Kailash Kora at 5,600 meters without any problems.*
*Amazing what a belief can do!'*
*M.V.S.*

So, this man had the experience of being sick at heights, which gave him the belief of being sick at heights. With PSYCH-K we can change the beliefs and because we engage the subconscious mind for the new beliefs, it also prepares itself physically to realize them.


## Insomnia

P.D.K. has attended the Basic and the Advanced Workshops. From his Dutch book *'Leven. Een zaak van zijn. Waarom onze problemen niet verdwijnen als wij ze oplossen, maar wel als wij oplossen'*, we translate the next passages about his working with PSYCH-K[6].

*'Results of processes of change cannot always be easily perceived although we can always find out if the belief in question tests*

"strongly". But it does of course matter whether someone had trouble with insomnia or whether there is another kind of anxiety. The person in question can easily diagnose a change in this. A director of a large international company, who travels a lot, came to see me because he had sleeping problems. After one session he seemed to be able to sleep soundly. More than a year later he came back to me. Now he used to wake up at about five o'clock in the morning, He did so because he had to go to the toilet and then he was unable to sleep again. When he left I asked him to let me know after one week how he was doing. After three days I received a mail that in the past three nights he had again woken up quite early to go to the toilet, but that he was able to sleep again immediately.

Another year later he had trouble to fall asleep again. This time we used the same belief statements as the first time, but we added: "I know that"... This time the Balance took a long time. But it seemed to work. Since then he has been sleeping well again.'

P.D.K.


**When mourning blocks you ...**

G.B. has attended the Basic, Advanced and the Divine workshops several times.

'A widow of 76 years old came to see me with the story that she still was feeling deep sorrow, at moments when the memories came up concerning her husband's death that occurred two years ago. She was convinced that the cause of this sorrow only had to do with her husband's death. After questioning her, it appeared that the sorrow had its origin in guilt feelings that had rooted after his death. It was about simple things from the time he was still alive. She had once refused him a glass of wine, because it might have made his illness worse. For two years she had not been able to open a bottle of wine, although she would have liked to do so. When she passed his favourite butcher's shop, she started crying, because she had refused him his favourite piece of meat, for the same reason. We did two Balances for inner peace (Stress Balances), where she could clearly relive these

situations. Two weeks later she called me quite relieved to tell me that she did not feel sorrow again in similar situations, and that she would like to continue with PSYCH-K. It is so nice to know and apply PSYCH-K.'
G.B.

## The feeling of panic stays away

'My girlfriend got a panic attack when seeing a road sign with the warning for a slope of 25% on our route in England. We did a Stress Balance for this and after 10 minutes the panic was gone. Sometimes she still sees ghosts from the last holiday, but the feeling of panic stays away!'
M.C.

Every one of us has his or her own desires. By means of PSYCH-K we can shape these. As soon as we have integrated a belief into our system, the subconscious mind will look for correspondences in the inner world and the outer world thus creating a new reality.

## Nice to practice PSYCH-K together and explore the possibilities

M.W. attended the Basic, Advanced and the Divine workshops. In the last two years she organized a three-day course in order to practice PSYCH-K twice. Plans for the coming years have already been made.

'The workshops and the Divine Retreats I have been able to attend so far, resulted in myself being touched by the people who are working with PSYCH-K. In June last year it resulted in the gathering of 14 PSYCH-K facilitators from the Netherlands and Belgium in Scheveningen.
For three days we worked with complete dedication, and every day new people arrived but we all hit it off from the first minute. Talking, Balancing, trying out new things in combination with PSYCH-K (for instance in combination with a real family set up). It was great. You can get new ideas and we all made huge progress.

*When you talk about "feeling", this is certainly a very important example of what can happen, if you allow the process to do its work.'*
*M.W.*

We do not completely know the possibilities of this process. We continue to explore and are surprised about these. If that process of discovery is being undertaken together, this is a real joy. Together we are creating a new world in which it is good to live. That brings us to the next chapter: 'PSYCH-K unleashes Love'.

# 12. PSYCH-K® Unleashes Love

*'There is only one Source, and it is in all things. The sooner you see the big picture, the more you get clear about the power of love and the illusion of separation.'* – Robert Williams

**A Testimony**

*'My experience with PSYCH-K*

*In March 2014 I started with the PSYCH-K Basic workshop with M.R. I attended the Pro workshop in May and the Advanced workshop in July.*

*In the past 10 years I attended several training sessions, among other things in shamanism and Eco therapy. While practicing I could considerably work on myself and gradually I had the wish to start my own practice or to co-operate in an existing practice. What prevented me from doing so was that I did not like the working methods of trainings. At the beginning of this year I read Bruce Lipton's book "The Biology of Belief" with a paragraph about PSYCH-K and from that moment I have experienced an emotional and spiritual roller coaster.*

*After the Basic workshop quite a lot of puzzle pieces fell into place. At last the inner trinity of body-mind-soul was manageable for me (in PSYCH-K this is called the "system"). Now I can connect with this system and I can continue clearing and reconditioning the disturbing values and norms from a protestant-Christian environment, in full cooperation with it. The rewarding and punishing God has already been dealt with and instead there came the spiritual approach to the Divine and the understanding of being connected with everything and everyone.*

While processing the course material of the Basic workshop all of a sudden this sentence received full meaning: "Let your soul establish contact with the Divine". I am connected with my soul and my soul is connected with the Universal Soul and so with the Divine. At last I have the feeling that I can concentrate on the here and now, knowing that we are connected with all that exists. Isn't this nice, no worries about reward or punishment, no worries about the hereafter.

This breakthrough also has further effect on a daily basis in the contact with people around me and more generally in my position as a member of society. I had the opportunity to proclaim the above in the Pro workshop last May.

In spite of these wonderful new insights I was upset for a couple of weeks after the Pro workshop. I said that I was in a Post workshop Depression, something like Post Natal Depression, which happens to certain women when they become a mother for the first time and are afraid of not being good enough when raising their child.
The course material of the Pro workshop made me realize that the possibilities of working on myself with PSYCH-K or of co-operating with others as a facilitator are almost infinite. This feeling is to be compared with trying to imagine the infiniteness of the universe. I often tried to do this but stopped, because it makes me feel dizzy.

But this did not succeed with the newly acquired insights about PSYCH-K; that dizziness did not leave. As a reaction I entered more deeply into the course material of the Pro workshop and tried, by doing Balances, to get more space in order to admit these insights. Finally I went through the whole process, peace and confidence settled in again and I started looking forward to the PSYCH-K Advanced. Looking back I should not have tackled this on my own; I should have asked the help of M.R. or my fellow students.

The Advanced workshop in July has not stopped the roller coaster experience with PSYCH-K, because this workshop had a lot to offer me as well. I thought I more or less understood how I could progress on my life path. My 65th birthday came up and I celebrated that with the runic character for Harvest (Jera); no longer toiling, but living here and now, etcetera. The experiences with the PSYCH-K insights supported this. But when during the workshop we did the Balance with Belief Points and Energy Focusing, I again and again muscle-tested weakly for: "I give my whole spirit to life and my whole life to Spirit".

I felt that this weak muscle test was correct, because this belief sounded to me as monastic vows and monasteries in my eyes are connected with the judging and punishing God and the Ecclesiastic Institution. At the same time this belief was so comprehensive that it again made me feel dizzy. While I am writing this, I have still not recovered.

This experience made me realize that apart from harvesting and working with the tool that has shaped itself during my life, I will continue to chop away limiting and blocking beliefs. Whenever they show up, I will overwrite them with positive constructive beliefs and keep asking for inspiration.

The way is the target! And this is true for PSYCH-K but not for any other method I know. Moreover I do not have to do this on my own, because facilitators increasingly keep networking with each other both in Belgium and in the Netherlands.'

J.H.

In J.H.'s testimony he describes the interaction between unity within ourselves, peace with others and acceptance of the divine. This is the structure of this last chapter. By applying PSYCH-K we are becoming lighter, one with ourselves, and love can flow again between us and openness will grow to what is more than we, people are. The Divine.

## Our system is one

As J.H. describes, with the word 'system' – a word that is said once or twice in every Balance – we mean the inherent human unity of body, soul and mind. A Balance has an effect on this unity: body, soul and mind are strengthened by it. By dramatically reducing the static our body relaxes, our mind becomes purposeful and open, and our soul becomes more unique and connected.

Peace in us means 'unity'. It is the driving force to streamline our subconscious database with what we consciously want and with what our superconscious mind directs us to. The focus lies on us here, on the relationships in and with ourselves.

We are also one with *each other* and with *the world*, which we live in. We express this unity with each other with the word 'peace'. It means being committed to the well-being of the other person, with all that belongs to him or her as a human being, in certain relationships. All that is not grafted onto peace will divide us or set us up against each other. It alienates us from whom we are and should be.

We usually call spirituality our aspiration for unity with the divine. We long to take up our role in the whole as this unique human being. By walking this road we receive ourselves as a gift one way or another. By fine-tuning to the divine – especially when the needs of the other person are crossing my own programme (Levinas) – we completely become ourselves: 'here I am'. There is an interaction: what we give unconditionally will be given back to us in equal measure.


**From separation to unity**

S.M. has attended the Basic, Advanced, Divine and the Health and Wellness workshops.

*'PSYCH-K came into my life at a moment that I had decided to take responsibility for my own feelings, but I did not know how to do this. At last with PSYCH-K I have a fine method to bring sustainable change into my life and my relationships.'*
*S.M.*

S.M. responds after he made his contribution to the book to add something:
*"There is something else I was thinking about after I read my testimonial and the piece you wrote, that followed it. I touched on it before. It is about responsibility: in English we have the word "responsible"*

in which I strongly hear "response-able". This is the essence of my testimonial: I now feel "able to respond". I can take responsibility. Often we remain in a powerless position, because we do not have the tools and possibilities (or we think we do not have them) to do something different than our habitual programming tells us (remaining a victim, feeling ruled by forces outside of ourselves)".
S.M.


K.V.O. has attended the Basic and Advanced workshops.


'Resentment has become a part of myself in the past months. Negative conversations, filled with reproaches, are haunting me. I know that there has to be a change from within. This is not healthy...

One morning I was doing the Balance "I forgive her". With every Balance I tested that it was necessary to do a visualization exercise about this. This visualization exercise is helping me to see, feel and experience what I want to achieve. For me it is a necessary element because otherwise things remain too vague. After this visualization exercise I continued to do the Balance. I felt much lighter and also clearer in the head.
When I met this woman that week, I was able to greet her sincerely. It had been months since I could greet her sincerely and could talk to her warm-heartedly. Phew! That is over...'
K.V.O.


When our inner unity is disturbed, we create drama around us.
In this book I have described three mechanisms that are responsible for the fact that we experience our body as an opponent and that we see each other as enemies: these are the sensory alarm signals, the perception of hostility, and the drama.
As a result of loss of control, sensory fear signals are separating us from the unity with ourselves and with others. They make us (energetically) expand our territory. This way we are increasing the anxiety in ourselves, because we are afraid of revenge.
Moreover, these sensory fear signals change our perception. We do no longer perceive the others as companions but as enemies, against

whom we have to defend ourselves. As soon as we no longer have peace with regard to the other person, there is something rotten in our own subconscious mind[1]. Fear of the other person legitimates our defence and we have come full circle.

Drama is the result of this defence. Whoever takes part in the drama, feels like a victim. In fact the participants are victims and perpetrator in turns, until the drama dies down. That usually happens by expelling a 'scapegoat'. Irrespective of the position we take in a group, from the place where we are, we continuously increase the tensions. It could be different. Whoever is in a Whole-Brain State, can more easily resist the dynamics of exclusion and scapegoating[2].

The three mechanisms lead us all back to a bodily misunderstanding: because our *own* body perceives alarm *in ourselves*, we do no longer experience ourselves as a unity. As soon as our inner unity is disturbed, we create drama around us.

Q.R.S. has attended all PSYCH-K workshops.

*'It was a week ago since I realized that everything I think I need or long for, IS all in myself already. I have it all in me nothing is outside of myself! I have done several PSYCH-K exercises like a Relationship Balance with "my true Self", even installed a belief like "Everything IS in myself, I AM everything, I am the source", done a Balance in order to go within my deepest source and from there to experience myself and the outer world. It is the same for love, recognition, life, truth, information, freedom, earth, God, ... everything is in myself. As soon as I think I need something from someone else or I am angry, I only have to go inside of ME...*

*Everything is changing now; all beautiful things are coming to me (expressions of love, texts concerning subjects I am dealing with, answers to questions, a telephone I ordered from the universe, etcetera).*

*For a couple of days the subject Unity came up.*
*I received a lot of insights... I understand that all anxiety springs from the idea of being separated and now I gather what is meant by "disease"*

and "being expelled from paradise" (Adam and Eve... Me)... I am doing this to myself. I must have created the belief and the illusion that I am separated from the SELF/ UNITY/ GOD/ UNIVERSE/ PARADISE. That is why I experience separation. I separated myself from mySelf.

I have done a Balance in which I said to my subconscious mind: "Go to the first time I felt separated (alone, sad, angry, empty, cold,) and nod when you are there." My subconscious mind sunk (or so it felt) into this feeling. I felt emotions underway,... and nothing... until I heard the words: "I feel so guilty!" There was no nodding of my head... but I saw an entrance. Then I started a conversation with whoever said this,(it felt female), like someone from another life. She had been angry and felt so terribly guilty that she did not dare to show herself to Me or to God (which is the same).
Now my head is nodding, so here is the origin... I explained to her that separation was intended and that she and I had experienced this quite long enough now. So everything is fine. She will be able to choose to see separation as a Gift so that she may feel gratitude... By experiencing separation we can now EXPERIENCE UNITY (the experience of light exists thanks to darkness). She is free to continue to live like this or to choose unity; I feel unconditional love for her. "YEEES, unity".
I feel love for separation, let it Be what it Is and choose my Truth of Unity... I feel myself going deeper, feel warmth within me, love, there is a lighter hue, it is wonderful and peaceful inside of me... Is this how Paradise would feel?

The next day, my reactions and thoughts are working really hard in order to try to convince me of my separation! Ha, awake and alert I react with unconditional love and say that these are old beliefs and patterns and that I am New and One.
I discovered what my Essence is all about, what really fills my heart with joy: others experience Themselves as Who they Really are. By giving what I enjoy most (experiencing myself as who I really am), I experience my true Self. How funny this all is.
I am all smiles for life and life is all smiles for me, this is so beautiful!'
Q.R.S.

What Q.R.S. describes are mystical experiences of peace and unity. They are at odds with day-to-day drama. Growing towards this is asking for conscious choices. We are free and responsible to choose separation or unity. Unity requires tuning in to the superconscious mind, to what in the long run is good for the realm in which we are moving. It is necessary to transform our subconscious database, so that it can automatically guide us into this direction of unity. This will be explained more, later.

*Connect with the superconscious during a PSYCH-K Balance*

## Consciously choosing peace freely and responsibly

I.K. only attended the Basic workshop.

*'Through PSYCH-K I became aware of the fact that I am not a puppet dangling from the strings of the Universe, but that I can really give direction to my life. More enlightening insights are found on my path slowly but steadily. This changes my life for the better both mentally and bodily.'*
I.K.

H.V. has attended the Basic, Advanced and the Divine workshops several times.

*'Every moment is an invitation to see what is happening as a pearl of wisdom. Every moment – also with experiences that I would not possibly choose myself, experiences that sometimes are really painful – is a new opportunity for transformation and growth. I want to take this chance. In fact the heart of the matter is to discover this time and again. This process has changed my experience of life. In that sense it is an invitation to really live consciously, to always see the potency of the moment.*
*In doing so I have been experiencing more and more how special the process is of establishing fortifying beliefs. In this I experience that the more space I leave for the whole experience, the more easily the essence of the limiting experience becomes clear and a new perspective may come into being.*
*This process also asks for real honesty. I have personally experienced in the last years that feedback from others is sometimes crucial in this.'*
H.V.

We are free people, we can freely – and responsibly – choose what we want to achieve in life. At least this is the illusion we cling to. Our behaviour is mainly determined subconsciously. The margin of our freedom is extremely small[3]. We can choose to readjust our subconscious motives; that is the freest choice we have.

When people come to see me for a first private session, I suggest starting looking at the fundamental beliefs that direct someone. The Core Belief Balance that I have discussed before examines whether someone is directed at construction or destruction[4]. If the relationship between both is disturbed – constructive basic beliefs have to test strongly, destructive ones weakly. We will first set this right. If the foundation is strong, we can trace and transform further nuisances. There is always an interaction between the growing self and peace with other people.

If we choose growth with other people, we need all the skills we have developed up till now in order to learn to exist in dialogue. In dialogue we meet each other and that is the highest we can achieve among human beings[5]. We stay close to ourselves and are open and curious to find out what guides the other person. In dialogue the other person can reveal himself and we can outgrow ourselves. Like Levinas we can say: 'here I am', ready to get along together.

The choice for dialogue and living together implies that we only live in our own territory and respect the space of the other person as irreducibly belonging to himself. Just like me, the other being has free choice and responsibility. That is what professor Burggraeve calls 'owing': 'our owing space to the other person makes us into responsible human beings'.[6]

We can also choose not to take responsibility. Being responsible ourselves implies that we can also choose the things that could harm our community and ourselves. Because this way others could be harmed, we have the right and even the duty to limit and transform the damage that arises as much as possible. At that moment giving to each other in surrogation is a contribution to the peace we are profoundly aspiring to.

With PSYCH-K we can assume our free responsibility completely, because we can either choose to remain in stress reaction or to act from a Whole-Brain State. If we completed the Basic and the Advanced workshops, we are able to put ourselves back on track – often in less than one minute.

It is still a choice, because we will have to do this over and over again. We can also choose not to apply PSYCH-K and let ourselves be sucked in the drama that presents itself. Whatever we choose, with this process we can carry the consequences of our choices in peace, and I mean in peace and not being attached to the drama.

Where or whenever, PSYCH-K remains a choice, a choice of the *conscious mind*. This is the power of our conscious mind: making choices and being responsible for them. We completely have to respect this choice in PSYCH-K, which is extremely important to me. I am a free human being and I want to be respected as such. I know that this is true for you, the reader as well.

Just like we ourselves can choose to grow, we can choose to contribute or not to others, by being at peace with them ourselves and/or by helping them come to a place of peace within themselves. We can also choose and decide that it is enough, that our contributing has been sufficient. We put ourselves in the first place then. Everything is possible; we are totally free and responsible time and time again. However it is not because we decide to take the space for ourselves today, that tomorrow we will not be completely ready for each other.

What is this all about? What are you longing for? What do you really want to achieve? In the PSYCH-K Balances these questions are constantly asked.


## Fine-tuning to the superconscious mind

T.G. has attended the Basic, Advanced, Divine and the Health and Wellness workshops.

*'For me PSYCH-K is a method that helps me become more and more united, consciously and subconsciously with myself and at peace with the others and with all that is. As soon as I am bumping into something,*

*I ask my superconscious mind if it is safe and appropriate to deal with it and I try to find out what it is that "is clinging" to it that I do not understand. For instance stress during work or in communication with others, incidents that are constantly playing in my head, things I become aware of and that I want to balance. This way I align with the Higher Self – for the connection with the All – and my subconscious mind is cooperating with the changes that are beneficial to me. Since I have been applying PSYCH-K it is really amazing to see how I have been able to grow both at an individual level and at the level of interactions with others and even at a spiritual level. I dare to live with far more dedication and I choose to learn to release my ego. Of course this is a choice to take my responsibility more and more. Not that easy! In this way PSYCH-K is a method that helps me guide my life in continuous harmony with the All – or whatever you may want to call it – with the Source that is guiding me and that I can follow by listening to the superconscious mind.'*
*T.G.*

Choosing to fine-tune to 'who or what knows what is good for us' (e.g. the superconscious mind), instead of starting from the ego is a conscious decision. It is up to us to decide to connect and work together with our highest energy or to refuse it. Within the spiritual development this choice is called a 'leap of faith' or a 'conversion'.[7] It often is the result of a shocking experience but some people make this choice on rational grounds or out of curiosity.

A similar choice is not necessarily a one-off choice. Whoever treads the spiritual way like J.H. has to make decisions again and again. Which God, which highest value or presence do you want to live for? Is our deepest motivation anxiety or love? Is our motivation directed at ourselves or at the other people? These are fundamental choices that determine whatever is possible in our life.
Earlier I told you that as a Catholic, I believed in one life and we have to make the best of it. Experiences have made me aware of the possibility of having several lives. It was a new choice to embrace this openness or to reject it. In other words I choose whether or not to connect with the highest value in my life and to determine the outlines of this presence.

What can the superconscious mind realize? It is only what fits my way of thinking, or is it really transcendent. Is it more than what I can think of? If for whatever reason I cannot grasp it, do I still want to choose this unknown realm?

For myself it is important to keep all doors open and to abandon myself to the benevolence of the superconscious mind. Because I believe and absolutely trust in these beneficial creative possibilities, they become real in my life. In the Bible this is called 'your faith has saved you'. Only that which we believe, lies within our possibilities. I have great faith in my life and everything is possible.

## Aligning our subconscious mind to the superconscious mind

Choosing the superconscious mind implies that I engage myself to Balance all that does not match this wisdom and these possibilities. I am part of the superconscious mind and I have my place in the whole. As I have explained in Chapter 5 'From drama to a learning opportunity', I am part of this creative capacity. Only, my beliefs (that have come from my life experiences) seem to stand in my way.

As I have written in this book, I am not free from disturbing reactions. Every situation is different thus generates other sensory signals and I am sure that I do have to transform lots of things. That brings me to the last piece of wisdom: learning to listen to the synchronicity and living from grace.

## Learning to listen to synchronicity

Listening to synchronicity implies that we take the succession of coincidences in our life seriously[8]. Apparently there are lessons for life in the incidents that occur all around us. It is important to really listen: to the intuition inside ourselves, to the coincidences we notice, to the presents we are being given. Everything is a learning opportunity.

This book was started at the moment that a journalist of a Flemish newspaper offered to write an article at the end of an introduction day. She received permission from the newspaper, but the editor-in-chief did not want to publish it right then. He said: 'We will publish it when there is a hype'. I chose to hear this as a stimulus rather than a rejection. The message therefore was: give more publicity to PSYCH-K. Will do!

In the words of thanks I will refer to 'smart coincidences' that have been the supportive foundation of this creation. By listening to all the messages, invitations and opportunities, while writing I have grown as a human being. I feel more open now, I dare to do more, I stand strong in my own power.

Because I am listening to the coincidences of life, I am receiving opportunities to develop myself and to be of service to life, to you... The more I do this, the more beautifully the coincidences present themselves. Life is so beautiful. Is it also beautiful to you? You own the choice... Go for it!

# A Word of Thanks

Dear reader, thank you so much for your interest. If you completely read this book until these words of thanks, I am glad that you remained interested by the information and the stories. I hope that it did you some good and that you found some hope and perspective. Thank you for accompanying me on this trip.

My gratitude goes to the 'who or what' – You, All – that offered me this opportunity. All my talents and discoveries I owe to You. Whoever or whatever you may be, thank you from the bottom of my heart.
Thank you so much, Rob Williams, for listening to what was given to you. Thank you for relaying PSYCH-K to each of us.

The history of this book is, as I mentioned before, one of synchronicity. It started at the end of an Introduction day. Thank you so much, Els, and thank you so much, editor-in-chief, to have pushed me into the book's direction.

We did a Relationship Balance with this book. During this Relationship Balance between the book and me, it showed that it 'would travel around the world'. So, this implied that I had to write for a larger audience. Thank you so much, Veronika.

Then came the realization that I had to ask Robert Williams to read through the book before the publishing, as he is the originator of PSYCH-K. He welcomed the idea. Thank you so much, Rob!

Someone told me that the finest thing she had done in her life was reading and correcting a manuscript. I suggested that she would proofread this book. She has gladly done so. Thank you so much, Mia!

The book is illustrated by Sam Geussens. This young creative artist bubbles with inspiration! Thank you Sam!

Several people have read the book before it could go to the publisher. Thank you so much, Bart, Hans, Helga, Fransien, Lut, Koen and Tinne! Prof. Roger Burggraeve read the texts of Levinas. Thank you Roger!

In order to have this book completed with the endorsement by Rob Williams, it had to be translated into English. Thank you so much, Jos, and thank you so much, Claire!
A Lady from London, called Su made the translation more fluent. Thank you Su!
Then a English-Dutch couple put their effort in post reading and correcting the translation. Thank you Sandra and thank you Louis!
Roeland helped with the further layout. Thank you Roeland!

Then it was time for designing the cover. Thank you Monique for a beautiful painting! The picture on the back cover was taken as I committed myself as a Co-changer with CHANGE. Thank you for the good recordings!
M.C. allowed me to print the testimony on the cover. Thank you for that!
Daisy and Liesbeth were a great help for the printing of this book. Thank you Liesbeth and Daisy!

We also needed a website to promote the books. Thank you Johan, Danny, Frans and co!

Thanks to the 77 people who have written down their experiences as a contribution. Thank you for sharing this part of your life, of your discoveries! Your contribution makes this book into a project that has been carried through together. It was extremely nice working with you! Thank you again and again!

I especially want to thank my most loyal loved one, Koen. You are my support and refuge. You have made it possible for me to write this book while in a beautiful spot in nature. Thank you so much!

We all together have made this book concrete and accessible to everyone. Thank you!

# *Notes*

## Introduction

[1] cRZ is called FARA now. Information Desk for Pregnancy Choices.

[2] Riemslagh, M. & Vanmechelen, B., *Abortus voorgoed voorbij? Een hulpverleningsmodel*, Leuven, Lannoo Campus, 2003, 156p.

[3] You can read this book as a personal story of me as a PSYCH-K Instructor. Each Instructor has his or her own story. We share the competence in teaching PSYCH-K workshops. I gladly recommend you to do the PSYCH-K workshop with the teacher that suits you the best. For more information see www.psych-k.com

[4] The term 'superconscious mind' comes from psycho synthesis. Roberto Assagioli created this term to describe our true core, the soul, the source of all creative inspiration. Psycho synthesis: Individual and Social, p. 2, (access 08.09.2014) http://two.not2.org/psychosynthesis/articles/psindivandsocial.pdf. "These tendencies and energies, which can be named *superconscious*, have relationships and interactions with the conscious personality which are curiously analogous – at a higher octave – to those of the lower unconscious urges. It has been ascertained that these higher energies are often repelled and rejected from the 'field of consciousness' for similar motives: lack of understanding, fear, preconceived ideas, depreciation, unwillingness to be disturbed or fulfil new inner tasks and to renounce selfish attachments and satisfactions."

[5] Williams, R., *PSYCH-K, The missing piece peace in your life!*, Colorado, The Myrddin Publications, 2009, p. 13-17.

[1] The so called 'Other Life' training is a three day training for people with unexplainable medical complaints such as chronic fatigue, fibromyalgia, compulsive disorders, ... given by Helga Verhoeven in The Netherlands. For more information see www.anderleven.nl

[2] That more than 10% of the people who followed a workshop in the Dutch speaking area wrote a testimonial about the results of PSYCH-K in their lives is a statement that PSYCH-K works. I really enjoyed the stories. I am very glad with them.

## 1. Beliefs determine our lives

[1] Lipton, B., *The Biology of Belief. Unleashing the Power of Consciousness, Matter & Miracles*, Carlsbad, Hay House, 2005, p. 97-98. "… the seemingly 'separate' subdivisions of the mind, the *conscious* and the *subconscious* are interdependent. The conscious mind is the creative one that can conjure up 'positive thoughts'. In contrast, the subconscious mind is a repository of stimulus-response tapes derived from instincts and learned experiences. The subconscious mind is strictly habitual; it will play the same behavioural responses to life's signals over and over again, much to our chagrin. How many times have you found yourself going ballistic over something trivial like an open toothpaste tube? You have been trained since childhood to carefully replace the cap. When you find the tube with its cap left off your 'buttons are pushed' and you automatically fly into a rage. You've just experienced the simple stimulus-response of a behaviour program stored in the subconscious mind.

When it comes to sheer neurological processing abilities, the subconscious mind is millions of times more powerful than the conscious mind. If the desires of the conscious mind conflict with the programs of the subconscious mind, which 'mind' do you think will win out? You can repeat the positive affirmation that you are lovable over and over or that your cancer tumour will shrink. But if, as a child, you heard over and over again that you are worthless and sickly, those messages programmed in your subconscious mind will undermine your best conscious efforts to change your life. Remember how quickly your last New Year's resolution to eat less food fell by the wayside as the aroma of the baking turkey dissolved your resolve?"

[2] Williams, R., *PSYCH-K. The Missing Piece Peace in Your Life!*, Colorado, The Myrddin Publications, 2009, p. 45-54. 'The Power and Biology of Beliefs, Toxic Beliefs Can Be Hazardous to Your Health'.

[3] Lipton, B., *The Biology of Belief. Unleashing the Power of Consciousness, Matter & Miracles*, Carlsbad, Hay House, 2005, p. 101. "In *Molecules of Emotion*, Pert revealed how her study on information-processing receptors on nerve cells membranes led her to discover were present on most, if not all, of the body's cells. Her elegant experiments established that the 'mind' was not focused in the head but was distributed via signal molecules to the whole body. As importantly, her work emphasized that emotions were not only derived through a feedback of the body's environmental information. Through self-consciousness, the mind can use the brain to *generate*

'molecules of emotion' and override the system. While proper use of consciousness can bring health to an ailing body, inappropriate unconscious control of emotions can easily make a healthy body diseased."

4 Williams, R., *PSYCH-K. The Missing Piece Peace In Your Life!*, Colorado, The Myrddin Publications, 2009, p. 55-65. 'Conscious versus Subconscious Beliefs. Two Minds are Better than One'.

5 Lipton, B., *The Biology of Belief. Unleashing the Power of Consciousness, Matter & Miracles*, Carlsbad, Hay House, 2005, p. 134. "Given the precision of this behaviour-recording system, imagine the consequences of hearing your parents say you are a 'stupid child', you 'don't deserve things', will 'never amount to anything', or are a 'sickly, weak' person. When unthinking or uncaring parents pass on those messages to her young children, they are no doubt oblivious to the fact that such comments are downloaded into the subconscious memory as absolute 'facts' just as surely as bits and bytes are downloaded to the hard drive of your desktop computer. During early development, the child's consciousness has not evolved enough to critically assess that those parental pronouncements were only verbal barbs and not necessarily true characterizations of 'self'. Once programmed into the subconscious mind, however, these verbal abuses become defined as 'truths' that unconsciously shape the behaviour and potential of the child through life."

In the interview with Bruce Lipton and Rob Williams of 10 July 2014, Lipton calls the subconscious mind a sponge that absorbs everything. You can find it here: http://www.freefullliving.com page Science.

6 Lipton, B., *The Biology of Belief. Unleashing the Power of Consciousness, Matter & Miracles*, Carlsbad, Hay House, 2005, p. 103. "Reflex behaviours may be as simple as the spontaneous kick of the leg when a mallet taps the knee or as complex as driving a car at sixty-five miles per hour on a crowded interstate highway while your conscious mind is fully engaged in conversation with a passenger. Though conditioned behavioural responses may be inordinately complete, they are 'no-brainers'. Through the conditioned learning process, neural pathways between eliciting stimuli and behavioural responses become hardwired to ensure a repetitive pattern. Hardwired pathways are 'habits'."

7 Lipton, B., *The Biology of Belief. Unleashing the Power of Consciousness, Matter & Miracles*, Carlsbad, Hay House, 2005, p. 97. In order to see Bruce

Lipton himself telling that our subconscious mind works as a tape recorder, you can also consult: http://www.freefullliving.com page Science.

Our subconscious mind is a million times more powerful than our conscious mind. 5 percent conscious against 95 percent subconscious behaviour.

[8] We can only be guilty inasmuch as we have not stopped our destructive operation. Our conscious mind is capable of stopping the subconsciously directed reaction through a command 'I do not want this'. Narváez, D., *Triune Ethics: The Neurobiological Roots of Our Multiple Moralities*, in *New Ideas in Psychology* 26 (2008) 1, 95-119.

[9] Lipton, B., *The Biology of Belief. Unleashing the Power of Consciousness, Matter & Miracles*, Carlsbad, Hay House, 2005, Addendum. "… I'd like to talk a little about one of these energy psychology techniques called PSYCH-K because I have personal experience with it, and I am confident of its integrity, simplicity, and effectiveness. (…) In the fifteen years since I witnessed that woman's quick transformation, I have seen other people rapidly improve their self-esteem and change their relationships, their finances, and their health using PSYCH-K. The PSYCH-K process is simple, direct, and verifiable. It utilizes the mind/body interface of muscle testing (kinesiology) … to access the self-limiting 'files' of the subconscious mind. It also makes use of left brain/right brain integration techniques to effect swift and long-lasting changes. In addition, PSYCH-K integrates Spirit into the change process, just as I have integrated Spirit into my understanding of Science. Using muscle testing, PSYCH-K accesses what Rob calls the 'superconscious' mind to make sure that the person's stated goals are safe and appropriate. These built-in safeguards allow this system of personal change to be taught to anyone who is interested in taking charge of their lives by moving out of fear and into love.

I use PSYCH-K in my own life. PSYCH-K has helped me undo my self-limiting beliefs, including one about not being able to finish my book. The fact that you are holding this book is one indication of the power of PSYCH-K!"

[10] For a brief explanation of the Core Belief Balance, see the Introduction on page 14. The testimony of A.X. in the next chapter concerns a Core Belief Balance.

[11] Lipton, B., *The Biology of Belief. Unleashing the Power of Consciousness, Matter & Miracles*, Carlsbad, Hay House, 2005, p. 57. The cell biologist Bruce Lipton understood that not only the genetic material, but also especially the activities of the cell membrane are decisive for the life of a cell. At a certain moment he realized that our human body functions as a multi cellular being,

which has contracted out certain cell functions to organs. To the brain the cell membrane function has been contracted out, the ability to make contact between the inner world and the outer world.

"To exhibit 'intelligent' behaviour, cells need a functioning membrane with both receptor (awareness) and effector (action) proteins. These protein complexes are the fundamental units of cellular intelligence. Technically they may be referred to as units of 'perception'. The definition of perception is 'awareness of the elements of environment through physical sensation'. The first part of the definition describes the function of receptor IMPs. The second part of the definition, the creation of a 'physical sensation', sums up the role of the effector proteins."

[12] Lipton, B., *The Biology of Belief. Unleashing the Power of Consciousness, Matter & Miracles*, Carlsbad, Hay House, 2005, p. 101, 106. "As more complex animals evolved, specialized cells took over the job of monitoring and organizing the flow of the behaviour regulating signal molecules. These cells provided a distributed nerve network and central information processor, a brain. The brain's function is to coordinate the dialogue of signal molecules within the community. Consequently, in a community of cells, each cell must acquiesce control to be informed decisions of its awareness authority, the *brain*. The brain *controls* the behaviour of the body's cells. This is a very important point to consider as we blame the cells of our organs and tissues for the health issues we experience in our lives."

In other words, our brain is finally responsible for the functioning of our organs, not the organs themselves. "Suppose you're working in a bank. The branch manager gives you an order. The CEO walks in and gives you the opposite order. Which order would you follow? If you want to keep your job you'll snap to the CEO's order. There is a similar priority built into our biology, which requires cells to follow instructions from the head honcho nervous system, even if those signals are in conflict with local stimuli."

If you notice inside your body some signals that you have to lay this book aside for a while in order to relax, but if you have learned that you should first read to the end of the chapter, this final belief, which has been stored in your subconscious mind (brain), will determine your behaviour. The fact that your body — for instance your eyes — is tired and wants to relax, is just the 'assignment of the branch manager'.

[13] Interview with Rob Williams: Kamp, J., *The Mind is the Doctor*, in *Ode, The Intelligent Optimist* September/October (2012).

[14] Lipton, B., *The Biology of Belief. Unleashing the Power of Consciousness, Matter & Miracles*, Carlsbad, Hay House, 2005, p. 103. "Humans and a number of other higher mammals have evolved a specialized region of the brain associated with thinking, planning, and decision-making called the prefrontal cortex. This portion of the forebrain is apparently the seat of the 'self-conscious' mind processing. The self-conscious mind is self-reflective; it is newly evolved 'sense organ' that observes our own behaviours and emotions. The self-conscious mind also has access to most of the data stored in our long-term memory bank. This is an extremely important feature allowing our history of life to be considered as we consciously plan our futures.

Endowed with the ability to be self-reflective, the self-conscious mind is extremely powerful. It can observe any programmed behaviour we are engaged in, evaluate the behaviour, and consciously decide to change the program. We can actively *choose* how to respond to most environmental signals and whether we even want to respond at all. The conscious mind's capacity to override the subconscious mind's pre-programmed behaviours is the foundation of free will. However, our special gift comes with a special pitfall." See further, note 6 to Chapter 4 'Stress and total exhaustion': Ibid., p. 103-104.

[15] TED Talk with Kelly McGonigal about the effects of our beliefs on stress and on our health condition.
https://www.youtube.com/watch?v=RcGyVTAoXEU
(access 10.12.2014)

## 2. PSYCH-K Works Quickly and Effectively

[1] This question: 'what do you want instead?' is well known by caretakers who are acquainted with solution-focused therapy. In Solution Focused Therapy this question is called 'the miracle question'. Sparrer, I., *Miracle, Solution and System. Solution-focused structural constellations for therapy and organizational change*, Cheltenham, Solution Books, 2007, p. 33-34. "Suppose you go home after this session... and you talk to your family, eat your evening meal and maybe do something else (...) and then at some point you become tired and go to bed (...) suppose... during the night... a miracle happens (...) and the miracle would be... that all the problems that brought you here today... are solved... suddenly... just like that (...) and that really would be miracle, wouldn't it? – (...) and you wake up early

the next morning – and no one tells you that this miracle has happened – how then would you know this miracle had occurred?" PSYCH-K follows a similar process as what happens in what we call the V(isual) A(uditory) K(inaesthetic) shaping of the future. The difference between solution-oriented therapies and PSYCH-K is that the latter intervenes directly on the level of the subconscious mind.

[2] Williams, R., *PSYCH-K. The Missing Piece Peace In Your Life!*, 3rd ed., Colorado, The Myrddin Publications, 2009, p. 31-41.

[3] Kinesiology is a science in itself. It is a way to remove tension from the body. Walther, S., *Applied Kinesiology*, SDC, Colorado, 2000, 628p. Craniosacral and foot reflexology are kinaesthetic therapies; they have nothing to do with PSYCH-K. PSYCH-K only uses muscle testing to establish communication with the subconscious mind; it is no kinesiology.

[4] Monti, D., et al., *Muscle Test Comparisons of Congruent and Incongruent Self-Referential Statements*, in *Perceptual and Motor Skills* 88 (1999), 1019-1028. Monti and his team examined 89 students. They pronounced 'my name is…' with their proper name and then 'my name is…' with a false name. The difference was significant. Using muscle testing, we become the trust worthiest results while pushing two seconds on the arm of the person; with about the pressure you would close a laptop.

[5] Hofmann, B., Stark oder Schwach, Selbst-Muskeltest als Entscheidungshilfen in allen Lebenslagen, KOHA, 2012, 150p.

[6] Hofmann B. *PSYCH-K im täglichen Leben. Für eine entspannte Kommunikation zwischen Bewusstsein und Unterbewusstsein*, KOHA, 2011, 174p.

[7] If we spontaneously focus on the auditory, our eyes are looking horizontally. That is why, as a listener, we are looking at the speaker. If we want to see images, our eyes spontaneously go up, to the visual field. If we stop in order to feel something, we tend to look down. That is the zone of the kinaesthetic field. This is what we know from NLP.

More info see: http://www.nlpu.com/Articles/artic14.htm (access 18.11.2014).

[8] McTaggart, *The Bond – Connecting Through the Space Between Us*, Carlsbad, Hay House, 2011, 336p.

[9] More about this in Chapter 7 'Surrogation'.

[10] Senge, P., et al., *Presence. Human Purpose and the Field of the Future. Exploring Profound Change in People, Organizations, and Society*, London, Nicholas Brealey Publishing, 2005, p. 159. "Synchronicity: The Field Knowing

Itself. Perhaps the most important aspect of crystallizing intent and prototyping is one that people rarely talk about. When people connect with their deeper source of intention, they often find themselves experiencing amazingly synchronistic events."

[11] Cross-crawls is one of the exercises in Braingym. For more information look at http://www.braingymbelgium.be/CMS/ Dennison, P. & G., *Brain Gym. Simple Activities for Whole Brain Learning*, Edu-Kinesthetics, 1986, 43 p.

[12] Williams, R., *PSYCH-K. The Missing Piece Peace In Your Life!*, 3rd ed., Colorado, The Myrddin Publications, 2009, p. 84-102. Real People... Real Results. Where the Rubber Meets the Road.

[13] Acquiring merit is a term used in the contextual therapy. By taking action we improve our relational world. Because we contribute to 'the whole' by taking actions, we as humans are being built up in our identity. Taking action – and this is an important part of a PSYCH-K balance – creates a solid relational identity. In an unspoken manner actions say: 'I know what I'm worth, because I invest in this world through my actions'. See Krasner, R., Austin, J., *Truth, Trust, and Relationships. Healing interventions in Contextual Therapy*, New York, Brunner/Mazel, 1995, p. 38-39. "'Merit' is a bilevel term that implies a condition of being, and an embodiment of action. In its noun form, 'merit' can be understood in individual terms. A person's life and existence per se carry uniqueness, singular value, dueness, and entitlement. I am, therefore I deserve. In its verb form 'merit' can be understood in relational terms. How you and I address each other earns value and deserves consideration by virtue of the choices and actions each one of us takes. I relate, therefore I owe. (...) In an ethical level, however, uncredited merit results in an injured order of existence, in skewed balances of give-and-take. (...) Merit is a self-motivating factor that addresses a self and a significant other."

## 3. Trauma

[1] Ledoux, J., *The Emotional Brain. The Mysterious Underpinnings of Emotional Life*, New York, Touchstone, 1998, p. 283-302, p. 285. "In sum, connections from the amygdala to the cortex allow the defence networks of the amygdala to influence attention, perception, and memory in situations where we are facing danger."

[2] Lipton, B., *The Biology of Belief. Unleashing the Power of Consciousness, Matter & Miracles*, Carlsbad, Hay House, 2005, p. 160. "Most human violence is neither necessary nor is it an inherent, genetic, 'animal' survival skill. We

have the ability, and I believe an evolutionary mandate, to stop violence. The best way to stop it is to realize (...) that we are spiritual beings who need love as much as we need food. (...) by realizing that Survival of the Most Loving is the only ethic that will ensure not only a healthy personal life but also a healthy planet."

[3] Taylor, S., *The tending instinct. How nurturing is essential to who we are and how we live*, Times Books, 2014. Taylor, Professor Psychology at the University of California, is a specialist in the realm of stress and health. Her book is trend breaking: who got a lot of love, has an easy social life and is socially highly rewarded. Who had a lack of care and friendship, has a more difficult path to go. When I first read this, I found this injustice. Now I know that we are the generation that can turn the destiny. We have all access to love and friendship: as soon as we establish our subconscious impulses towards that love, it comes towards us.

[4] Between square brackets there is a text that I inserted for the clarity of the reader.

[5] Riemslagh, M., *(In)Correcte Gespreksvoering. Fundamenteel en empirisch onderzoek naar de ethiek van het gespreksproces*, Puurs, UniBook, 2011, II. http://www.vrijvoluitleven.com/images/over-ons/AlgemeneConclusie.pdf

[6] Riemslagh, M., *Constructieve Counseling? Destructief recht in professionele gespreksvoering*, Leuven, Acco, 2012, 228 p. The book is not translated in English.

[7] Ron Hubbard came to this conclusion already about 1930, not me.

[8] There are several therapies that make use of this increased attention, for instance focusing and EMDR.

[9] How this works in anaesthesia. Here we do not have memories either, because the clustering of the sensory signals is chemically interrupted.

[10] During my research this was a shocking conclusion: as soon as we are in a state of alarm, our memory is no longer reliable. Riemslagh, M., *(In)Correcte Gespreks-voering. Fundamenteel en empirisch onderzoek naar de ethiek van het pastorale gespreksproces*, Puurs, UniBook, 2011, II, p. 335-346.

[11] In Chapter 5 'From Drama to Learning Opportunity' I will examine this behaviour more deeply.

[12] Conspiring with the friend next to me is also part of defensive behaviour.

[13] Film of Bruce Lipton on my web page

www.freefullliving.com/en/science.html.

[14] In this situation we react from the centre of fear, our animal survival mechanism. So we miss all our human characteristics. Ivan Boszormenyi-Nagy has studied this mechanism and described it as 'destructive right'. Riemslagh, M., *Constructieve Counseling? Destructief recht in professionele gespreksvoering*, Leuven, Acco, 2012, p. 32-44.

[15] Darcia Narváez calls this the 'I do not want to' possibility of the conscious mind. With our conscious mind we can stop the spontaneous (subconscious) defensive impulse. See also two articles that I published about this matter. Riemslagh, M., *Beveiligingsdrang, gehechtheid of verbeeldingskracht. Het verband tussen de structuur van onze hersenen en het verloop van pastorale gesprekken*, in G. Van Edom (ed.), *Lichaam en levensadem. Pastorale zorg voor de hele levende mens*, Antwerpen, Halewijn, 2010, p. 169-188.

[16] From my research it appears that the dogmatic assertion of our Belief that the other is the cause is actually in itself an indication of the opposite. Shocking, but true.

[17] The effects of well-known traumas are now medically recognized and classified in the SM IV as a syndrome: the post-traumatic stress syndrome or PTSS. For seven years I studied this matter as a result of the reactions that women showed after an abortion.

[18] Riemslagh, M., *(In)Correcte Gespreksvoering. Fundamenteel en empirisch onderzoek naar de ethiek van het pastorale gespreksproces*, II, Puurs, UniBook, 2011, p. 330-346. Riemslagh, M., *Constructieve Counseling? Destructief recht in professionele gespreksvoering*, Leuven, Acco, 2012, p. 144-163.

[19] To my own regret I have to come to this conclusion. Although I spent several years of my professional career on the verbal counselling of people...

[20] V. Lamme, *De vrije wil bestaat niet. Over wie echt de baas is in het brein*, Amsterdam, Bert Bakker, 2010, p. 147.

[21] Unless in therapies of regression that may eventually retrieve the origin, but cannot however disarm it!

[22] The speed of our subconscious mind is at least a million times faster than that of the conscious mind. And that is just as well. If a lion comes up to us, we do not really have time to think on how to handle the situation for the best.

[23] I am skilled in Psychodrama, in Bibliodrama, I did a two year training in contextual therapy and was a supervisor for this training. I did an introduction in systemic therapy, did a training in PRI (Past Reality Integration), I became skilled in the Theory of Presence, did a coach training, did a short training in

Resolution Focused Psychotherapy, and I became a PMA (Progressive Mental Alignment).

During my education as a CPE Supervisor I was in contact with EMDR, Brain training, Transactional Analysis, Theme Centered Interaction, Creative Therapy and Music Therapy. After this I became a Reconnective Healing Practitioner and only then I became a PSYCH-K Facilitator and Instructor.

[24] The Ethical Committee of the K.U.Leuven approved the research and all the criteria for qualitative research where met. Riemslagh, M., *(In)Correcte Gespreksvoering. Fundamenteel en empirisch onderzoek naar de ethiek van het pastorale gespreksproces*, I, Puurs, UniBook, 2011, p. 127-156.

[25] Riemslagh, M., *Constructieve Counseling? Destructief recht in professionele gespreksvoering*, Leuven, Acco, 2012, p. 45-2116.

[26] In my research I have used the term 'defensive'. In most psychological literature the term 'reactive' is used. Defensive expresses the attitude of the person who has to defend himself. Reactive stresses the impulsive – direct, triggered by the subconscious mind – action of the person as a reaction to the environment. Both terms are interchangeable.

[27] Reference to the interview with Bruce Lipton and Rob Williams of 2014, July 10. Bruce says that from the moment our attention weakens, our subconscious behaviour takes over.

[28] Korthuis calls sensory signals with an alarm code a bad cluster in Korthuis, *Desirable Power, Take control of your life, health and relationships*, Orlando, BCE Institute, 2006, p. 173. "Also matters as the outburst of an angry parent, receiving calamitous news, being confined into a small space, a stay at the hospital and more of these painful and fearful events can cause a bad cluster. Whether or not a bad cluster appears, differs from person to person and from event to event. It depends on the situation, your background, constitution, health, age and several other aspects."

[29] The fastest PSYCH-K Balance takes more time for someone who has only participated in the Basic workshop than for someone who has also attended the Advanced workshop. After a Basic workshop the fastest Balance can still take one minute.

## 4. Stress and Total Exhaustion

[1] That parts of our brain are inactive in a stress situation is to be seen on EEG. A picture is to be found in Chapter 10, where the effectiveness of PSYCH-K (and the business variant PER-K) is being shown on the basis of research. Fannin, J. & Williams, R., *Q EEG Reveals Interactive Link Between The Principles of Business, The Principles of Nature and the Whole-Brain State*, in *Neuroconnections* (2011) Fall, 1-9.

[2] Because my father had become lame at one side – and I worked as a nurse then – I was quite fascinated by the literature about how our brain works in connection with our thinking and feeling. The basis about how it works I found in the book of Damasio, professor of neurology at the University of Iowa. Damasio, A., *Descartes' Error – Emotion, Reason and the Human Brain*, New York, Penguin Books, 1994, p. 249, 251. "'This is Descartes' error: the abyssal separation between body and mind, between the sizable, dimensioned, mechanically operated, infinitely divisible body stuff, on the one hand, and the unsizable, undimensioned, unpushpullable, nondivisible mind stuff; the suggestion that reasoning, and moral judgment, and the suffering that comes from physical pain or emotional upheaval might exist separately from the body." (...) "The truly embodied mind I envision, however, does not relinquish its most refined levels of operation, those constituting its soul and spirit. From my perspective, it is just that soul and spirit, with all their dignity and human scale, are now complex and unique states of an organism. Perhaps the most indispensable thing we can do as human beings, every day of our lives, is remind ourselves and others of our complexity, fragility finiteness, and uniqueness."

[3] Narváez, D., *Triune Ethics: The Neurobiological Roots of Our Multiple Moralities*, in *New Ideas in Psychology* 26 (2008) 1, 95-119.

[4] Narváez, D., *Neurobiology and the Development of Human Morality: Evolution, Culture and Wisdom*, New York, W.W. Norton, 2014.

[5] Riemslagh, M., *Beveiligingsdrang, gehechtheid of verbeeldingskracht. Het verband tussen de structuur van onze hersenen en het verloop van pastorale gesprekken*, in G. Van Edom, *Lichaam en levensadem, Pastorale zorg voor de hele levende mens*, Leuvense Cahiers voor Praktische Theologie 12 (201), 173-191.

"Narváez continues to build on the foundation that our brain roughly speaking consists of three big structures that are mutually linked and connected with each other in an evolving way. The basis, the unquiet reptile brain, is situated most centrally and composes the *hardware*. Around this we find the visceral-emotional limbic nervous system, the mammal brain that came into evolution in the sedimentary era. Since that time we have been living in groups so that mutual attachment offers the biggest guarantee of survival. The latest developed somato-cognitive human nervous system is mainly to be found in the brain cortex. Because thinking processes are connected with emotions, this *software* enables complicated procedures like reacting empathically, distinguishing ambivalences and making judgments. Conform with the activities of these three brain structures we can speak of hot-tempered instinct (reptile brain), behaviour triggered by emotions (limbic system) and what we call freely acting by choice or free will (thinking informed by emotions).

Narváez claims that brain activity and operations are in fact not yet ethics. We can only talk about ethics, as soon as the motivation that steers the behaviour is raised to the highest leading norm by the person."

[6] Narváez, D., & Lapsley, D., *The psychological foundations of everyday morality and moral expertise*, in D. Lapsley & C. Power (eds.), *Character Psychology and Character Education*, Notre Dame, University of Notre Dame Press (2005) 140-165, p. 159. That is why a climate of group support is necessary to teach ethical behaviour. Whoever continuously finds him/herself in a stressful environment, receives little chances to develop his or her most human side. In that case there is rather a supply of self-security behaviour.

[7] Lipton, B., *The Biology of Belief. Unleashing the Power of Consciousness, Matter & Miracles*, Carlsbad, Hay House, 2005, p. 103-104. "While almost all organisms have to actually experience the stimuli of life first-hand, the human brain's ability to 'learn' perceptions is so advanced that we can actually acquire perceptions indirectly from teachers. Once we accept the perceptions of others as 'truths', *their* perceptions become hardwired into our own brains, becoming *our* 'truths'. Here's where the problem arises: what if our teachers' perceptions are inaccurate? In such cases, our brains are then downloaded with misperceptions. The subconscious mind is strictly a stimulus-response playback device; there is no 'ghost' in that part of the 'machine' to ponder the long-term consequences of the programs we engage. The subconscious works only in the 'now'. Consequently, programmed misperceptions in our subconscious mind are not 'monitors' and will habitually engage us in inappropriate and limiting behaviours. (...) Perception 'controls' biology, but as we've seen, these perceptions can be true or false."

[8] Think of a lemon and find out what will happen.

[9] Iacoboni, M., *Mirroring People – The New Science of How We Connect With Others*, New York, Farrar, Straus and Giroux, 2008, p. 267-268. "When we encounter each other, we share emotions and intentions. We are deeply interconnected at a basic, pre-reflective level. This we now know, and this *fact* seems to me a fundamental starting point for social behaviour that has been largely neglected by an analytical tradition that emphasizes reflective behaviour and differences between people."

[10] Ibid., p. 271. "We have evolved to connect deeply with other human beings. Our awareness of this fact can and should bring us even closer to one another."

[11] Riemslagh, M., *(In)Correcte Gespreksvoering. Fundamenteel en empirisch onderzoek naar de ethiek van het pastorale gespreksproces*, Puurs, UniBook, 2011, II, p. 404. "Now we know that in the brain only the actually present sensory signals can be activated. If a counselling partner tells a story of which the sensory stimuli do not match the data in the pastor's brain, they cannot be 're-traumatized'. But if he/she has stored similar sensory fragments in a threatening situation for him/her, the pastor can be tackled considerably by the story of a counselling partner. If he/she has decided to accept the counselling partner in everything he/she is, the pastor can take this opportunity to do his/her own homework."

[12] Lamme is professor of cognitive neuroscience at the University of Amsterdam. Lamme, V., *De vrije wil bestaat niet. Over wie echt de baas is in het brein*, Amsterdam, Bert Bakker, 2010, p. 147, 206. Free translation.

"There they are again, these thoughts. Full of recklessness and overestimation of oneself the thinking 'I' does not hesitate to wave aside the true backgrounds of our behaviour. Where the hell do these ideas always come from? And how is it that the thinking 'I' seems to have this stupid idea that it determines our choices?" (…) "The belief with the left hemisphere talks about the reasons of the behaviour of the right hemisphere is therefore at least remarkable. Gazzaniga concludes that in the left hemisphere there should be more than just the capacity to produce language. Apparently there is also a mechanism here that tries to summarize, or better interpret, all behaviour of the person. He calls this the 'brain interpreter'. Freely translated I would say 'the chatterbox'. I have freely translated this as 'the conscious mind telling stories'."

[13] On the initiative of C.C. I insert this former description. These are her own words.

[14] In the Netherlands there is the 'Alexander Concept', a three day training of 'Ander Leven' free translated as 'Other Life', during which people with unexplainable complaints learns to stop this stress response. They choose to train their subconsciousness to function differently. In group – and the function of the group is very important – they learn during three days to stop the self-undermining stress responses.

[15] Parentification is a term first used by I. Boszormenyi-Nagi. What he means is that the parents do not take up responsibility and the children have to be "parents" to their parents; the result being that children do not know their own boundaries/space. They have not been able to explore their limits in a safe environment.

Michielsen, M., Van Mulligen, W. & Hermkens L., (eds.), *Leren over leven in loyaliteit. Over contextuele hulpverlening*, Leuven - Amersfoort, Acco, 1998, 288p. Parentification burdens the exchange, a normal life situation between free people.

Ducommun-Nagy, C., *Ces loyautés qui nous libèrent*, Éditions Jean-Claude Lattès, 2006, p. 35-44. – Free translation: "the human brain (....) is equipped for special tasks: cooperation and exchange. The brain can discern who is worthy of trust and who could be a traitor but especially it is equipped to keep the relational score. It is programmed for exchange, the capability to trust and loyalty. This capability originated before we were capable of entertaining complex communities and before our religions and great philosophical currents were developed."

[16] Some would call these holes in the aura or an energetic field too large.

## 5. From Drama to a Learning Opportunity

[1] Seale, A., *Create A World That Works. Tools for Personal & Global Transformation,* San Francisco, Red Wheel/Weiser, 2011, p. 15.

[2] Girard, R., *The Scapegoat* [1982], Translated by Y. Freccero. Baltimore, Johns Hopkins UP, 1986, 236p.

[3] I did not know the phenomenon. Clients in my practice told me about it. Austermann, A., Austermann, B., *Das Drama im Mutterleib: der verlorene Zwilling,* Königsweg Verlag, 2006, 228p.

[4] That is why all stress reactions together are called the *vanishing twin syndrome*. You can find more about this in Chapters 8 and 9.

[5] The text was read by L.'s mother, so everything that is written here, is correct.

[6] 'Doing' stress is medical language. In medical education diseases or symptoms are 'done', we don't 'have' them nor 'are' we the illness. In Chapter 9 'A Healthy Mind in a Healthy Body' we come back to his language.

[7] In an email M.T. explains "You can change 'butchered' into 'divided' feeling. 'Butchered' is not a word from the dictionary, it only formulates my personal feelings."

[8] To get acquainted with the meaning of surrogation in PSYCH-K see Chapter 7 'Surrogation'.

## 6. PSYCH-K Principles and Philosophy

[1] We know what is in our higher good through making contact with the superconscious mind.

[2] The body is producing an effect, because of an epigenetic (mind) signal playing through the body.

## 7. Surrogation

[1] Riemslagh, M., *(In)Correcte Gespreksvoering. Fundamenteel en empirisch onderzoek naar de ethiek van het pastorale gespreksproces*, Puurs, UniBook, 2011, I, p. 61-69.

[2] Levinas, E., *De plaatsvervanging*. Translated into Dutch introduced, with notes created by Theo de Boer, Baarn, Ambo, 1989, p. 14-15. In his introduction De Boer states (now translated into English): "The face of one's fellow man, who is persecuted and oppressed, is the place where our being is shocked in its autonomy. The face owes this ability to the Infinite itself, which leaves a 'track' in an unpredictable manner, which is difficult to understand. We can also say that the infinite 'ordinates' the other towards the face. The Other is therefore written with a capital letter. In the direct religious language, which Levinas uses in his Jewish scriptures, it is said that God has a secret Alliance with the humiliated. " In this book I write 'the other' always in lowercase.

[3] Comment of J.A. Van der Ven on Burggraeve's contribution to the expert seminar After You on 11 February 2010.

(http://theo.kuleuven.be/page/seminar_afteryou/ toegang op 31 juli 2014).

4   Levinas, E., *Ethics and Infinity. Conversations with Philippe Nemo* (translated by R. Cohen), Pittsburgh, Duquesne University Press, 1985, p. 97. "To say: here I am [me voici]. To do something for the Other. To give. To be human spirit, that's it."

5   Levinas, E., *Difficult Freedom. Essays on Judaism*, translated by S. Hand, Baltimore, The Johns Hopkins University Press, 1990, p. 294. "The orientation towards the highness of the Other [...] is like a grading in being itself. The above does not indicate a turning into nothingness [néantisation] but a 'more than being', better than the happiness of the social relation."

6   Riemslagh, M., *(In)Correcte Gespreksvoering. Fundamenteel en empirisch onderzoek naar de ethiek van het pastorale gespreksproces*, Puurs, UniBook, 2011, I, p. 53. So I suspend myself, my behaving to the other as if I know him, my appropriating of the other and treating him as if 'I know' him, and I give the other one the possibility to speak for him or herself.

7   Hansel, G., "Autrui est 'visage', non pas dans le sens d'un visage 'vu', d'un visage pouvant se fixer sur une photographie ou dans la mémoire, mais expression, discours. 'Visage' qui est d'emblée et tout à la fois parole, demande, supplication, commandement, enseignement. Et dès lors, le 'visage' oblige; il exige réponse, aide, sollicitude, compassion. Et nous arrivons ainsi au terme peut-être le plus employé par Levinas: la responsabilité à l'égard d'autrui."

http://ghansel.free.fr/WebTalmud/levinas.htm (access on May 12, 2007).

8   Levinas, E., *Is ontology fundamental?*, in *ID., Entre Nous. Thinking-of-the-Other*, London/New York, Continuum, 2006, 1-10, p. 6. "I have spoken to him, that is, I have overlooked the universal being he incarnates in order to confine myself to the particular being he is."

9   Levinas, E., *Difficult Freedom. Essays on Judaism*, translated by S. Hand, Baltimore, The John Hopkins University Press, 1990, p. 293. "The disproportion between the Other and the Self is precisely moral consciousness. Moral consciousness is not an experience of values, but an access to external being: external being is, *par excellence*, the Other. Moral consciousness is thus not a modality of psychological consciousness, but its condition. At first glance it is even its inversion."

10   Ibid., p. 295. "The ultimate sense of such a responsibility consists in thinking the I in the absolute passivity of the Self – like the very act of *substituting* oneself for the other [l'Autre]; of being his *hostage*, and in this

substitution not only being *otherwise* but, as freed of the *conatus essendi, otherwise than being."*

[11] Levinas, E., *La substitution*, in *Revue philosophique de Louvain* 66 (1968), 487-508, p. 500. "It is a responsibility of the ego for what the ego has not wished, that is, for the others. This anarchy in the recurrence to oneself is beyond the normal play of action and passion in which the identity of a being is maintained, in which it *is*. It is on the hither side of the limits of identity. This passivity undergone in proximity by the force of an alterity in me is the passivity of a recurrence to oneself, which is not the alienation of an identity betrayed. What can it be but substitution of me for the others? It is, however not an alienation, because the other in the same is my substitution for the other through responsibility, for which, I am summoned as someone irreplaceable. I exist through the other and for the other, but without this being alienation; I am inspired. This inspiration is the psyche." (...) "In this substitution, in which identity is inverted, this passivity more passive still than the passivity conjoined with action, beyond the inert passivity of the designated, the self is absolved of itself. Is this freedom? It is a different freedom from that of an initiative. Through substitution for others, the oneself escapes relations. At the limit of passivity, the oneself escapes passivity or the inevitable limitation that the terms within the relation undergo. In the incomparable relationship of responsibility, the other no longer limits the same it is supported by what it limits. (...) In this most passive passivity, the self liberates itself ethically from every other and from itself."

## 8. Peace in Relationships

[1] Lipton, B., *The Honeymoon Effect. The science of creating heaven on earth*, Carlsbad, Hay House, 2013, p. 98-100. "While no mechanism has been identified to account for the rapidity of behavioural changes that result from these practices, the fact is that the changes are real and long lasting. Personally, I am most familiar with the PSYCH-K belief change process developed by Rob Williams. I know PSYCH-K's energy-balancing technology is effective because it radically changed my life. More important, over the last few years I have heard from hundreds of people around the world who have used PSYCH-K to successfully take charge of their lives."

[2] The underlying theoretical framework that is being used in this chapter is that of contextual therapy. I was trained in this method myself and I have been a supervisor for the education. In note 6 you will find the basic works.

I refer to my doctoral research Riemslagh M., *(In)Correcte Gespreksvoering. Fundamenteel en empirisch onderzoek naar de ethiek van het pastorale gespreksproces*, Puurs, Unibind, 2011, I & II, 680p.

Perhaps the Relationship Balances are so apparent to me, because I have been trained in psychodrama. A Relationship balance is a bodily shaping and correcting of a relationship.

[3] The popular booklet of the Japanese, Masaru, E., *The Hidden Messages in Water*, Atria Books, 2004, and the first published double-blind research into the effect of intention on the formation of water crystals, Radin, et al., *Double-Blind Test of the Effects of Distant Intention on Water Crystal Formation*, in *The Journal of Science and Healing*, 2 (2006) 5, p. 408-411, gives some evidence that the water from which we came into being, directly reacts to the power of words.

[4] Lipton, B., *The Biology of Belief. Unleashing the Power of Consciousness, Matter & Miracles*, Hay House, 2005, p. 135. "Again I go back to cells, which can teach us so much about ourselves. I've said many times that single cells are intelligent. But remember, when cells band together in creating multicellular communities, they follow the 'collective voice' of the organism, even if that voice dictates self-destructive behaviour. Our physiology and behaviour patterns conform to the 'truths' of the central voice, be they constructive or destructive beliefs."

[5] Bertau, M.-C., *On the Notion of Voice: A Psycholinguistic Perspective*, in *International Journal for Dialogical Science* 2 (2007) nr. 1, p. 133-162, en Bertau, M.-C., *Voice: A Pathway to Consciousness as 'Social Contact to Oneself'*, in *Integrative Psychological and behavioural Science* 42 (2008) 1, p.92-113 convey psycholinguistic research into the way in which meanings are being transferred between people. The most important thing is that the one who is listening exactly takes the words of the other one into his mouth and lets them vibrate in his own body, so that they are being 'tasted' by the whole system. If we work with beliefs, it is always the partner who has to choose the words that exactly fit him or her.

[6] How these sensory alarm signals come into being has been extensively discussed in the third chapter about trauma.

[7] Boszormenyi-Nagy, I., *Grondbeginselen van de contextuele benadering*, translated by N. Bakhuizen, Haarlem, De Toorts, 2000; Boszormenyi-Nagy, I. & Krasner, B., *Tussen geven en nemen: over contextuele therapie*, translated by N. Bakhuizen, Haarlem, De Toorts, 1994; Boszormenyi-Nagy, I. & Spark, G., *Invisible Loyalties. Reciprocity in Intergenerational Family Therapy*,

Hagerstown, Harper & Row, 1973. In stagnating or blocked relationships it is beneficial to bring to life again this dynamics of giving and receiving, receiving and giving.

[8] The 'cell material' doesn't carry the beliefs. The beliefs are in the 'field of consciousness' and express themselves through the body. It is an epigenetic phenomenon.

[9] Riemslagh, M., Vanmechelen, B., *Abortus voorgoed voorbij? Een hulpverleningsmodel,* Tielt, Lannoo, 2003.

[10] 'The child that was not born' is the term that we use to indicate that pregnancy always implies a child; it is indeed a 'budding child'.

[11] AKP is the Dutch abbreviation of General Periodic Inspection, the annual compulsory check on a car in the Netherlands. Prior to such an inspection, all defects will be repaired.

[12] For the four levels of change, see Chapter 5 'From Drama to a Learning Opportunity'.

## 9. A Healthy Mind in a Healthy Body

[1] Until 2014 this workshop is organized in the Dutch-speaking region only every two years. PSYCH-K facilitators who want to attend this workshop sooner, have to travel for it.

[2] From Bruce Lipton there is a film in which one can see that the subconscious mind is working like a recording device. Getting three similar sensory signals has the effect of pushing the 'rewind' button. The subconscious mind goes back to 'then'. You can watch the film at http://www.freefullliving page Science

Lipton, B., *The Biology of Belief. Unleashing the Power of Consciousness, Matter & Miracles*, Hay House, 2005, p. 135-136. "In reality, the subconscious is an emotionless database of stored programs, whose function is strictly concerned with reading the environmental signals and engaging in hardwired behavioural programs, no questions asked, no judgments made. The subconscious mind is a programmable 'hard drive' into which our life experiences are downloaded. The programs are fundamentally hardwired stimulus-response behaviours. Behaviour activating stimuli may be signals the nervous system detects from the external world and/or signals that arise from within the body such as emotions, pleasure, and pain. When a stimulus is perceived, it will automatically engage the behavioural response that was learned when the signal was first experienced. In fact, people who realize the automated nature of this playback response frequently admit to the fact that their 'buttons have been pushed'."

[3] The technique of regression that we used was PMA. Starting from the acute agony that the woman felt during a flush, all other sensory signals were revived in the subconscious mind. This happens because she went back from trauma to trauma. This procedure makes this technique quite painful and quite dangerous. Because the actualized stressors may be so vehement, they may cause physical damage. PMA still has more disadvantages, that is why I think it is unjustified to use this technique any longer.

[4] Lipton, B., *The Biology of Belief. Unleashing the Power of Consciousness, Matter & Miracles*, Hay House, 2005, p. 140. "As we've seen, the mind plays a powerful role in controlling the biological systems that keep us alive."

[5] Chopra, D., *Quantum Healing: Exploring the Borders of Mind/Body Medicine,* Bantam, 1997, p. 248-249. "The vital issue is not how to win the war but how to keep peace in the first place. The West has not arrived at this insight, or comprehended that the physical manifestation of a disease is a phantom. The cancer cells that patients dread and physicians battle against are just such phantoms – they will come and go, raising hopes and despair, while the real culprit, the persistent memory that creates the cancer cell, goes undetected."

[6] Lipton, B., *The Biology of Belief. Unleashing the Power of Consciousness, Matter & Miracles*, Hay House, 2005, p. 140-141. "The futility of battling with the subconscious is a hard message to get across because one of the programs most of us downloaded when we were young is that 'willpower is admirable'. So we try over and over again to override the subconscious program. Usually such efforts are met with varying degrees of resistance because the cells are obligated to adhere to the subconscious program."

[7] Williams, R., *PSYCH-K. The Missing Piece Peace In Your Life!*, 3rd ed., Colorado, "The Myrddin Publications, 2009, p. 21. "The problem is that insight, even combined with action and willpower, is seldom sufficient to make lasting changes. Knowing the cause of a problem will not change its effect.

The limitations of insight.

My experience in practicing insight-based talk-therapy was fairly typical of other practitioners of the art. After weeks or even months of talking about the problem, gaining new insights into its cause and specifying new behavioural strategies, little change took place. Put another way, *after all was said and done, more was actually said than done.*

The fact is that mainstream psychotherapy has been looking in the wrong place for answers it needs to solve the problem." (...)

"The keys to meeting the challenges of the human mind aren't usually found where the light shines the brightest (at the conscious level of insight). Although insight may shed light on the origins of a problem and provide some constructive strategies for redirecting your life, it seldom changes the situation or the dysfunctional behaviours.

In the dim of the alley of the subconscious mind is where the real keys to lasting change can be found."

[8] Riemslagh, M., *(In)Correcte Gespreksvoering. Fundamenteel en empirisch onderzoek naar de ethiek van het pastorale gespreksproces*, Puurs, Unibind, 2011, II, p. 338.

[9] On the basis of repeated experience I have learned to distrust my definite stories. It is painful to recognise, but they do not correspond. They are stories that show me in the best possible light (I am the victim) and the other one(s) or the situation take the role of the perpetrator. In psychology the mechanism underlying the definite stories is called a mistake of attribution. "This is the error of ignoring situational factors and overconfidently assuming that distinctive behaviour or patterns of behaviour are due to an agent's distinctive character traits. In fact, there is no evidence that people have character traits (virtues, vices, etc.) in the relevant sense. Since attribution of character traits leads to much evil, we should try to educate ourselves and others to stop doing it." Harman, G., *Moral Philosophy Meets Social Psychology: Virtue Ethics and the Fundamental Attribution Error*, in Proceedings of the Aristotelian Society 99 (1999) no. 3, 315-331, p. 315. The problem with such attributions is that they impede seeing what is really going on.

I am inviting you to check for yourself how your definite stories are. You can test this very simply through kinesiology. If your body goes into stress during the story, you know that it is not completely true.

[10] See also the experience of 'I cannot do this on my own' in Chapter 2 'PSYCH-K Works Quickly and Powerfully'.

[11] Church, D., *The Genie in Your Genes. Epigenetic Medicine and the New Biology of Intention,* Elite Books, Santa Rosa, 2009, p. 236-237, p. 237. Church tells the story of a woman in a Basic workshop is liberated from years of pain after a car accident. He also quotes a former president of the Union of

Psychotherapists of Colorado: "'PSYCH-K is clearly the most amazing tool for effective personal change that I have ever encountered'. Other testimonials report cessation from various fears and phobias, allergies, depression, weight problems, and a variety of organic diseases."

[12] As mentioned before, applying PSYCH-K is a free choice of the person in question. If someone does not want to discover what impediments are possibly hidden in his or her subconscious mind, it is the choice and the responsibility of the person in question. By applying PSYCH-K only with people who choose this, we respect and honour his or her conscious mind.

[13] During a Ted Talk, Elly McGonigal, a health psychologist, discusses the research into beliefs concerning stress. The astonishing result is that whoever thinks that stress is bad for one's health, comes off more badly than whoever is convinced of the opposite. Within PSYCH-K stress is a signal of old impediments that can be cleared. You can see the film at https://www.youtube.com/watch?v=RcGyVTAoXEU (access on November 10, 2014)

[14] Lipton, B., *The Biology of Belief. Unleashing the Power of Consciousness, Matter & Miracles*, Hay House, 2005, p. 106.

[15] Numerous books have been written about the enneagram. In the Netherlands and Flanders we use beliefs from the ennegram in order to embed these into the subconscious mind. Therefore we use the enneagram in combination with PSYCH-K.

[16] Moseley, B. et al., *A Controlled Trial of Arthroscopic Surgery for Osteoarthritis of the Knee*, in *The New England Journal of Medicine*, 347 (2002) 2, p. 81-88. Prof. Moseley tells his story at http://www.dailymotion.com/video/xex9wu_the-placebo-effect-knee-surgery_tech (access on November 10, 2014)

[17] Lipton, B., *The Biology of Belief. Unleashing the Power of Consciousness, Matter & Miracles*, Hay House, 2005, p. 140. "... we must realize that no amount of yelling or cajoling by the conscious mind can ever change the behavioural 'tapes' programmed into the subconscious mind. Once we realize the ineffectiveness of this tactic, we can quit engaging in a pitched battle with the subconscious mind and take a more clinical approach to reprogramming it."

[18] Lipton, B., *The Biology of Belief. Unleashing the Power of Consciousness, Matter & Miracles*, Hay House, 2005, p. 107-113.

[19] Ibid., p. 113.

[20] Ibid., p. 114.

## 10. PER-K, PSYCH-K at the workspace

[1] Riemslagh M., *Eindelijk: van een 'opvliegerig' naar een 'warm en open gesprek', dankzij PSYCH-K*, in *Coachend Vlaanderen*, www.issuu.com, 1 (2012) 1, p. 5-8. The English version, *'At last: from a "hot-tempered" to a "warm and open conversation"'* can be downloaded at http://www.freefullliving. com,page Science

[2] Fannin J., Williams R., *What Neuroscience Reveals about the Nature of Business*, in *The International Journal of Management and Business* 3 (2012) 1, 3-22.

[3] Fannin, J. & Williams, R., *Q EEG Reveals Interactive Link Between The Principles of Business, The Principles of Nature and the Whole-Brain State*, in *Neuroconnections* (2011) Fall, 1-9. This article shows that PSYCH-K and PER-K can bring someone in about ten minutes from a stress brain into a Whole-Brain State. When we can use our whole brain, we can function in an optimum way, we can use our ratio and our emotions.

[4] Fannin J., Williams R., *What Neuroscience Reveals about the Nature of Business*, in *The International Journal of Management and Business* 3 (2012) 1, 3-22, p. 17-18.

[5] Whoever has attended a PSYCH-K workshop, is a PSYCH-K facilitator; who has completed a PER-K workshop, is a PER-K catalyst.

## 11. Infinite Possibilities

[1] Telephone conversation 30 July 2014.

[2] To repeat: when we are practicing PSYCH-K with someone, he or she is our partner. If someone comes to see an independently working person for counselling or a session, this person is a client. While we are working with the client, we consider him or her as our partner. This partnership is essential to PSYCH-K. The other person determines the content; the facilitator knows the procedure (Balances).

[3] 'I do my best and my best is good enough' is one of the standard beliefs that are embedded in the Basic workshop. Whoever has practiced PSYCH-K, will have to smile while seeing this sentence, because while integrating it, a heavy burden of stress is falling from our shoulders. We do not have to commit or strain ourselves, doing our best is good enough.

⁴ Coelho, P. *The Alchemist*, Harper Collins Publishers, 2013. This sentence is repeated several times in the book: Kindle version locations 322, 323, 494, 539, 1106, 1394 of 2154.

⁵ Within the Christian tradition we find references to Two Bible stories, Mt 7,7 and Luke 11.9, where we read: "Ask and you will be given. Search and you will find. Knock and the door will be opened to you." Because during PSYCH-K we are making contact with the higher conscious mind, every Balance is like a question, a knocking and receiving and finding. We will often receive gifts that we did not expect.

## 12. PSYCH-K Unleashes Love

¹ Chapter 3 'Trauma'.

² Chapter 5 'From Drama to a Learning Opportunity'.

³ Lamme, V., *De vrije wil bestaat niet. Over wie echt de baas is in het brein*, Amsterdam, Bert Bakker, 2010, p. 146. Free translated as: "Where a direct, 100% causal relationship between history and choice is no longer to be recovered, there seems to be room for something like free will. But who sees how strong the effects are of even small manipulations in (recent) history, cannot but conclude that the space for free will is not actually there. In our head genetics is fighting the experiences implanted in the brain for every percent that they can put in the scales of a decision. There is no room there for a factor that does not depend on that history. Free will does not exist, and is not necessary at all." I agree with Lamme, only with PSYCH-K there is really room to change our rooted experiences. That however is a conscious choice. It is a small margin, but a very important one.

⁴ The testimony at the beginning of Chapter 3 is the result of this Balance.

⁵ Riemslagh M., *(In)Correcte Gespreksvoering. Fundamenteel en empirisch onderzoek naar de ethiek van het pastorale gespreksproces*, Puurs, Unibind, 2011, I, p. 65-74, p. 65. Philosophically the dialogue is based on Buber's writings. "For Buber a meeting is a contact between two people where both become aware of their *uniqueness*, because they address each other in their *being* and they *let themselves be touched* by the *being different* to the other person in such a way that both *know themselves to be accepted* as this human being."

⁶ Comment by J.A. Van der Ven on a contribution by Burggraeve to the expert seminar *After You* on 11 February 2010 http://theo.kuleuven.be/page/

seminar_afteryou/ (access on December 14, 2010). Burggraeve determines 'responsibility' as 'what we owe to the other' as well as 'taking our personal responsibility'.

[7] The word 'conversion' may call up old devotion or the overwhelming power of sects. Etymologically speaking, it means that we turn away from the old ways and find a new way. We always convert 'to' something and not away from something. The 'conversion' we want to express in PSYCH-K is from being attached to our old role of victim to a future that we are co-creating.

[8] Chopra, D., *The Spontaneous Fulfillment of Desire: Harnessing the Infinite Power of Coincidence*, New York, Three Rivers Press, 2003, 301p.

# Bibliography

Austermann, A., Austermann, B., *Das Drama im Mutterleib: der verlorene Zwilling*, Königsweg Verlag, 2006.

Bertau, M.-C., *On the Notion of Voice: A Psycholinguistic Perspective*, in *International Journal for Dialogical Science* 2 (2007) 1, 133-162.
Bertau, M.-C., *Voice: A Pathway to Consciousness as 'Social Contact to Oneself'*, in *Integrative Psychological and behavioural Science* 42 (2008) 1, 92-113.

Boszormenyi-Nagy, I. & Spark, G., *Invisible Loyalties. Reciprocity in Intergenerational Family Therapy*, Hagerstown, Harper & Row, 1973.
Boszormenyi-Nagy, I. & Krasner, B., *Tussen geven en nemen: over contextuele therapie*, vertaald door N. Bakhuizen, Haarlem, De Toorts, 1994.
Boszormenyi-Nagy, I., *Grondbeginselen van de contextuele benadering*, vertaald door N. Bakhuizen, Haarlem, De Toorts, 2000.

Chopra, D., *Quantum Healing: Exploring the Borders of Mind/Body Medicine,* Bantam, 1997
Chopra, D., *The Spontaneous Fulfillment of Desire: Harnessing the Infinite Power of Coincidence*, New York, Three Rivers Press, 2003.

Church, D., *The Genie in Your Genes. Epigenetic Medicine and the New Biology of Intention,* Elite Books, Santa Rosa, 2009.

Coelho, P. *The Alchemist*, Harper Collins Publishers, 2013.

Damasio, A., *Descartes' Error – Emotion, Reason and the Human Brain*, New York, Penguin Books, 1994.

Dennison, P. & G., *Brain Gym. Simple Activities for Whole Brain Learning*, Ventura, Edu-Kinesthetics, 1986.

Ducommun-Nagy, C., *Ces loyautés qui nous libèrent*, Éditions Jean-Claude Lattès, 2006.

Fannin, J. & Williams, R., *Q EEG Reveals Interactive Link Between The Principles of Business, The Principles of Nature and the Whole-Brain State*, in *Neuroconnections* (2011) Fall, 1-9.

Fannin J. & Williams R., *What Neuroscience Reveals about the Nature of Business*, in *The International Journal of Management and Business* 3 (2012) 1, 3-22.

Girard, R., *The Scapegoat* [1982], Translated by Y. Freccero. Baltimore, Johns Hopkins UP, 1986.

Harman, G., *Moral Philosophy Meets Social Psychology: Virtue Ethics and the Fundamental Attribution Error*, in *Proceedings of the Aristotelian Society* 99 (1999) 3, 315-331.

Hofmann, B., *PSYCH-K im täglichen Leben. Für eine entspannte Kommunikation zwischen Bewusstsein und Unterbewusstsein*, Burgrain, KOHA, 2011.
Hofmann, B., *Stark oder Schwach, Selbst-Muskeltest als Entscheidungshilfen in allen Lebenslagen*, Burgrain, KOHA, 2012.

Iacoboni, M., *Mirroring People – The New Science of How We Connect With Others*, New York, Farrar, Straus and Giroux, 2008.

Kamp, J., *The Mind is the Doctor*, in *Ode, The Intelligent Optimist* 18 (2012) September/October.

Korthuis, *Desirable Power. Take control of your life, health and relationships*, Orlando, BCE Institute, 2006.

Lamme, V., *De vrije wil bestaat niet. Over wie echt de baas is in het brein*, Amsterdam, Bert Bakker, 2010.

Ledoux, L., *The Emotional Brain. The Mysterious Underpinnings of Emotional Life*, New York, Touchstone, 1998.

Levinas, E., *Ethics and Infinity. Conversations with Philippe Nemo* (translated by R. Cohen), Pittsburgh, Duquesne University Press, 1985.
Levinas, E., *Difficult Freedom. Essays on Judaism*, translated by S. Hand, Baltimore, The Johns Hopkins University Press, 1990.
Levinas, E., *Is ontology fundamental?*, in *ID., Entre Nous. Thinking-of-the-Other*, London/New York, Continuum, 2006.
Levinas, E., *La substitution*, in *Revue philosophique de Louvain* 66 (1968), 487-508.
Levinas, E., *De plaatsvervanging.* Vertaald, ingeleid en aantekeningen door T. de Boer, Baarn, Ambo, 1989.

Lipton, B., *The Biology of Belief. Unleashing the Power of Consciousness, Matter & Miracles*, Carlsbad, Hay House, 2005.
Lipton, B., *The Honeymoon Effect. The science of creating heaven on earth*, Carlsbad, Hay House, 2013.

Manna, J. & Hellinger, B.,

Masaru, E., *The Hidden Messages in Water*, Atria Books, 2004.

McTaggart, *The Bond – Connecting Through the Space Between Us*, Carlsbad, Hay House, 2011.

Michielsen, M., Van Mulligen, W. & Hermkens L., (eds.), *Leren over leven in loyaliteit. Over contextuele hulpverlening*, Leuven - Amersfoort, Acco, 1998.

Monti, D., et al., *Muscle Test Comparisons of Congruent and Incongruent Self-Referential Statements*, in *Perceptual and Motor Skills* 88 (1999), 1019-1028.

Moseley, B. et al., *A Controlled Trial of Arthroscopic Surgery for Osteoarthritis of the Knee*, in *The New England Journal of Medicine* 347 (2002) 2, 81-88.

Narváez, D., & Lapsley, D., *The psychological foundations of everyday morality and moral expertise*, in D. Lapsley & C. Power (eds.), *Character Psychology and Character Education*, Notre Dame, University of Notre Dame Press (2005) 140-165.

Narváez, D., *Triune Ethics: The Neurobiological Roots of Our Multiple Moralities*, in *New Ideas in Psychology* 26 (2008) 1, 95-119.

Narváez, D., *Neurobiology and the Development of Human Morality: Evolution, Culture and Wisdom*, New York, W.W. Norton, 2014.

Nicolai, N., *Overdracht en tegenoverdracht bij traumabehandelingen*, in P. Aarts & W. Visser (eds.), *Trauma, Diagnostiek en Behandeling*, Houten - Diegem, Bohn Stafleu Van Loghum, 1999, p. 1-20.

Radin, D., et al., *Double-Blind Test of the Effects of Distant Intention on Water Crystal Formation*, in *The Journal of Science and Healing* 2 (2006) 5, 408-411.

Riemslagh, M. & Vanmechelen, B., *Abortus voorgoed voorbij? Een hulpverleningsmodel*, Leuven, Lannoo Campus, 2003.

Riemslagh, M., *Beveiligingsdrang, gehechtheid of verbeeldingskracht. Het verband tussen de structuur van onze hersenen en het verloop van pastorale gesprekken*, in G. Van Edom (ed.), *Lichaam en levensadem. Pastorale zorg voor de hele levende mens*, Antwerpen, Halewijn, 2010, p. 169-188.

Riemslagh, M., *(In)Correcte Gespreksvoering. Fundamenteel en empirisch onderzoek naar de ethiek van het pastorale gespreksproces*, Puurs, UniBook, 2011, I.

Riemslagh, M., *(In)Correcte Gespreksvoering. Fundamenteel en empirisch onderzoek naar de ethiek van het pastorale gespreksproces*, Puurs, UniBook, 2011, II.

Riemslagh, M., *Constructieve Counseling? Destructief recht in professionele gespreks-voering*, Leuven, Acco, 2012.

Riemslagh M., *Eindelijk: van een 'opvliegerig' naar een 'warm en open gesprek', dankzij PSYCH-K*, in *Coachend Vlaanderen*, www.issuu.com 1 (2012) 1, 5-8.

Seale, A., *Create A World That Works. Tools for Personal & Global Transformation,* San Francisco, Red Wheel/Weiser, 2011.

Senge, P., et al., *Presence. Human Purpose and the Field of the Future. Exploring Profound Change in People, Organizations, and Society,* London, Nicholas Brealey Publishing, 2005.

Sparrer, I., *Miracle, Solution and System. Solution-focused structural constellations for therapy and organisational change,* Cheltenham, Solution Books, 2007.

Taylor, S., *The tending instinct. How nurturing is essential to who we are and how we live,* Times Books, 2014.

Walther, S., *Applied Kinesiology,* Colorado, SDC, 2000.

Williams, R., *PSYCH-K, The missing piece peace in your life!,* Colorado, The Myrddin Publications, 2009.

## Request for Review

If you enjoyed this book, I would appreciate if you could possibly leave a review on Amazon.

That would be very helpful!

Thanks a lot in advance,

*Marina Riemslagh*

Made in the USA
Lexington, KY
27 March 2015